How Small Business Trades Worldwide

HOW SMALL BUSINESS TRADES WORLDWIDE

▼

Your Guide to Starting or Expanding a Small Business International Trade Company Now

John Wiley Spiers

Seattle Teachers College Press

Seattle   Hong Kong

How Small Business Trades Worldwide
Your Guide to Starting or Expanding a Small
Business International Trade Company Now

Seattle Teachers College Press

For information address:
Seattle Teachers College
5902 East Mercer Way
Mercer Island, WA 98040
USA

www.seattleteacherscollege.net

ISBN: 0-595-19955-0

Printed in Hong Kong

For the Spiers Girls . . . salvet me Deus!

Contents

LIST OF ILLUSTRATIONS

FOREWORD

How Small Business Trades Worldwide is a step-by-step approach to starting your own import business, with a view to eventually expanding into exporting as well. Although there are many approaches to international trade, the methods laid out in this book represent the experience of an actual practicing importer; this is work he has done since 1974, lectured on since 1984 at dozens of colleges, has advised others to do in his consulting practice, and what he continues to do himself.

This book will explain why so many people have become international traders, what importers know, and how you too can become an importer. You will be guided through what is necessary and sufficient in selecting products, finding suppliers; licensing; working with governments, bankers, Customs brokers, carriers, and insurers; financing, costing and pricing, and gaining orders for your goods or services—all from an expert whose seminars on the subject are highly rated for his experience, candor, information and humor. This book also assumes you wish to travel, and would like to work out of your own home to start. Although the book is directed at those who want to earn a living at this work, the tips on informal trade procedures and start-up marketing will be invaluable for anyone wishing to trade as a sideline.

This book is about working in international trade, and focuses on trading as an entrepreneur to limit the scope to those who would organize and operate a small international business, and enjoy the benefits of the work.

For those with a great idea, you will see how to most fully develop your idea and market. Most people have no idea what to trade; for them this book is unique in that it shows you how to come up with a great idea.

For those hoping to find a job working with an international trading company, this book will clearly define the various roles people play in a trading company, enabling the reader to identify the ideal position in such a company and discuss the position knowingly during a job interview. Indeed, by following the research steps outlined in this book for those wishing to start their own businesses, a prospective employee will be able to identify the potential problems and opportunities any given business may be facing, and use that knowledge to secure a position. The steps outlined will also serve anyone working with a medium or large company who has been charged with beginning international operations.

Once you have completed the book, you may take a free quiz at www.johnspiers.com to test your knowledge. If you pass the quiz, you will be invited to join an internet e-mail group dedicated to small business international trade discussion. In this way you gain free access to the author and several hundred others (as of December 2000) like you.

The advantage the author has over most others in starting his own business is his years of experience working as an international trader. Now this experience, the advantage, is available to you in this book.

PREFACE

At some point in most careers one considers the idea of starting a business. Some people want to pursue a dream, some figure they can beat the boss at his own game, and for some people unemployment forces the issue.

Surely there is no safer investment for your time and money than self-employment. Surprisingly, for many who start their own businesses, making money is not always the prime motivator. Nonetheless, recent books such as The Millionaire Next Door provide some remarkable information about self-employment: 80% of the millionaires in the USA are "first generation"—meaning they became so in their own career—and some two-thirds of the working millionaires are self-employed (20% of US millionaires are retired); the self-employed are four times more likely to be millionaires than those who work for others—it seems the most common career move in becoming rich is to become self-employed.

US Customs tells us most international traders are small businesses, and world trade continues to grow rapidly. Given the improvements in transportation and communication worldwide, inevitably now small business in USA has some international component—some more than others.

This book is written to show you how to build a business, takes you through the steps so you will know you can do it, and is structured so you may take positive steps after each chapter toward building your business. Surely you will finish the book before your business gets started, but by the time you finish the book, not only should you feel "ready to go," but actually be on your way.

World trade is different from the domestic variety, and small is different from large business. Small business international trade has some specific challenges which this book illumines and solves.

Starting a business is necessarily disruptive…but to what extent? Like the tennis pro who shows you how to get great improvement out of small changes, this book assumes you desire economy of motion and minimal risk.

For those who desire to engage directly in world trade, and for those who are hired to do so, this book explains how small business trades worldwide.

ACKNOWLEDGEMENTS

A book that took fifteen years to write and is based on experience will have very many acknowledgements to make indeed, and cannot thank everyone…so I will work chronologically to hit some highlights:

• First, there is Charles Manca of Manca Imports in Seattle who hired me on and promoted me quickly to buyer, there I learned the mechanics of international trade;

• next, to Raymond Leung of Hong Kong who taught me the economics of international trade and has been a generous business partner;

• in those early years of semi-annual trips to China I met many remarkable people—such as Madame Wu, the political commissar for one of the corporations with impossibly long names popular at the time—for having a sense of humor;

• for the anonymous Dutch fellow who said after a long evening of comparing career notes said "you can do better…";

• Ted Van Doorn of Vandor Imports in San Francisco, for teaching me how small businesses compete on design, and trusting me with the general management of his company (which I dare say proved to be a good move on his part);

• sometimes a word of advice can open vistas, and Lefty Stern and Robert Bolman both of the Bay Area made comments on business financing and marketing, respectively, that have proven sturdy over the years;

• Ray Smardon and Austris Rungis taught me more about labor relations in four months of the International Longshore and Warehouse Union master contract talks than most people get to learn in a lifetime;

• my sabbatical from work put me back in school which opened up teaching as a means for learning - and the continuing education directors for being they who keep education alive in these present dark ages when vandals have control of the schools;

• Skip Ellsworth for showing me how to teach;

• starting one's own business involves innumerable people and I owe the various retailers who taught and encouraged me, such as Sue Grosz; designers such as Dan Chen, Chris Bolton, Gary and Marilyn Pelzman and Lowell Herrero for their excellent contributions;

• Jerry Murphy for export business insights; Bill Spiers, R.J. Steinberger, Dennis Ragsdale, Margaret McCullough, Jim Smith, Greg Van Gaver;

• Betty Tong Lau of the Seattle Public Library proved again that something is wrong when people so valuable are not paid better (I've never heard her complain, though);

• James Helwig at the Unites States Department of Commerce, International Trade Administration introduced me to the National Trade Data Bank, while Dan Giavina of the same organization showed me how to extract the data simply;

• John Hicks, MBA, JD, for business organization advice, banker John Gordon for finance advice, banker Brenda McKelvey for being unique among bankers by being frank about letters of credit;

• Linda Lorentz for insights into US Customs;

• Tom Ratfield for his wide experience in distribution;

• the N S Gustin sales organization for doing the hard part (actually getting orders);

• John Wiedmier, Ken Wiser, Bob Keeler, and the Romanos for allowing me to test some theories (with happy results) on exporting agriculture;

• Hal Glatzer helped me in early drafts of this book, and my father the English professor who had to endure proofreading these, and who with my mother provided many tips and improvements;

• Leslie Ehle for assuming this book would be first rate in all ways and editing the final draft with this presumption paramount;

• and readers Bolinas Frank, Christina Fyve, Kathleen Rybicki, Mitch Odom and Jeff Slye for spotting errors in the first printing and kindly bringing them to my attention.

Finally, one does not start a business or write a book without the family along for the ride, whether they like it or not, so special thanks to my wife and daughters for their patience, indulgence and occasional sense of humor.

CHAPTER ONE:

▼

THE FIELD OF INTERNATIONAL TRADE

Your value as an importer at the small business level is to build markets in the United States for suppliers overseas, and your role in the United States is to bring innovative products to the market. As an importer you have products better made (and sometimes made better) overseas. Although the cheap-labor argument is popular, by far the main reason we go overseas is to take advantage of another country's excess: importers exploit another nation's excess management capacity, excess production capacity, excess credit capacity, or any combination thereof. And furthermore, this excess we exploit comes from our top three sources for imported products: Canada, Japan and Germany. These three countries also happen to be our largest customers for US-made products. By selling us better-made or lower cost items, people overseas are able to earn money to buy our better or lower-cost items, a business in which we may engage as exporters.

There are 350,000 importers in the United States bringing in some $656 billion worth of goods each year (and growing). The top 1,000 of those importers account for 61% of the total import value—some $400 billion, or an average of $400 million each.[1] That leaves the remaining $256 billion in imports spread among 349,000 importers, or a rough average of $734,000 each in importation value. Assuming normal profit margins we can assume the "average" importer has sales of $1–2 million dollars per year, but keep in mind start-up companies are part of the set making up the average. As you can see, although relatively few huge corporations handle nearly two-thirds of all imports, for almost all importers, importing is a small business.

Importers find that for the more difficult work in business—the more critical work, developing products and manufacturing—it is preferable to work with foreign suppliers. This is not to say United States suppliers are not qualified; to the contrary, it is clear the United States capability is superior to the rest of the world in almost any area. The problem is United States manufacturers are often too busy, too afraid of liability, or simply too expensive overall to be relied on. On the other hand, foreign suppliers are eager and able to work with importers on developing products for the United States market, if for no other reason than the USA is the largest market in the world.

Importing ultimately allows an interest in a vague idea to be pushed forward with the help of talented people resulting in products on store shelves that consumers are delighted to buy and to use.

And in spite of all the talk of overpaid CEOs at America's largest businesses, owners of US small businesses are usually far better compensated than the CEOs of major corporations![2]

---

1. United States Customs Service, FY 1997 Trade Enforcement Plan, part eight, "audit/compliance assessment."

2. "When it comes to pay, heads of little firms can outdo top CEO's," *Wall Street Journal* (July 21, 1993): A1.

And there is an intangible area I find attractive: international business is based on relationships, not on the Uniform Commercial Code as it is in these United States. Legal problems exist only in the law, among lawyers. Business people experience business problems. Too many business people make the mistake of converting business problems to legal problems by calling a lawyer when they have a business problem. In so doing, the business people give up their power and turn it over to lawyers. It is taught in the US business schools—if a problem arises, call a lawyer. It is silly to blame lawyers for a failing among business people.

In international trade, there is no legal jurisdiction covering two companies in two countries. Therefore, as it was domestically perhaps a century ago in the United States, if there is a business problem in international trade, it remains a business problem. In over twenty five years in this business, I have never retained legal counsel.[3] Certainly there have been problems, but they have always been settled at the business level. In essence, small business international trade affords us all the resources and excitement of building our own business, with none of the distraction of legalism.

As mentioned, the basis for international trade is relationships. These relationships are based strictly on the quality of your work and its future potential. Keep this in mind, because this premise is helpful when thinking of solutions to problems in this business, as you will see.

A critical part of importing as a small business, selling, we leave in the hands of independent sales representatives. As you shall see these experts focus on performance and results, and are not inclined to legalistic recourse either.

International trade has grown rapidly over the last decade largely due, I believe, to the improvements in communications and transportation

---

3. Curiously, San Francisco advises people starting business as step number one to "Consult with attorney." *Getting Business Started: Entrepreneurs Guide to Doing Business in San Francisco*. It is copyrighted 1990 by Pacific Bell, a huge conservator corporation, which proposes to advise people on starting up a business.

worldwide. It is just too simple to find the best place in the world to have a product made, and once found, too easy to move it from there to here. People formerly forbidden access to the rest of the world are now free to trade, and they are capitalizing on their new-found freedom. Freedom is good for business: Hong Kong is freer than the United States (as of this writing), and has five times per capita the billionaires of the United States. All the countries freed as socialism fell (in both its fascist and communist versions) still have governments and rules and regulations, but the citizens generally ignore the governments. The practical effect is, economically speaking, those people are as free as the people of Hong Kong.

The days of the import company on top of the warehouse in a port city are over, too. Again, the improvements in communication allow me to have my offices in my home in a mountain town (near skiing and lakes) and my warehouses in a distribution center in another state.

For all of these reasons and more, small business international trade has probably the widest demographic spread of any occupation. It doesn't matter who you are.

Overview

The practice of international trade is near universal. Texaco and I import. Boeing Commercial Airplane Company and I export. From tiny to huge, international trade cuts across all commodities and services, all countries, and all kinds of people. Within the narrow scope of small business international trade, let's review the players: the service sector, the importers, the exporters, and the commission agents.

The service sector assists you in handling the nuts-and-bolts in an international trade transaction, the rules, regulations, logistics, packaging, labeling, and all the technical questions you have specific to your product. Such experts as the bankers, the Customs brokers, the steamship lines, the insurance carriers, and so on have a vested interest in seeing you succeed. By sharing their specialized knowledge and experience, you will proceed with the transactions, and that is where they get paid: by handling the actual logistics. All of these people teach you what you need to know and how to handle your product before your first transaction, at absolutely no cost to you. That first transaction may be at least a few months away, or maybe a year, and therefore you learn a tremendous amount from these experts in the meantime. They in effect become your continuing education program as you proceed. Also, the rapid changes in law, communication and transportation make information on logistics, rules and regulations obsolete too quickly for the importer to remain abreast. Therefore, the importer relies heavily upon the knowledge and experience of these experts. The importer focuses on the important task of developing markets, products and sources. In later chapters I will discuss specifically who these service sector people are and how and when you work with them.

The next area is the importer. With an idea for a product or a vision of a potential market that ought to be exploited, importers buy products from overseas, take title to (ownership of) the goods, bring them into the United States and distribute.

Exporting is the mirror image of importing. Importers find their customers at home, exporters find their customers overseas. Therefore importing may seem easier than exporting, because the hardest thing to do in business is gain your customers.

Also, as your suppliers become more confident in you, they will begin to ask you to source American-made products for them. For instance, a supplier of baskets in Hong Kong requested American cigarette filter material from me. The Hong Kong company had the distribution rights for filterless Chinese cigarettes in Hong Kong, and demand was growing in Hong Kong for filtered cigarettes. Although I have never dealt in cigarettes (at least not since the fifth grade), it is easier for the Hong Kong merchants to contact me regarding cigarette filter material than to follow the standard yet more formal process of contacting a US Foreign Commercial Officer at the US Consulate in Hong Kong. Although these US officers are quite competent, they are too busy with many such requests. My supplier can expect full attention from me to his request. So whether it is a request for some component of the product they are producing for you, or simply some US made product they can distribute in their home market, or some unusual request like cigarette filter material, when you satisfy foreign requests for US made products, you are exporting. Of course, you may wish to begin business by exporting, and after laying out international trade fundamentals in the early chapters with a view to importing, we will devote a chapter to specific strategies for small business exporting.

The last area is the commission agent. A commission agent simply operates among various factories in the United States and around the world, and various end users in the United States and around the world. Commission agents put together deals and earn a commission of typically two to five per cent of the value of the transaction. Whereas the importer takes title to the goods and adds a profit margin, a commission agent never takes title to the goods, only handles the paperwork required for the agreements to buy and sell. This work appears especially attractive to newcomers in international trade, because all one needs to begin is a telephone and a fax machine, and a set of trade directories from around the world.

People hear of the real-life exploits of commission agents such as a friend of mine. A typical deal would be the time he sourced electrocardiogram machines for a major Japanese hospital group. He found the best place in the world to have electrocardiogram machines made to Japanese specifications was in Mexico. He earned a commission of a few percent for his efforts on the multi-million dollar deal he put together

Novices hear such stories and imagine a life of jet setting from exotic locale to exotic locale, eating sushi, drinking pina coladas, and working about forty five minutes a year, quickly amassing a fortune. Naturally it is not so easy.

The fellow in this example was educated for the work but it was by virtue of his long years developing markets worldwide for a small electronics manufacturer that led him to his present success. To be a commission agent you must have a strong reputation in a fairly narrow field and be known and trusted by both the buyers and the sellers, and in the information flow to hear about the requests-for-bid that starts the process.

Commission agency has been described as almost a semi-retired position. After one has gained a reputation for knowledge and integrity in a fairly narrow field, one can profitably begin this kind of service. Later we'll see a more realistic approach for us.

The Role and Value of the Importer

The importer is at the center of a large network of companies engaging in support services. You engage in the essential activity of buying and selling products. The people you propose to buy from, and the people you propose to sell to, know well your role and value. The best of these have many potential importers they can work with and support. If you do not know your role and value, they will not elect to work with you. In this sense, your work is competitive. It is critical to your success to clearly understand the role and value of the importer so you may provide it. Furthermore, you must communicate this role and value in every conversation, letter, fax, email or other communication. You will be judged based on the quality of your work and, as you will see, it takes remarkably little to be judged worthy.

The Basis of Competition

"Importing is a matter of having American products made cheaper overseas and selling them for a profit in the United States." This is a commonly held belief, and it is true for some very large companies under certain conditions. But for the start-up or small importer, nothing could be further from the truth. Indeed, I confidently predict that if you start up an import company competing on the basis of price, you will fail.

If price is not the competitive advantage for the small importer, then what is?

To answer this question, I will draw on the seminal work of this era's foremost business theoretician, Peter F. Drucker.

Drucker wrote a book entitled *Innovation and Entrepreneurship*[4] in which he laments the failure of US companies to be as competitive in world markets as they ought to be. He holds up as ideal the examples of the only two large businesses he can name that innovate, the 3M and Johnson & Johnson companies. These companies do enjoy a leadership position in markets worldwide. But these companies follow a pattern that mimics a paradigm played out daily between what I will call innovators and conservators. In essence, innovators compete by introducing new benefits in the form of goods or services, and conservators compete by lowering prices on those benefits and making them eventually available to virtually everyone.

Perhaps you've noticed this phenomenon: a small, innovative company develops a product and introduces it to the marketplace. The product is new inasmuch as it includes innovative features that are beneficial, but not so new as to overwhelm and put off prospective buyers. Since the product is innovative and different, it is what is called "price blind." Price blind means the consumer cannot hold this innovative product up against the old standard product and figure out what the price difference should be on the innovative product. My glassware is price blind: nobody knows what cold-strike phosphate opalescent glass should sell for, so $29.95 retail each for a tumbler is no surprise, it is simply information. Few people know the cost of materials difference between a seventy-nine cent wineglass at K-Mart and a forty-five dollar crystal wineglass at Neiman Marcus is about three cents (certainly there are production cost differences).

The product being price blind, the innovator may charge a premium price. Indeed, the innovator, being a small company, must charge the premium to cover the expenses of starting up a company, as we will see in detail later. But let's first review how an innovator gets started.

---

4. Peter F. Drucker, *Innovation and Entrepreneurship* (New York: Harper & Row, 1985).

In the mid-sixties Oregon track coach Bill Bowerman and team member Tinker Hatfield decided they needed a better running shoe.[5] This reflected a change in thinking, something the MBAs refer to as a "psychographic shift." There are demographic shifts (the US population on average is getting older; Mexico's is getting younger), geographic shifts (the migration of US citizens from northern states to southern states after World War II), and psychographic shifts. The first two are easy to follow by simply reading census reports. The psychographic shift is more difficult, and considered the most profitable to exploit. In any event, the track coach and athlete began thinking in terms not so much of the high-performance athlete, but high performance equipment as well.

We put a man on the moon, we were fighting a high-tech war in Viet Nam, Jean Claude Killy wins the downhill gold medal on special skis, and in popular culture James Bond was getting out of tough situations not due to his moral superiority, like Ivanhoe, but because of his gear.

Since your gear could account for 2/10ths of a second over your opponent, and an Olympic gold medal in track could land you a million dollar Marlboro cigarette endorsement contract, the coach and athlete badly wanted special shoes—shoes with EVA foam, a space program material that used in shoes allowed an athlete to run longer, faster and jump higher.

The coach and runner took the idea for better shoes to Jack Purcell, Converse, Wilson and the other US sport shoe makers who welcomed them. Unfortunately, these conservator companies could not proceed without a half-million dollars up front for developmental costs, a million dollar advertising budget, and an agreement that, if the product did well, the conservators would own 51% of the new company.

Disappointed, this team decided to make their own shoes and were shocked to find how easy it was. Upon appearing at track meets in their new shoes, the athletes drew the attention of other athletes envious of any

---

5. Christopher Boehme, *Compass* (November 1989): 26.

advantage another athlete might enjoy. "Where did you get those shoes? We've never seen such shoes." "We made them," goes the reply. "Why make a pair of track shoes?" "For the beneficial features of course," and the other athletes want the shoes as soon as they understand the benefits. This is in essence the genesis of every product in every thriving start-up company. The product provides a value, a benefit not yet available. And since you've probably figured out by now I am referring to the start of a company called Nike, I'll point out you need to watch for the experience the founders of Nike had: when the other athletes asked the coach and athlete if they would be willing to make a pair for them, the reply was yes, but since they are made one pair at a time, we have to charge you some $35 (this when most track shoes were going for $5 a pair). When the other athletes readily agreed to that premium price, Nike was born.[6]

And keep in mind the extra $30, the price premium, covers essentially seventy-five cents worth of E V A foam.

Charging a premium price does not necessarily make your product the most expensive. In a twist on charging a premium price; in 1968, Honda had a model at $1,300 positioned to compete against a Peugeot at $2,300. Was Honda competing on price? It would seem so, until you realize Peugeot was making about $300 per car and Honda about $500 per car. When few can be sure what your price *should* be, you can pretty much charge what you want.

Eventually the conservators, the large companies, spot the innovative product that has been introduced to the marketplace. They are able to conduct a valid and reliable market study to determine the potential sales if they were to offer the innovative product themselves through their distribution channels. For many novice entrepreneurs the idea of

---

6. Nike is an importer. It manufactures nothing; Nike exploits excess management, credit and production capacity overseas for shoes it designs and markets. Some public relations people at Nike actually believe Nike exploits cheap labor overseas!

a conservator stepping into the market is a nightmare. But like most nightmares it has no basis in fact and is nothing to fear.

But conservator companies do "appropriate" (in the sense of taking) the products and ideas of smaller companies and make them their own. Conservators appropriate ideas in one of three ways: they buy the innovator, they steal the idea outright, or simply come up with a better version and charge a lower price. Ought the innovator not fear this simple fact of life with a concern that the creativity, work and investment will be wasted? Should the innovator not take steps to protect this investment?

The reality is as follows: after determining a given innovative product has profit potential, the conservators will apply their economies of scale not only in manufacturing but in finance and distribution as well as others areas. Not only can a conservator manufacture less expensively (Econ 101, the more you make, the less the per-unit cost), conservators get their financing, marketing and distribution cheaper than innovators. By applying these formidable economies of scale to a given product, the conservator is able to move in on the innovator and steal the lion's share of the market. The innovator does not have these economies of scale, so the innovator cannot compete on price.

But this activity does not harm the innovator. The conservator has lowered the price of the item and made it available to a group of people—a "target market segment" in the lingo of the business schools—that could not or would not pay the premium price the innovator originally charged. In effect, the conservator is serving a market that the innovator could not serve, for lack of the resources that are at the command of the conservators. The innovators market share is a tiny subset of the entire market (Fig. 1). But with wide profit margins, and a multi-trillion dollar economy, the US market is the premier generator of new businesses.

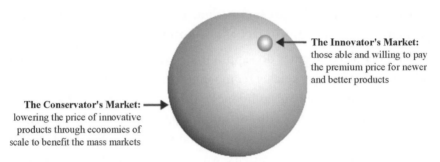

Fig. 1. Innovator's and conservator's markets

In this respect the conservators provide an extremely important service in our economy: they make the benefits of material goods available to ever wider markets. Think of how exclusive the transistor radio, the personal computer, the cellular phone and fax machine once were. The innovator first serves the privileged, the wealthy and the resourceful (and frankly, who better to act as guinea pigs?). By lowering the price of the innovative product, the conservator makes available to the middle class and poor the benefits the innovator introduced (and has proven to be safe and effective). In this way access to the benefits of innovative products become universal.

In 1982, the computer and software to run a $4 million import company cost $140,000, required a climate-controlled room, took three people to operate and the software did not work. Now far more computing power can be had in a laptop with a fax/data modem included with far superior and complete software for around $1,000 or less. How did these fabulous benefits become near universal? Because of the paradigm played out between the innovator and conservator.

Indeed, 400 years ago one of the richest men on earth was King Henry VIII. He enjoyed exotic foods, wore silk from China, was learned in Greek, Latin, philosophy, mathematics; his security was second to none; he could travel widely, had the best medical care (at the time), went to church daily, and had chamber music with every meal. Today, all of these benefits can be enjoyed by virtually any US citizen. Is this because we all became as rich as King Henry VIII, or is it because markets brought the cost of those benefits down to where virtually all of us have access to them? Do we all need to get as rich as Bill Gates, or do we need to have the access—the price that is—fall to where we can enjoy the benefits he enjoys? This is essentially the argument of what is known as the Austrian school of economics, not to be confused with liberal or conservative, Democrat or Republican. Simply put, material progress is price reduction, and free markets provide price reduction and the ever-widening access to material goods. (And the only event that stops this process is government intervention; indeed, price increases can always be traced back to government intervention.)[7]

Price reduction can come in two ways: lower the price on a standard item, or adding features and selling at the same price point. For example, the computer you can buy today at $2,000 has far more features than $2,000 computer of a year ago.

Now this may cause you to feel hot and passionate for free markets, until you realize that the free market may lead a conservator to lower the cost of YOUR product to benefit the great masses! So, do you "protect" your idea?

The innovator must never take steps to protect his idea, such as patents or trademarks or any other method. If you do, the conservator will simply redesign, and no doubt improve upon, your original idea, making that original design obsolete. After bearing the tremendous expense of "protecting" your idea, it will become worthless. Those successful small businesses you admire got customers first before anything else. Of the millions of patents issued, almost none of them become products for sale, and of those extremely few that do, almost none ever turn a profit. Patents are very recent and very Western in conception. Before wasting

---

7. Even if economics bores you, the Von Mises Institute teaches such commonsense solutions to business problems you ought to review their literature. Contact them at Auburn University, Auburn, AL 36849, (334) 844-2500, or www.mises.org

your time and money, get customers for your products first, and then you can turn over your hard-earned money to patent attorneys and such if you wish.

Once Bill Gates tried to buy an innovative company called Intuit, which sells a software program called Quicken. Although you would expect from his reputation Mr. Gates would simply steal the product, he in fact made an offer that delighted everyone associated with Intuit. The government, however, maintained that life as we know it would end if the deal went through, and vowed to fight it, so Microsoft withdrew the offer. Mr. Gates still did not steal the idea. He did worse, to my mind. Microsoft improved a product of theirs similar to Quicken, and priced it very attractively—free to anyone who wanted it.[8]

Regardless of how the conservator has lowered the market price on the innovative product, since the innovator cannot compete on price, is he not "done for"?

The innovators role is to innovate, to come up with innovative product. And no innovator is a one-trick pony. As a product matures in its life cycle, and is "stolen," the problem the innovator faces is not, "What will we do next?" but, "Which of these 500 great ideas we have thought up during this process will we work on next?"

Indeed, as an innovator, if your ideas are not being stolen it is because they are worthless. And conservators had better be constantly looking for good ideas to steal or they will not last. The US automakers are an excellent example.

To illustrate the innovator/conservator paradigm is the case of Apple Computer. In 1976, Apple introduced the personal computer to the marketplace. Jobs and Wozniak, Apple's founders, have a letter from executives turning their idea down when they offered it to Hewlett Packard.

---

8. Timothy L. O'Brien, "Microsoft to offer new Money package free for 2 months," *Wall Street Journal* (July 21, 1995): B8.

IBM certainly had the capital and technological resources to introduce a personal computer that year if they had wanted to do so. But in 1976 there was no interest, and Drucker explains why: no mainstream conservator company executive is going to risk his 9–5, weekends free, country club membership, good salary, health insurance and pension plan on a risky venture. That work is best left to the people like Jobs and Wozniak, literally working out of a garage, who introduce a beneficial new product to the marketplace. Indeed, conservators are usually public companies owned by the shareholders who buy stock in the companies with their savings. It would be unconscionable for these companies to risk innovation. (But what about such blue chip companies as 3M and Johnson & Johnson mentioned earlier? In both instances, the innovators in these companies are set up outside the corporation.)

After an innovation such as a personal computer does gain popularity, then the conservators step in, as IBM did, with their version of the PC. And when they moved in, they took the lion's share of the PC market. But this is a very important point to remember: IBM did not introduce the PC until 1981. As fiercely competitive as the computer business is, Apple was virtually alone in the market for five years! In that span Apple had plenty of time to organize, build up capital, and most important, to develop new products. After IBM stole the lion's share of the PC market, the then-new Macintosh line assured the survival of Apple Computer.

As a side note, study the sales of Apple products at the time IBM stepped in. Did Apples sale drop? Not at all, they skyrocketed! Until someone analyzes this event thoroughly, take my best guess: before IBM stepped in, governments, insurance companies, banks and health care organizations would not dream of buying a personal computer. After IBM blessed the idea, then everyone considered both the Apple and the IBM. 80% chose IBM—but 20% of those who would have never considered a "toy" computer chose Apple. And that 20% represented brand new business, and a huge increase for Apple.

As this paradigm suggests, and to answer the question posed earlier, a start-up importer cannot compete on price. We have neither the capital nor the distribution capability. Competing on price is the role of the large conservator. Competing on design is the role of the small innovator, the competitive advantage of the entrepreneurial, start-up importer. This relationship is symbiotic: it encourages and rewards new product introduction, yet assures the eventual universal access to the products.

If you are like me, and cannot draw a straight line or make a circle, how can you possibly compete on design? As you will see in the chapter on finding products, we innovators need only the idea. The world is flush with excellent designers, all underpaid, and most willing to work on a royalty basis. And, as you will see later, the best legal protection for your product is to have the designer "own" the copyright.

Sourcing Products

Later I will explain the specific steps an importer employs to find a product and to determine the best place in the world to have it made. For purposes of introduction, let's assume we have gone through that process and have found our factory.

The research process will yield names of companies able to make your product. Sometimes the company is the actual factory producing the goods, but usually the company overseas is only an agent representing factories capable of producing your products.

The idea of an agent between the importer and the factory makes many entrepreneurs uneasy. Another middleman adds to expense and makes you less competitive. But agents provide two critical faculties in international trade: bilinguality and red-tape expertise. Agents speak the language of the country of origin and English. Agents fill out the documents required by the government of the country of origin to export goods, and produce the documents required by the United States government to import the goods into the United States.

Bilinguality is a must. Usually factories are expert in production, but are not expert in communicating with the people worldwide for which they produce. Rarely do Americans have competent foreign language abilities, and when they do, it is usually true that the foreigner communicates in English better than the American communicates in the foreign language (two years of college Japanese and two months in Tokyo does not make one "fluent" in Japanese, as is claimed on many resumés). English is used because comprehension is best in English for all parties concerned. Because of agents, it is not important for you to speak a foreign language or hire anyone that does. English is the language of international trade, and it is spoken in virtually every trade center worldwide. Communication by every air traffic controller worldwide is in English (except in Montreal).

Beside bilinguality, the agents prepare documentation. Unz & Company is an East Coast printer that produces government form blanks for the international trade community. Their motto is: "international trade moves on paper."[9] This is apt, and you will learn the critical importance of having the paperwork in order when you experience your first importation. Missing or incorrect documentation can lead to delays, costly bond requirements and even seizure of your merchandise.

If you ask these overseas agents what they charge, they will swear that for you they work for free. Of course this is not true. The agents will get a price from the supplier, add on a commission for their services, and present their own price to you. You will see only the price the agent quotes.

But these agents are not unlike travel agents. Whether you go directly to the airline or to the travel agent, you generally pay the same for the ticket. If the factory had to hire the bilingual and red tape talent, the factory would have to factor in those costs in their price to you.

---

9. The Customs Modernization Act is enabling US Customs to communicate via Electronic Data Interchange, or simply put, you can file your documents via computer with Customs. The costs of such capabilities are dropping to where small businesses may connect. By 2002, all transactions may be paperless.

A final added advantage is the flexibility you enjoy with an agent. If a factory overseas begins to suffer a slip in quality control or some other unforeseen difficulty, an agent can quickly line up an alternative source. You would be hard-pressed to do that yourself, and follow up in a timely manner, and from the US.

Ultimately, it is the importer's goal to make contact and develop a relationship with whomever can best facilitate delivery of the merchandise. It does not matter if this is factory-direct or via an agent.

With the best factory (or agent representing that factory) in the world cooperating, we can now offer the item for sale.

Marketing

A primary concern when starting your company is how you will sell your products. You are free to import and retail, import and sell via mail order, import and sell door-to-door, or import and sell at flea markets. We will explain how to import and wholesale your products.

But first a special word about selling on the internet. The internet first lowered the cost of communication, then lowered the cost of research. To try an internet "pure-play"—that is, a business that is only web-based—is proving nearly impossible. Many of the claims about internet benefits (low cost, easy, part-time) are simply false, and the reality of online promotion efforts makes the medium a sheer money drain. Where once it was held that internet businesses would drive retailers out of business, it is now clear retailers who have some adjunct web activities are the ones surviving, not the pure play internet websites. As a fundamental principle to be viable on the internet as a business, one must offer capabilities that otherwise do not exist. If you can define what that capability might be, then perhaps you have a chance. Mass-customization of educational courses is a capability that did not exist before the advent of the internet. Mass customization occurs when the instructor, who is master of content and delivery and well versed in student needs, develops a course that is mass-customized—that is, tailored to each student.[10]

Why would anyone develop a plan to go where the customers are not? Who is selling music CDs profitably on the web, or furniture or groceries? Even the pornography vendors are not making money. On the other hand, the Wall Street Journal is profitably selling immediate news delivery not otherwise available. And if this is not convincing, consider the fact that as of 4th quarter 1999, less than 1/2% of retail sales took place on the internet. In other words, 99.5% took place the old-fashioned way, through stores. Why sell where it costs more, takes more time, and your customers do not go? If you are not convinced, and simply must sell on the web, then do a search for your products at www.google.com, and find the 3,794 online stores that sell exactly your product. Treat them like customers. Sell to as many of those stores as you can. And in six months, when 3790 have gone out of business, you can study the four remaining stores and discover what makes a successful store, and copy a winner.

Wholesaling (selling to retailers) is the simplest, most effective, easiest to organize and control, lowest in risk and least expensive way to market products in the United States. Survivability is best and the profit and growth potential is best. Importers must be able to buy certain minimum quantities from suppliers overseas, and wholesaling is the most likely way of generating demand at least equal to those minimums.

A business that hopes to import and retail as one at the small business level creates certain schedule and capital conflicts that make such a venture unlikely to succeed. Importing and selling mail order presents unnecessary

---

10. We synthesize: *Forbes ASAP* (February 21, 2000) features a theme of "Voices of the Revolution" in which Jay Walker of Priceline.com is quoted as saying, "At its best, the Internet offers capabilities that don't exist otherwise." (pg. 94) Ken Lay of Enron is also quoted as saying, "The internet is not a gimmick, it provides companies an enormous capability to go directly to the customer and tailor-make the product, moving from mass production to mass customization." (pg. 86)

risk inasmuch as the catalog or advertisement is an up-front expense without any assurance of success. You must also buy your merchandise in advance or run afoul of the federal laws requiring you to deliver goods against a mail order within thirty days or offer the customers their money back.

The trick—the number one rule in fact—is never buy anything without orders in hand to warrant the purchase. Only when we have orders in hand do we commit to an importation of our goods. The details will be covered in the chapter on selling imported products.

The import/wholesale distribution channel chart (Fig. 2) shows how independent sales representatives are tied in to the importer, providing a link between the retailer and the importer. Independent sales representatives ("reps") are private agencies contracted by importers and American manufacturers to offer their products for sale to the representative's customers, the retailers. Reps are independent of you, and they are independent of each other.

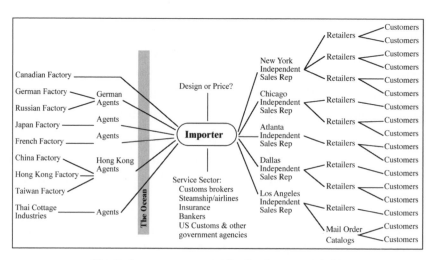

Fig. 2. A common source/distribution network for
importing as a small business

Independent sales representatives tend to cover a geo-demographic region. For instance, you might have an independent sales representative in Los Angeles covering retailers in Arizona and California from the Mexican border to Bakersfield. Another, separate independent sales representative in San Francisco covering from Bakersfield to the Oregon border and Nevada. Still another independent sales representative in Seattle would cover Washington, Oregon, Alaska, Idaho, and Montana. And so on until every major market in the United States is covered. As your company starts up, by working with independent sales representatives, you are able to have your products displayed by professionals in every major market in the United States while you work at your kitchen table.

This marketing structure exists for every industry. Any product you can conceive has a marketing and distribution channel in place now. The independent sales representatives are looking for new products to offer their customers, customers who will in turn become yours. There is no need to reinvent the wheel and develop a way to sell your products. Where to find the very best independent sales representatives for your products and how to work with them will be covered in the chapter on selling your product.

An order is a legally binding contract on the buyer and the seller specifying what goods are to be shipped where on what date. It may include details such as naming by what means the shipment is to be made. The shipment is the fulfillment of that contract, otherwise known as "the sale."

Independent sales representatives gain orders on behalf of the importers and manufacturers by showing the importer's samples. Importers ship directly to the customer, and the customer then pays the importer. The importer pays the independent sales representative a commission on the sales generated against an order, almost always after the sale has taken place, and sometimes after your customer pays you, the importer.

Some Concerns on The Diagram

The importer is at the center of a rather large network of manufacturers, agents, designers, bankers, brokers, government agencies, independent sales representatives and retailers. This structure may first appear formidable, especially when one considers importing as a small business, but keep in mind that all of the people in this diagram have a vested interest in helping you succeed, and none of them are paid until you engage in an actual buy-sell transaction. They are all experts in one part of the picture, and by relying on and working with them you are able to pull together the big picture and realize your goals of importing profitably.

Although you pay no fees to any of these associates until a transaction takes place, once a transaction does take place you will pay them. To earn enough to pay your expenses you mark up the price of the goods you import. Markups vary from industry to industry; in the gift and housewares industry the standard markup is 100% (50% profit margin). If a product costs $ .80 each in Kuala Lumpur, you may pay another $.20 each for shipping, fees, and other assorted costs associated with getting the product into your warehouse ready to ship to your customers. If so, then we say the product has a "landed value of $1.00." If the standard markup in your industry is 100%, then take the landed value of $1.00 and double it to $2.00. The independent sales representatives will offer it in turn to the retailers for $2.00 (wholesale value), and thereby earn their commission when you ship direct to the retailer against the order the representative gained. The commission is a percentage of the wholesale price.[11] The retailer will pay you directly for the merchandise you ship. The retailer, in the gift and housewares product group, will mark the item up at least 100% as well, to $3.95, at least. This is the price at which the ultimate consumer purchases the item.

---

11. Commissions vary from industry to industry. I have seen everything from 2% to 24%. Gift and housewares is 15%, garment 8%. In the chapter on research you will see how to find out what it is for your industry.

You will note a five times progression from first cost to retail (0.80 to $3.95). This is in part the reason prices of products look so cheap overseas. If you were to import the product into the United States and distribute it, you would find that it would go through the same five times progression. The standard distribution channel is always the most efficient, and therefore the least expensive. If there was a more efficient way, somebody would have introduced it and you would be using that way. Innovation in distribution is extremely rare in history. So you have no choice but to use the standard in place and incur the natural costs, costs your competitors incur as well.

The item that costs you a dollar you sell for two dollars. Since one dollar is cost of goods, the other dollar is gross profit. Out of the gross profit you will pay everybody involved, and have a net profit for your efforts. (We will cover this issue in depth in the chapter on costings).

Markups vary from industry to industry, and they are simply a reflection of the costs of doing the particular business. It is the nature of the competitive marketplace that costs and markups are standardized. (To discover the markups used in your industry, you may consult a book carried in every business library called Robert Morris & Associates Guide to Key Business Ratios, or ask other wholesalers).

Profits reflect risk. As a rule of thumb, the more essential the item, the more efficient the distribution channel, the less risk and the lower the markup. The less essential the item, the less efficient the distribution, the more risk involved, and therefore the higher the profit margin. Wheat is essential, it has a tight margin. Flowers are not essential, they have a four hundred percent markup.

Summary

Now that you are familiar with an overview of international trade and the role of the small business importer, let's now discuss the value of the importer. As noted earlier, the importer is in the center of a large network of dedicated professionals, all of whom have a vested interest in helping the importer succeed. An importer's value to the service sector people is easy to see: they earn a fee with each transaction. The designers earn a royalty when designs they created sell. All of these people serve the importer. The interest level of the various players will tend to match yours. By far most important to you are the suppliers and the sales representatives. To gain their cooperation you must be able to communicate your value clearly.

The value you provide to the independent sales representative is that you bring innovative products to the representative. Consumers go to retailers looking for newer and better products; retailers are going to the independent sales representatives looking for the same; and the independent sales representatives turn to the importers and manufacturers for such products.

Store buyers spend about 20% of their time buying 80% of their product, and about 80% of their time buying only 20% of their product. 80% of their products are the old standbys, the perennial products that sell steady and sure, like white T-shirts and penny-loafer shoes. To secure these items, the buyer merely places a reorder. But to remain attractive to their customers, any given retailer must keep updating the product selection with new and different items. Although these are only 20% of their products, it is so difficult to come up with such products that it takes 80% of the buyer's time. Every conversation an independent sales representative engages in eventually comes around to what is new or what is next. As an innovator your value is to provide these products to an eager market.

As an innovator your value is to build markets in the United States for overseas manufacturers. The products may be your designs, but the factory makes money manufacturing your designs and selling them to you. The United States is still the target market for the rest of the world, and although we are only some 1/15th the world's population, we consume over 1/5th of the world's production. You may be a start-up or small company, but even a small company in the United States can generate worthwhile orders for foreign suppliers. The suppliers overseas were recently enough small businesses themselves, if not still, and know well how small businesses can grow if properly conducted.

Too many people feel that starting a small business is somehow a less-than-legitimate occupation, and one must engage in corner-cutting and rule-bending to be successful at the small business level. This is not true, and certainly insulting to the thousands of successful small businesses that are thriving by providing a value. The value small business importers provide is solid and clear. It is critical to your success that you know it and communicate it; it is the basis for your relationships in business. Every conversation or communication with an independent sales representative or customer ought to stress how what you are doing is achieving the goal of new and better products. Every conversation or communication with suppliers overseas ought to stress how what you are doing is achieving the goal of building markets in the United States for your ideas, but products they in fact produce.

By exploiting the excess production, management and credit capacity of foreign manufacturers, the small business importer introduces innovative products with a demonstrable benefit to US retailers eager for newer and better products. The foreign manufacturers are delighted to have a US citizen building markets in the US for their excess capacity. A wide range of service sector people assist and guide you with a view to earning fees on an actual transaction. The actual transactions take place after you have proven a market exists. You are compensated as the transactions multiply.

The details of how to accomplish all of this follow. Next let's look at how to found the company and set up to communicate worldwide.

CHAPTER TWO:

――――――――▼――――――――

ORGANIZING FOR WORLD TRADE

Although money is not necessary to start your business, some people sometimes have a little money set aside for the purpose, and are eager to use it to make some sort of progress. Combine this with the commonly advised strategy of building an image for your company early on, and the natural result is start-ups often waste time and money before they know what business they are in. Until you can name your customers and answer why they will buy from you, spending any amount of money on anything related to the business is a waste.

Before you try to decide what computer to buy, how much space you need, what letterhead style you ought have and any of the other questions that will come up, ask yourself: will this help me gain customers?; If so, how? If you walk into a computer store, because you are starting a business, the help you get will depend on how clear you are about what you need. Do you need a computer at all, yet? As of this writing, you can easily save $100 for each week you wait. More importantly, the longer you wait, the better you can define what you need.

Fig. 3. Bizarro cartoon

An office of some sort, fax machine, fancy business cards, extravagant letter-head and so on does not cause people to buy from you. As you start this business, ultimately it is the quality of your work that people assess to determine whether they will work with you. Although the role and value of the small business importer is important, let's nuance this view with a useful attitude I call "the benefit of your insignificance." As a start-up business, we are insignificant inasmuch nobody knows and nobody cares about our business. If we do the work, it is important; if we don't, someone else will. On the other hand if a natural disaster wiped out the US auto industry one day, no more autos or parts, the disruption would create havoc. But if our business were to disappear off the face of the earth, our customers would fill their shelves with other products. This truth may be dismaying, but there is another side to the same coin. The benefit of your insignificance also means you need not spend any money on looking important, and you may freely gain help from larger competitors.

Everyone has a favorite restaurant that is fairly new, the decor a little haphazard, but popular since the food is so good. These are referred to as "hole-in-the-wall" restaurants. Later these restaurants grow more profitable and then upgrade with linen tablecloths and maybe valet parking. Like the restaurant, make sure your customers will support your efforts before you spend money being fancy.

You must never misrepresent yourself as being any more than you are. The people you will come to meet and admire the most will be the very ones who can spot the real from fake instantly. People will want to help you as a start-up business. We are no threat to the thriving and established. They know what it is to start up and pay your dues. These "elder siblings" in the industry you choose are normally delighted to pass on sales leads, advice and ideas if you honor them with straight talk and plain dealing. If you act like a big shot, there will be little incentive for anyone to help you. The fastest way to get the best people to turn their backs on you is to ask them to sign a non-disclosure agreement. You might as well start out by saying, "I will sue you someday." For reasons I will explain later, no one will steal your new ideas.

On the other hand, even larger competitors will welcome a small but serious effort to join the club. It will be the content of your effort, not any filigree on your image that will make or break you. As someone once said, "your work will speak for itself...don't interrupt."

Stated positively, we save every cent we have for one purpose: gaining customers. A benefit of our insignificance is every time we are faced with an expense, we can ask, "Does this gain us any customers?" As we shall see in this chapter, few expenses are warranted in starting up your company.

Business Incubators

A "business incubator" is some sort of organization the purports to provide the means for small businesses to get the assistance they need to start-up and grow. Often they provide bookkeeping services, photocopy machines, advice, and meeting rooms. I hope the concept of "business incubator" will die out now that dot.com people have proven no amount of money or talent can be directed at a business and incubate it. They are usually nominally free, but they cost too much and promise too much. Perhaps now the massive taxes paid to support such efforts will be returned to the small businesses it is taken from and we can avoid this malinvestment. At any rate, avoid working with anything or anyone who claims to provide "business incubation services." If they had any reasonable success rate they would lead their promotion with any such claim; none do.

Any business incubation services I've ever needed I found at Kinko's copy shops and Office Depot and Starbucks. Bookkeeping services come from the excellent software that is inexpensively offered. All the advice you can stand will come from your customers.

Communications

As you start your business, you will contact overseas suppliers regarding your product. Initially you make contact with overseas companies by mail. Suppliers overseas receive many letters from all over the world seeking production of merchandise. These letters range in potential from serious to ridiculous, and overseas suppliers are adept at separating the serious from the silly. The first test they apply to an inquiry is the letterhead test: does this (your) company look like it has potential to buy from us? Passage or failure of this test depends on how your letterhead looks and what it says. The second test, the content of the letter, will be covered in the chapter on finding the best place in the world to have your product made. For now, let's talk only about how your letterhead looks.

One of the first considerations in starting a business is naming your company. In the '70's there was much written about properly naming your company; whether it was better to be called Bob's Button Company or Advanced Fastening Systems. Image seemed more important than substance.

In naming your company I recommend you use your name, and only your name. At the small business level, your name ought to identify who you are, not what you do. What you do may change over time. My company is simply called John Wiley Spiers Company. The reasons for doing so are many: in international trade, relationship is everything (note the many successful, old-time companies named after the founder). If you put your name on the line, you communicate you plan to live and die by the agreements you make. Overseas, this sense is particularly strong. You apparently plan to do this the rest of your life. You need not file for a fictitious name registration, because you will not be using a fictitious name. When doing research, some information sources (like competitors) are slow to share information with a company with "international" or "import" in the name. Using only your name, you can appear to be anything at anytime. When people see just "Calvin Klein" they know it is a clothing company.

More practically speaking, if you change your mind about what you are doing, you don't have to change your name. For instance, there is a successful import company called Merchant du Vin in Seattle. Anyone would assume that the company is a wine importer, but they would be wrong. Initially the company imported wine, but found far greater success importing beers. Now the company is almost exclusively a beer importer, yet named Merchant du Vin. Having spent a small fortune promoting this brand name, the principals feel stuck with it. They pay extra to explain the name in their Yellow Pages listing.

How about a logo (or trademark) for your company? I believe logos are a waste of time and money. Even if you design your own logo, it usually requires the extra cost of color in printing. Logos in no way enhance your image; no one works with you because of your logo. Often enough, they look silly, and communicate to others that the holder has a poor sense of priorities, inasmuch as money was put into a logo and not into getting customers. Huge corporations, the conservators, may need logos because they are selling to mass markets which include the illiterate or foreigners who make selections based on the trademark (the original use of logos).[12] But a small company communicates value through relationships or not at all.

Certainly, in a sense, image is important, but not in the sense commonly held. Your name should convey who you are, not what you do. What you do may change in time. The "right" image cannot be conveyed with linen paper and fancy logos, or an outlandishly named company.

The rule of thumb for developing letterhead is "less is more." Quotes from Kahlil Gibran and flowers in the margin of your letterhead do nothing for your company. Keep it simple; choose a plain type style and have a typesetter layout your name, address and so on. To create the artwork for a professional letterhead, envelope and business card should cost no more than $30. Printing is variable, but many print shops have package deals. We recommend you select their simplest offering if you go this way.

Cheaper yet is to simply select one of the standard template letterhead styles that come in the word processor of every computer. Within a few minutes you can easily lay out and print off a perfect letterhead.

Use black ink on white paper for your letterhead. The paper ought to be standard size, twenty pound weight. I use the cheapest Office Depot has to offer. No need to use any special lightweight international letterhead. The airmail postage for a letter is charged for the first half ounce—that is, up to three pages of twenty pound weight. Three pages is too much information in a letter overseas, so you might as well use twenty pound weight.

---

12. See *Ogilvy On Advertising* (New York: Vintage Books, 1985): 95.

I assume the reader wants to be as economical as possible to start, so I recommend starting your company out of your house or apartment. In ten-plus years of working out of my home, with my home address on all my business correspondence and in directories, I have yet to have someone show up at my door wanting to do business. The post office does not care if you have the word "company" after your name on the letters addressed to you. Although your street address is listed on your letterhead, nobody overseas (or in the US) knows or cares if the address is in a residential area. If you like, you may use the word "suite" instead of "apartment" in your address. As you will see later, most customers buy through independent sales representatives, not directly with you.

Many people believe they must get a post office box when starting a business. It is a waste of time because you must go to the post office to pick up your mail when the letter carrier would gladly bring it to your home, and it is a waste of money because you must pay rent on a post office box. The letter carrier is delighted to carry your outgoing mail to the post office for you. Remember to spell out the city and state in your address. Use Memphis, Tennessee instead of Memphis, TN. Your potential supplier will try to find you on a map, and not many maps list a place called TN.

Always use "USA" or "United States of America" in your address. You cannot be serious about international trade and forget to mention what country you are from. America is a country of immigrants and many towns in America are named after another one in "the old country."

Also, your contact overseas may know where Los Angeles is, but the foreign mail sorter may not be able to read "Los Angeles." The sorter may only recognize "USA" or "United States of America."

Use your home, private phone number (including area code) and list it on your letterhead and cards. It is permissible to list your home phone on your business stationary, but you may not answer your private line with a company name. There is a heavy fine for doing so, and there are many cases where where the phone company has taken such cases to court and won. Simply answer your private line with your name, eg "John Spiers here." This conveniently matches the name of your company, and if the call is not personal but business, the caller is happy to have reached the owner of the company (as well as the bookkeeper, the janitor, the national sales manager). Also, avoid mentioning the word "company" on your answering machine for the same reason.

Why not just get a business line? A business line will cost at least $40 a month more than a personal line. The only advantage you gain is a listing in the yellow pages. Nobody is going to call you up and ask you to sell them something; you will get orders only by selling yourself or contracting independent sales representatives to do so for you. Instead of paying the phone company $480 a year for a useless Yellow Pages listing, put that $480 into a trip to New York to contract another sales representative. This is a far more effective use of resources. And instead of picking up a new expense, you can now write off part of your home phone as a business expense.

Also, private lines can take advantage of the 5 cents per minute (or less) nationwide long distance; often, flat rates are not available for business lines.

Fax and email are fast becoming the standard method for communicating internationally. By 1990, over 50% of the telephone traffic between Japan and the United States was by fax. Although your first correspondence with an overseas supplier ought to be by letter, subsequent correspondence can be by fax.

If the phone company in your area has "custom ringing," you may have both telephone and fax capability on one line. Custom ringing is a telephone company service that gives a single line telephone two phone numbers. Each phone number has a separate ring pattern. One number dialed will ring two long and one short, and the other will ring two shorts. You can buy a device that can "hear" these rings electronically and direct the calls to the correct device, either fax or telephone. For the purpose of those who want to have both a fax and a telephone on one line, custom ringing allows a person to give one custom ringing number as a phone number and the other as a fax number.

Alternatively, if custom ringing is not available in your area, then you may buy a device that can sort out incoming fax transmissions from voice transmissions and direct the transmission to the correct device. There are many makes of these devices on the market, and they run around $100, but the money you save on installing, taxes and maintaining a second line may be well worth it. Also, your home computer can be easily turned into a fax machine. Do a search on the internet for this topic and it will yield the current options.

Either way, you can still use a telephone answering machine with these devices. Therefore, it is possible (and very economical) to have a fax, phone, and telephone answering machine on one private line.

In some underdeveloped areas of the world, communication is by telex. A telex is a typewriter-like communication device in which you type in a message and it goes out to another such typewriter somewhere else in the world where the message is printed out immediately. It had been a very common communication tool in international trade, but it is being displaced by the use of fax and email. Unfortunately, fax machines depend on telephone service, and there are still vast parts of the world that have poor phone service so the telex is the preferred quick communication device. However, to get a telex set up in your house will probably cost you about $300 installation charge and plus something like $150 a month for the line charge. Visit the website for Western Union (www.westernunion.com) and study their Cablegram options for access to communications via telex from your home, without the equipment.

And currently, displacing all of the above electronic communication devices, is the computer phone, or internet phone. Working with an internet service provider, people with a computer set up with a microphone can call any other such computer and communicate 24 hours per day, seven days per week for the basic $20 per month internet access fee. This of course is mind boggling, but as the cost of doing business goes down, so does the price of material benefits.

We'll talk more about computers in the chapter on organizing the operations.

Licensing

The first thing you need to know about licensing your import business is that there is no such thing as a license to be an importer. No agency—government, private or otherwise—issues a license to be an importer. No one will ever ask to see your license to be an importer because such licenses do not exist. Ironically, a federal license is required to export. A freight forwarder, an export version of the Customs broker, will automatically provide the license if you plan to export.

A "license" is required to *sell* goods, imported or otherwise. A federal license may be required to sell some federally controlled items (for instance, weapons, explosives, drugs, and liquor), but the license is required to deal in the product, whether or not imported. To determine if you need a federal license, a Customs broker will advise you after he has seen your product.

The whole issue of business licensing is actually a misnomer. The "licenses" are in actuality registrations with lawful tax collecting agencies. You are not getting a license to do business, you are registering your business to pay taxes. It is more correct to say, "My business is registered with the state," than, "My business is licensed by the state." For the purposes of this chapter, I'll stay with the term "license" as commonly used. If you already have a business license, you do not need another for this business. When it comes time to report your business activity, you will simply mention these efforts in the same report.

The laws differ from state to state, but most states require any business operating in the state to register with the state, and this means you. Usually this is a matter of simply filling out a form with your name, address and phone number and a description of your business activity. There may or may not be a nominal fee, but some states, like California, want a start-up business to prepay the expected taxes. In this instance, refuse on the grounds that your start-up company will probably not have any revenue the first year while you do your research for the business. This is not only economical, it may be true. Give yourself the benefit of your insignificance.

Why bother getting a state license at all if a forecast lack of revenue obviates the need? A state registration is your ticket into the trade shows in your state for your industry. Such trade shows are closed to the general public. (If there is no state license in your state, then a license with the highest licensing authority, such as the county, is required as proof to enter the trade shows).

Some industries have heavier restrictions on who can enter the trade shows, and may require stronger proof of business activity, such as copies of purchase orders to your benefit or a business checking account. Of course you cannot yet produce purchase orders, but you can get a business checking account, of sorts, good enough for the purpose at hand. Business accounts have hefty fees for activity and bounced checks, etc, whereas personal accounts are lighter in this area. So how to get a business account without the heavy fees associated with it? In your personal supply of checks you have a check reorder slip. Say the new starting number in the upper right hand says "5001." Cross that out and write in its place "10,001." Next, after your name on the check, write the word "Company," and mail it in to the bank. In two weeks what appears to be business checks will arrive, and your problem is solved for about $7.00. Then take the reorder form included with these new checks, cross out the word "company" and replace what will say 10,251 with 5001, and send it to the bank. In about two weeks, you'll have a continuation supply of your personal checks.

You need be licensed only in the state in which your office is located, not in any other state to sell in those states. The states cannot regulate interstate commerce; therefore, simply by demonstrating you are operating out of another state (show a drivers license), you can enter trade shows in other states to do business. In some states, some counties have licensing requirements, although this is unusual.

The most common license is the local (city or town) license. Wait until revenue is coming into your company from the sale of merchandise before you get a local license, since you are not required to do so until then, and the local licenses usually have yearly fees to pay and do not otherwise benefit your company.

There may be zoning restrictions against operating a business in a residential area. Almost all localities have a variance option for those who are operating a business that has no customers coming to the premises, if the address is used only for the bookkeeping and communications. First get the conditions for the variance and then determine if you meet the conditions.

You don't need licenses to be able to write off the expenses of starting up your business. For more information contact a local Certified Public Accountant. Often one- and two-person offices have fair rates and specialize in small businesses. Do not be afraid to seek a license; the more companies on the tax rolls the better from the point of view of the licensing agency. And remember, most states tax revenues regardless of the profits.

Once you are licensed, you will be sent tax forms to report your business activity. How often you report will depend on the size of your company. Perhaps you will get the forms monthly, perhaps quarterly, and for very small companies, perhaps yearly. Naturally, report any sales activity you had, but be sure to report even if you have had no sales activity. You may report zero activity, and you must if you want to keep your license active. Most states assess a fine for failure to file, even if business activity is nil.

When licensing, you must declare the legal structure of your company. Will you operate as a sole proprietor, a partnership (if so, what kind), or perhaps a corporation? People assume they must talk to a lawyer about these concerns, and for conservator companies this may be the case. But it is certainly not the case for the innovative, start-up company.

Protecting Yourself

Some lawyers advise people to incorporate to limit their liability. Although as a legal principle the advice may be sound, as a practical matter the advice is silly. I don't practice law, but I do practice importing and distribution of products, and have done so since 1974. The liability from which you supposedly gain protection by incorporating is generally in two areas: product liability and financial liability.

The courts have held the importers have full product liability on the legal fiction the importer is the manufacturer, simply because no one can sue a foreign company.[13] It is possible to be sued, but as a practical matter, being sued is exceedingly remote for the small business. First and foremost, your company and personal assets are probably too slim to warrant the interest of the kind of lawyers that gain their income from encouraging such suits.[14] Again, there is a benefit to your insignificance. And second, the likelihood that you are going to develop a product that maims or kills is, as you rarely hear lawyers say nowadays, de minimus.

Product liability insurance is a better way of protecting yourself, but this is usually cost-prohibitive for the start-up importer. A friend of mine began importing quartz movement clocks from Japan. After selling small amounts to major customers, the orders began growing tremendously.

---

13. In a family fight, a Mitsubishi television was unwittingly damaged by a thrown bottle of cologne that imperceptibly cracked the screen and doused it with cologne. After the altercation had died down, a woman turned on the television and it exploded, killing her. Mitsubishi of Japan, the manufacturer, was not sued. Mitsubishi of America, the American importer, was sued.

14. "Of the 49 named plaintiffs in Milli Vanilli cases , at least 41 appear to have preexisting relationships with lawyers, most of whom worked at firms specializing in class-action cases." "Class Action Lawyers Brawl Over Big Fees in Milli Vanilli Fraud," *Wall Street Journal* (October 24, 1991): A1.

The risk managers at the department stores demanded the buyers gain proof of insurance coverage from the importer.

The reality of the marketplace demands product liability insurance for the larger thriving company. Even though a department store has no liability for merchandise purchased from an importer, an aggrieved party will name both the importer and the department store in a lawsuit. The hope is the department store will make some sort of settlement out of court, even though there is no liability. Just the cost of extrication from a lawsuit can be daunting. Therefore, stores require popular vendors to have product liability insurance so plaintiffs will have enough money to gain from you, the vendor, leaving the department store out of the suit.

Minimum coverage for a product liability policy is one million dollars. The premiums range tremendously. By not gaining liability insurance for the first few years of your business, you are able to pass the first hurdle in getting liability insurance. The insurance salesperson will ask how long you have been in business, and how many lawsuits have you had for the product. To be able to state you have been in business for three years and have had no lawsuits is of great benefit when the insurance company is considering your premium.

And when you shop for insurance, shop around aggressively. My friends with the quartz clocks were quoted insurance premiums of everywhere from $24,000 down to $210 per year for a million dollars in coverage. In this area, it truly pays to shop.

In the area of financial liability, incorporation will not protect you either. It is the entity that loans you money, such as a bank or supplier, that has the strongest claim on your assets. Phone companies, box sellers, computer vendors are all unsecured creditors. If you go out of business they will certainly attempt to collect from you, but they often find it easier to write off the relatively low amount of your debt than to actually sue. Certainly there are repercussions in not paying these people; you can expect it to be very difficult to get credit in the future or phone service without a deposit if you fail to pay your bills. But these unsecured creditors cannot take your home away, in spite of the fact that collectively the debt you have run up may be substantial.

It is the bank, or in some instances the supplier, that will have the largest amount at stake. But before they lend you dime one they will require that you sign a perfected security agreement, giving themselves first right to all your assets, both company and private. Whether or not you are incorporated, this perfected security agreement, or a UCC filing, allows them to take your personal assets if need be, rendering incorporation useless except for tax reasons. Bankers are not in the business of risk, and they will exercise an "abundance of caution" to see their assets protected.

In summary, the decision whether to be a sole proprietor, corporation or partnership is something you ought to decide with an accountant, given your particular situation, not a lawyer.

Summary

This chapter is more about attitude than information. I get more heated debate on this topic than any other, which I understand completely, since most of it is contrary to what we have learned, and some of it seems self-contradictory. For example, above I argued, "Never misrepresent yourself," and then I go on to instruct you how to contrive from your personal checking account a business checking account.

Two points: what I present here is what I was taught, and learned, from the most successful people I have met. I cannot claim credit for these ideas—I am just passing them on. I found them useful; you can take them or leave them. But before you do, you may perceive a pattern. In international trade, we do not have the benefit of the Uniform Commercial Code of the United States, we only have relationships. Just as lawyers are taught to think like lawyers, we need to learn to think like traders. On one hand we must deal forthrightly; on the other hand, we must be sharp enough to refuse to be taken. I ran a red light in Cancun one night and neither paid the officer directly nor received the ticket from the arresting Mexican police officer.[15] It is not a trick, it is an attitude. On the small point of business checking accounts, there is really no difference in the cost to the banks as far as personal or business checking goes. What is happening is the government dictates the rules to banks on customer relations for personal accounts, but the banks are free to pass on the costs to businesses. It is up to you whether you will play that game.

If we seem particularly impecunious in this chapter, it is because most start-up companies waste valuable resources in precisely the start-up phase. Communications facility is tremendously important when you start out, but it does not have to be fancy or expensive. Simple, clear and inexpensive is always best. Now that we are licensed with the government, and we have what it takes to communicate worldwide, let's do what is most fun: find the best products to sell.

---

15 The common practice of paying a policeman directly has led to much slander of the Mexican system. It is said because police officers are so poorly paid they must take bribes. Although the issues are complex, simply note that under the legal theory dominant in Mexico, a policeman is paid lowly and expected to exercise judgment when issuing tickets. The theory is called subsidiarity. Compare this to the United States where police officers, judges and others are constricted by "mandatory actions" which result in many injustices.

Chapter Three:

▼

Finding the Best Products to Sell

The single, most crucial factor contributing to success in international trade at the small business level is a love for, a passion about, the product or service in which the trader engages. This is contrary to the widely held belief that importing is a matter of going overseas, finding something "cool" that has not yet been imported, and then making a living (or at least paying for travel) by importing the item.

Nor is doing a market study to determine what product is best for you a viable option at the small business level. A market study is a scientific effort that gives a valid and reliable proof that a market exists, and the nature of that market. Such studies require disciplined, highly educated researchers and enormous financial reserves. If the study is not valid and reliable, it is merely anecdotal, and worthless. Conservators hire MBAs to conduct market studies, and this is appropriate to the conservators. At the small business level we simply cannot do a worthwhile market study. But then, a market study is not necessary if the orders we receive for our products are equal to or greater than the minimum production requirements of our suppliers. How we accomplish this we will detail in the chapter on selling your products.

The key to thriving in international trade is drawing on your background to develop products that solve problems. This concept builds on the already mentioned role and value of the small business importer, and understanding this will allow you to develop your company faster, cheaper, and more profitably, while having more fun than otherwise would be possible.

The most exciting part of the business is to bring your products into the marketplace and to receive orders from perfect strangers all over the United States, and even around the world. This is especially gratifying when those products were also your ideas (more or less, as you will see). We must target the right customer, or risk wasting our time and money on efforts that have little or no long term value to us. There is little profit in a one-time deal; real wealth is built on long term relationships and repeat sales.

Product and customers go hand in hand, so we have an added problem of deciding *which* customers to approach. The right product must go to the right customers.

Getting to this point requires you start and follow a certain path. First, I will dispute some commonly held errors in international trade strategy; then outline the advantages of working within your milieu to come up with a product; and third, lay out the concrete steps of how you take a product from an idea to designers, and then to samples ready to market.

The Fantasy of Import Product Selection

Over twenty five years of experience tells me importers thrive when they draw on their interests in developing products; a decade of teaching tells me most novices think they will thrive finding something "cool" overseas to sell in the United States. It is unlikely and unreasonable to either find a product overseas to sell in the United States, or to make cheaper overseas something selling well in the United States, as I mentioned in the first chapter and will demonstrate further. So, we must come up with our own products to sell, just as do all other small importers who grow and thrive.

But can't we just get passionate about something cool we find overseas? No, because being self-employed, we are compensated for the value we provide in the marketplace. If anyone can find something overseas to sell here, everyone can, and will. Your input is low, your risk is low, your profits are low, your likelihood of thriving is low.

The fantasy has two adherents: the wanderer and the opportunist. The wanderer believes he will travel to some exotic location and stumble upon some fascinating product that will sell well in the United States. The opportunist believes he can thrive by simply looking at government trade data on what imported product is hot and profitable and sell that. Certainly people can wander, and certainly people can look up what is hot and profitable, but both of these methods lead nowhere.

How about exploiting trade leads from various sources posted on the internet? Trade leads are usually generated by people who do not have a market and answered by people who do not have a product. Millions are issued, nearly none matter. Serious traders follow the steps we outline in the next chapter. But for now we face the problem: which comes first? The customer or the product?

The problem may have its genesis in an fundamental error as to who the right customer is for an innovative small business. Let's compare Wal-Mart and Gump's. Wal-Mart is well known, and Gump's is a single specialty store in San Francisco.

Large retailers appear to be attractive to a small business since they can place large orders and do eventually pay their bills. What could be simpler than to sell a million dollars worth of some wonderful foreign item to Wal-Mart and earn an easy fifty thousand dollars profit? (Expecting better margins? Good luck!) This is not an uncommon plan, and Wal-Mart is so inundated with requests to consider products that they have a web site devoted to potential vendors.[16]

Before I go any further, let me assure you I am a devotee of Wal-Mart, I know when to shop there and for what, and have relied on the store for some of my most prized possessions. I pity the misunderstanding folk who reject Wal-Mart, and I completely accept the Wal-Mart argument that they improve the standard of living of every community they enter. In essence, since people save money shopping at Wal-Mart, serious money over time, the same customers take their savings and spend those savings in other upscale stores in town. There is no defense against Wal-Mart if as a retailer you try to compete on price; but the reality is small retailers who move up market when Wal-Mart arrives generally thrive in Wal-Mart's shadow.[17]

Having said that, let me say Wal-Mart is an extremely unlikely customer for the small business international trader. So many people approach Wal-Mart as vendors that Wal-Mart has formalized a process for responding.

For new businesses like ours, there is the Wal-Mart Innovation Network (WIN), which is not an invention development or marketing service. To quote from the www.wal-mart.com web site, "WIN services are limited to providing inventors with a commercial feasibility analysis (evaluation) of their invention or new product idea. WIN does not provide research services for its clients, and it does not develop or market inventions for its clients. The responsibility for development, licensing or commercialization is solely that of the inventor/innovator. We do, however, at our option, provide a no-cost referral service to members of the WIN Innovation Network and other sources of management and technical

---

16. Given how web site addresses change, my web site maintains updated links to companies cited here, and at the end of the book you will be provided my web page address, as well as the means to join a "listserv" of past students of mine.

17. The theme is repeated many times in the press; for an example see "The Irrational Antitrust Case Against Wal-Mart," *Wall Street Journal* (October 20, 1993): A15.

assistance." And further, "During the period of 1991 to 1998, WIN provided preliminary evaluations of approximately 4,500 inventions. A recent sample of 400 ideas/inventions/products evaluated by WIN (1/1/99–4/30/99) received the following recommendations:

28% Not Recommended

23% Very limited and cautious development

23% Limited and cautious development

5% Recommended with reservations

12% Recommended for other channels of distribution

8% Recommended for Wal-Mart review

1% Other

This sample contains a significant number of near market-ready products submitted by manufacturers which may cause a positive bias in the data."

So Wal-Mart tells you right up front your chances, assuming you have a good-to-go product, are maybe 8 in 100 that you will even be referred to Wal-Mart for consideration. 92 out of 100 are rejected immediately. That is to say, of 100 new companies wishing to sell to Wal-Mart, 8 are recommended to Wal-Mart. Wal-Mart did not comply with my request for a percentage of how many recommended vendors of those eight are actually selected as vendors. My question after that would be, how many of those eight that are selected as vendors ever turn a profit selling to Wal-Mart.

Wal-Mart helpfully includes this note on their web site:

INVENTOR ALERT: State and federal investigations into abuses in the invention promotion industry continue. It appears that only about 1 in 1,000 inventors make a profit of $1 (one dollar) or more when utilizing the services of invention promotion firms, but pay fees frequently as high as $12,000.

And then, this:

> Many new products are not suitable for review or introduction through large discount/mass merchandise stores. Pursuing improper channels of distribution can lead to serious consequences. Thus, we try to steer you in the right direction. Please refer to paragraph #3 of the Innovation Registration Disclosure page for a summary of recent evaluation results. Results may vary over time depending upon the nature of inventions/innovations submitted to WIN.

I could not agree more, and that is why this book focuses on finding the proper, the very best sales channel for your products. But what does paragraph #3, noted above, say?

> As noted in our Registration & Disclosure forms, the fee for an invention evaluation is $175 in the United States and $195 elsewhere; checks must be in US dollars (the extra $20 covers the cost of air postage outside of the US). The fee for a product assessment is $200 in the U.S. and $220 elsewhere.

See why Wal-Mart is the most successful retailer in history? They will let you pay at least $175.00 for you to find out what they already know, and that is it is extremely unlikely they'd be interested in your product. And further, they will consider foreign supplier's products as well, for $20 more. So the supplier overseas, for whom you are trying to sell his product, can very easily go directly to Wal-Mart. What value would you provide to either the foreign supplier or Wal-Mart selling to Wal-Mart?

Wal-Mart has shelf space that must produce a certain amount of profit or the Wal-Mart mission fails. The most likely candidates for Wal-Mart are items already popular—that, as the Wal-Mart slogan goes, can always be priced less than elsewhere since "We Sell for Less." Kim Carter in Wal-Mart's Supplier Development emailed me this note on 19 July 2000: "In response to your e-mail, no, Wal-Mart is not for every product. We offer products for everyone at the lowest price available. In our Supercenter we offer one stop shopping from Grocery to Automotive to Apparel."

"Products at the lowest price available" implies the product is available elsewhere too, at a higher price. Naturally, well-known items fit the bill. The start-up importer does not have the economies of scale to support the Wal-Mart mission.

Look at the problem from another angle: certainly, million dollar orders from Wal-Mart are not unheard of, although necessarily the item would have to be popular—some sort of commodity item such as a flashlight, jar of peanut butter or a sweatshirt. On a million dollar order, Wal-Mart would be risking time and opportunity cost in hopes you would perform, not to mention advertising dollars spent and whatever other promotional work Wal-Mart might engage in. My guess is Wal-Mart would expect to gain sales of $1.6 million on the one million dollar purchase from you. Since this is a commodity item, you are likely to take perhaps 5% for your trouble, or $50,000.[18] The supplier likely has some $800,000 cost of goods at risk here, and a $150,000 profit. Now think about this scenario: why would the buyer and the seller put so much at risk so you, someone unknown and untested, could earn $50,000? It may seem like a great idea to you, but it makes zero business sense from the perspective of Wal-Mart and your supplier overseas. Too risky, especially when a deal of this size means they can easily find each other without you.

Wal-Mart does allow some latitude for a single store to buy from a vendor, but this rather diminishes the charm of a huge order Wal-Mart might have had in the mind of the entrepreneur. Here is how Wal-Mart states the program:

> Local Purchases Program
>
> If you are interested in becoming a supplier for your locally-based Wal-Mart Store or Supercenter and do not want to distribute product on a national level,

18. Bill Bonner mentions in his dailyreckoning.com online newsletter, "Hussman Econometrics, as reported by Richard Russell, calculated that S&P earnings have grown at an average of 5.7% over the last 40 years." Meaning overall, competition keeps profits within a certain range. Any excess profits are "corrected" by competition.

you then explore/apply to our Local Purchases Program. You may acquire the Local Purchase Supplier Guide at any Wal-Mart store from the Store Manager. This guide includes step-by-step instructions and requirements needed to become a local supplier with Wal-Mart Stores, Inc. Merchandise presented for resale must first be approved at store level and then authorized by a purchasing agent at the Wal-Mart Home Office. All final decisions are made by this agent and if approved, only then would you receive a supplier number.

And although having Costco or Levitz or another of these mass merchandisers as a customer is certainly image-enhancing, it can also be a business killer. I know many start-ups that failed before they could turn a profit because they sold to such mass-merchandisers. And it is not just small businesses: the mighty Kroehler Manufacturing Company, founded in 1892 and once the largest furniture maker in the USA, began selling to Levitz in 1972. Kroehler sales jumped up, but profits dropped, eventually going negative, and by 1983 Kroehler was out of business.[19]

Let's compare that to Gump's (at www.gumps.com). Gump's is a San Francisco-based retailer of fine gifts and housewares. They have one store and a catalog. They sell well known brands such as Baccarat and unknown names such as Carl Rotter. One nice water glass at Gump's might sell in the $150 price range. Some people might view that as expensive, but Gump's is not expensive, when you consider the amazing talent and workmanship that went into the product. As they say, "you couldn't make it for that."

In the history of mankind, those artifacts we consider examples of our finest art and culture are very often produced in very difficult circumstances. In cuisine, the truffle is considered de luxe, but truffles would never have entered our diet if people were not so desperate at one point as to steal food from pigs. Beer, cheese, and popcorn were all mistakes. Lute fisk likewise. Celadon pottery, silk garments. Many other products are created when a problem is perceived and a solution painstakingly created.

---

19. Milton Moskowitz, "The Money Tree: Kroehler Checks Out of Furniture," *San Francisco Chronicle* (September 15, 1983).

Either way, the most appropriate venue to introduce such products, whether discovered accidentally or painstakingly created, is not the Wal-Mart and other huge mass retailers. Gump's is an example of just one store, in one industry, gifts and housewares. There are thousands of such stores across the USA in gifts and housewares. They have counterparts in every other industry: clothing, autos, footwear, foodstuffs, jewelry, skin care and boating. Larry Sands sells $30 million a year worth of eyeglass frames, which run from $300 to $18,000. There are specialty gloves which sell for $2,000. If you can conceive of a product that solves a problem, there is a store that is appropriate for selling the item.

Gump's is a favorite of mine since it is a leader in my industry, but also because of a certain skill they maintain. When exotic items first emerged in history, say celadon, it was the royalty who first enjoyed it. Now such items appear first in stores such as Gump's. And as a practical matter, you might have to expose your risk credit-wise some $100,000 to support a Wal-Mart transaction and yield some $5,000 gross profit; a $10,000 risk from Gump's would normally yield you the same $5,000 gross.

In reality, whether you have sales of $5,000 or $5 million, you will likely make no net profit your first year. The reason is simple. Your first year every cent you make goes to pay for the infrastructure to support the level of sales you enjoy. You must use that income to pay for the computers, training, travel, meals, product development, meeting representatives and so on, seemingly ad infinitum. Although you may have a wonderful time traveling and eating exotic meals, and the tax write-offs are useful, there will be no profits. The profits come in subsequent years when you sell more of the same and allied products through those very same channels, the channels you paid for your first year.

It does not matter if the wanderer can get a product that sells well if one cannot get the makers to redesign the product as the market in the United States demands. All customers demand improvements on all products as they reorder. If you cannot, you customers will dwindle, and all of your work setting up the business will be wasted.

Likewise, the opportunist tries to sell some hot product, and if lucky, the regular distributors will step in and do what they need to do (lower prices) to cut the opportunist out of the market. Can you really expect a business that spent time and money developing a good business to stand by and take no action as you try to step in and scoop up profits from their customers?

In the mid-90's the Iomega Zip Drive was hot. Epson had an apparently identical "zip drive" introduced at $50 less than the Iomega model. Next the Epson zip drive came free with any computer purchase. Talk about competing on price! Obviously, Iomega, the company that introduced the Zip Drive, is still making profits, while Epson is working with razor-thin margins. And so it goes with hot products; unless you introduce the product, it is unlikely you will be profitable.

There is another lesson from the Iomega Zip Drive. It is an imported item, but it was designed in the United States. As a matter of fact almost everything imported into the United States is designed in the United States. Surprising? Let's look at the top three imports, dollar value, by category, of items imported into the United States: office equipment (such as fax machines, computers, scanners, copiers), clothing, and automobiles. You may not be surprised to learn the clothes and Apple Computers imported into the United States are designed here, but you may be surprised that every foreign automobile manufacturer in the world that sells in the United States has design facilities in the United States. The hot selling Mazda Miata was designed in Venice, California by the son of the man who designed the '59 Cadillac. It is axiomatic, if you want to sell it in the United States, it has to be designed here.

Indeed, all the products you think of as "foreign designed" were likely designed especially for the US markets, and likely designed here. The Giorgio Armani suits you get in Milan are not the same as the ones you get in New York, the Seiko watches in Asia are different the Seiko watches sold in the United States[20] (and not just different time zones). Nutella is formulated differently for the US market.

Please don't be disappointed, because as you will see, the reality is far more interesting. But to proceed, not only must office furniture from Italy be designed for the US market, the reverse is true too. I have a friend who exports apple juice to Japan. I teased him for the ease of that job (squeeze the apple, package the juice, and off it goes), and he corrected me: the Japanese prefer a slightly tarter, cloudier apple juice than United States consumers, so he must "redesign" the apple juice for the foreign market. On the other hand, Snapple bombed in Japan in spite of a multi-million dollar ad campaign and cooperation of Japan's top food and beverage retailer. The reason: "(Snapple)...wouldn't change its drinks to suit local tastes."[21]

One can argue importing is the business of studying US consumer complaints; exporting is the business of studying foreign consumer complaints.

But these are major items: furniture, cars, watches. Many readers plan to import native handicrafts, and the "native" aspect is precisely the selling feature. Well, I began as a buyer of native handicrafts. In fact, one of the first companies I ever did face to face negotiations with was one known as CCNPABPIECSB, or China National Native Products and Animal By-products Import Export Corporation, Shanghai Branch. The product I was buying was baskets, a Chinese handicraft for some 5,000 years at least. Although the Chinese workmanship was first-rate, and the materials were beautiful, we redesigned practically every basket for the United States market. The Chinese designs evolved to suit needs in China; they did not

---

20. Wal-Mart imported Seiko watches designed for overseas customers, and Seiko refused to honor warranties. Seiko said watches made for sale outside the U.S. are "of lower quality." *Wall Street Journal* (December 3, 1993): A12.

21. Norihiko Shirouzu, "Snapple in Japan: How a Splash Dried Up," Wall Street Journal (April 15, 1996): B1.

suit needs in the United States. For example, a basket the Chinese used for collecting clams on the seashore we in the United States employed as a planter basket, except it did not fit the common pot sizes in the United States. We redesigned the basket for the United States market. I recall a basket we redesigned to be a single-serving bread basket. This confounded the Chinese—a single serving breadbasket? Did we in the United States not understand the concept of "meal," wherein a group gets together and shares? We assured the Chinese the sample proved popular, and indeed it sold well. Here again was something the Chinese themselves would never have designed.

I am told the Sunni Muslims would never employ the color green in a carpet, because the color is reserved for Allah. On the other hand, the Shi'ite Muslims are more than happy to include the color in carpets for the Western markets.

There are wood carvers in Cameroon that have art books full of various African tribal carvings. You simply dictate the tribe you want represented, the size and motif, and the artists will skillfully reproduce what you like.

A friend of mine designed picture frames and specified stone and coral materials. Although the picture frames were her designs, she was inspired to use the materials mentioned because she saw them employed to attractive effect in furniture. It never occurred to the supplier in the Philippines to use his production capacity to make picture frames, but given the sales to the United States for these frames, he was delighted she thought of it.

Let's take a small diversion to make a profitable point. Let's assume we do travel to some exotic location, say Peru, and wander into a remote, sleepy village that makes the most gorgeous alpaca wool sweaters. The designs are beautiful, the colors attractive, and the prices are, of course, no barrier. Although this village is remote, and has never been approached before, they have seen money and you are able to buy a few dozen of these sweaters.

You return home, using your $400 federal tax exemption[22] at the border to bring the items in duty free, and the leading retailers you approach all applaud your taste and select a few of the sweaters you proffer (I realize this fantasy is getting out of hand, but let's proceed to the point). A month later you call the retailers and ask if they would like more, because if so, you will go back to Peru and get more. The answer is yes the retailers want more—except (and this is the cold reality) they will take more only if the pattern that was on the red sweater is featured in blue. They have new fall colors they want worked into the line; dozens of people tried on the white sweater, but complained of the collar design, so that must be changed. As you see, everything comes back to design, and redesign.

A simple truth in this business is orders mean nothing. You will quickly learn stores throw out test orders like confetti: the only meaningful kind of order is a reorder. This means the retailer's customers liked the product, which means the retailer likes your product.

This is also why you cannot sell candles one year and t-shirts the next year and expect to ever make a living. In essence you would be building one business and abandoning it before it could pay off.

This leads us to the classic problem of the fad. In the mid 1970s a fellow by the name of Gary Dahl imported rocks from Mexico upon which were painted the faces of animals. These were boxed cutely and sold as pets, hence the name "Pet Rock."[23] No one disputes this fellow sold millions of dollars worth of pet rocks in a little less than a year. What people don't realize is Mr. Dahl made no money. He certainly can still get a cup a coffee

---

22. This amount changes occasionally, and from United States Customs website you'll find a section called "Know Before You Go," which outlines current rules for travelers. I recommend it highly.

23. Although the Pet Rock story is an American classic, it needs to be retold here because so many new importers are recent immigrants and have never heard of the Pet Rock. As I relate the story in class, these immigrants eyes grow wide as it dawns on them: if the Pet Rock sells here, just think what they could do!

from someone who wants to hear the story again, but he got no economic gain. Quoting from an article, Mr. Dahl said, "I wish I had all the legal fees back that I spent to trademark the Pet Rock worldwide."[24] Every cent went to paying for an infrastructure, including patents and trademarks, for which there was no continuing market. (Conservators are not beyond fads. For instance in 1994, consumers were treated to items you could see through: Ivory clear dish washing soap, Clearly Canadian soft drink, Crystal Pepsi, Ban Clear deodorant, Palmolive clear dish washing soap, Mennen Crystal Clean deodorant, Rembrandt Mouth Refreshing Rinse, and Miller Clear—a transparent beer!)[25]

Yet people will still argue it can be done. Certainly products are imported into the United States, directly from the host country, and sell well. For example, the board game Trivial Pursuits, Evian water, Godiva chocolates, the wok, Arnott Cookies, and so on. I am sure you can come up with your own examples. In every instance the item was actually spotted by a professional buyer who folded the item into an already existing line of items. For instance, Trivial Pursuit was a hit in Canada for years before it was introduced in the United States—by Selchow Richter, the company that markets the board game Scrabble. And so on through the other items. To assume you can find, in the rare instances it might happen, something cool overseas no on else has spotted is to presume you will beat professional buyers at their own game. Unlikely.

If you visit any swap meet in the United States, you will meet people with quite a lot of clever and inexpensive gadgets imported in bulk from overseas. You may even share the appreciation for the product the importer has, and wonder why especially at these prices, the importer is selling the items in such a miserable venue. Usually these swap meeters bought some product from overseas, off the shelves of the supplier, and tried to sell in

---

24. Josephine Novak, "Consumer Corner" New York Times News Service (date unavailable).

25. Kathleen Deveny, "Anatomy of Fad: How clear Products Were Hot and Then Suddenly Were Not," *Wall Street Journal* (March 15, 1994): B1.

the United States. What they didn't realize is these products have already been sold to saturation in the United States, and there is no longer any profitable market left. Yet the supplier overseas still has a warehouse full, and is only too happy to separate a fool from his money. With the internet, the process has been quickened.

I can take guests on a sad tour of Seattle where people have garages full of unsalable items: one with a load of "Slim Tea" (drink this and lose weight); Indian carpets with no customer; satin gung fu shoes, and so on.

But what about importing antiques? Certainly there cannot be a requirement to design antiques in the USA. This would be an exception to the rule, except...I imported "imitation antique" rugs from China. The rug was woven thinner, using an old pattern and then washed in tea to age the rug. The Chinese weren't trying to fool anyone; these were tagged clearly as to the fact they were imitations, but I saw similar rugs in antique stores being sold as the real McCoy.

Also, in Seattle and other cities, there are antique importers that seem to bring in an endless stream of armoires. After twenty years of watching these items sell, and marveling at the apparent limitless supply of these items from England, I happened to watch an episode of "This Old House," the home remodel show on government television. In this episode, the remodel of a flat in London was the task. At one point the host said, "You Europeans don't use closets like we do, you use furniture—armoires and such. Will you build in closets?" To which the Londoner replied, "No, we'll use furniture, antiques as a matter of fact." The show host suggested that might be rather expensive, but the Londoner assured him, no, and off they all went to the antique factory. Yes, a factory where they make antiques, to your specification. How can this be?

The first antique armoires imported into the United States proved so popular soon there was a shortage. Enterprising Englanders came up with a plan: make armoires out of old and ancient moldings from buildings torn down around England, and use the wood to fashion new "antiques." The wood is old, but the fashioning into furniture of the old wood is current. Therefore molding from a demolished Regency-era building could be made into an "antique" home entertainment center. Now am I not denigrating the legitimate antique importers, which are more akin to art dealers than importers. But "antique" is a loose term, it seems sometimes. The point is, if there is demand in the United States, then the factories will emerge to meet the demand, even for "antiques." And if a factory overseas wants to sell in the United States, then it has to have designs meant for the United States. And, these items enjoy duty-free status under US Customs rules since the chief value is the antique wood, so the items are legitimately imported as "antiques."

Many people try to decide what product will make them rich. The rewards enjoyed by an entrepreneur are in direct relationship to the value provided. One can import jewelry handmade at the seashore and enjoy modest success. One may develop more attractive glassware and retire early. One may invent photocopy machines and grow quite rich. Still another may develop software that makes boring and redundant record keeping simpler, faster, cheaper and more accurate and become a billionaire *toute de suite*. Your monetary success will reflect the value you provide in the marketplace.

It is surprising though how few, if any, successful people began their enterprises with a desire to get rich. Certainly they expected to make money, but the driving motivation for most successful entrepreneurs was the desire to develop and market the product. All of the top players in the computer industry have claimed their success was a surprise to them. The many successful people I have spoken to in international trade echo this. I suspect it is a universal trait.

And while on the topic of fantasies, at my seminars often people will explain how they really intend to eventually import product B, but for now want to import product A, because they can make a killing on product A, and then use the money from product A to begin to import product B. This is nonsense, since efforts required on starting company A are wasted when you begin to import product B. You must be efficient to survive, and it is far better to start with what you truly want to do and build only from there.

How Those Importers Thriving Developed Product

If not from wandering through exotic locations, or from consulting trade data on hot selling imports, what is left? We come back to what historically works, and that is a product proceeding from the founder of the company. The best place to begin when developing a product is with yourself. Most people are initially unaware of it, but there is no richer source for marketable ideas than a field in which you presently work. But how does one come up with an idea? You have already, many times in your life. Let me explain.

"*Why don't they just...?*" You fill in the blank. Have you ever, in your life, been doing something and become frustrated with the less-than-clever process involved? Have you thought of a better way of doing something, or had a better idea? Of course you have, and that is the beginning of the process of coming up with a product that launches your company.

In the mid-1950s a woman who immigrated from Europe went into a pharmacy in Oakland to buy a card for a friend ill in the hospital. She looked at the various offerings and was very disappointed. The woman had an advanced art degree from the Sorbonne, and what was available in the way of greeting cards made her nauseous, especially the sentiments regurgitated on the inside of the card.

"*Why don't they just* put details of public domain Renaissance art on the front of the card and leave the inside blank for someone to write his own sentiments?" The woman and her husband founded Marcel Schurman company to do just that, and the company is still successful, thriving and growing, with the second generation in command. Indeed, they have some 100 retail stores named Papyrus.

Mrs. Fields noticed how everyone loves hot, gooey chocolate chip cookies fresh out of the oven and said "*Why don't they just* bake these in street level stores and sell them this way?"

Roy Raymond founded Victoria's Secret because he was uncomfortable buying lingerie for his wife and designed a store with her targeted to, well, pleasing men.

These are famous examples and I could go on forever relating stories of companies thriving yet of which you've probably never heard: Old World Christmas selling top quality ornaments; Crest selling specially produced dinner ware for private yachts and corporate jets; Chukar Cherry to share with the world the delights of dried cherries; Vandor to get the creativity of US designers marketed on useful everyday items; World Music to promote foreign music distribution in the United States, to name a few.

There is no solution that cannot be improved upon. As you will note with every example, no item is completely new, it is merely an improvement on an existing standard. You must watch for the experience of frustration that causes you to say, "*Why don't they just…,*" and you become "they" and get to work.

The idea likely will not be too revolutionary. In Seattle there is an ice cream company started by the Morse brothers called Fratelli's (Fratelli means brothers in Italian, they wanted an "imported" feel to their name; Haagen Daz is a made-up name by a New Jersey outfit). The Morse brothers were making homemade ice cream and putting ripe summer fruit in it. As you can imagine, it was delicious, which led one to exclaim, "Why don't the ice cream companies just put seasonal fruit in ice cream?" "Why don't we?" replied the other. And so the company was born. As the company grew rapidly, the founders were invited to speak at small business promotion functions. Often after their talks, participants would come up and say, "Fresh fruit in ice cream was my idea, too." The Morse brothers would point out the difference: the Morse brothers put out an effort, they actually did the work. They actually developed a formula, called an ice cream factory, negotiated production of their recipe, worked out the packaging and developed a customer base. The reason some people are successful is because they take the next step after a great idea: they find out what needs to be done. And then they do it. Today the company grows by putting only the freshest candy canes in their ice cream at Christmas, and only the freshest crushed Oreo Cookies in February.

If you are a landscape laborer, then that is the field you ought to observe for possible products. If you are a homemaker, the home is your best bet. If you are a teacher or a dentist, your workplace is ripe for exploiting. Whatever field you are in, opportunities abound for spotting products with tremendous potential.

The Process

On a flight to San Francisco I sat next to a house builder en route to Las Vegas. By specifying a certain type of plumbing fixtures for the homes he built and outperforming his competitors, he won the trip all expense paid (including $500 gambling cash). Eventually we discussed developing products and the house builder made the statement that he did not believe there was any need for product development in his field, because there was no need for change!

I asked if he experienced any problems in his work, and he replied no. I asked him to name the most frustrating event in house building. He thought for a moment and related how, at the end of the construction process, when the building is completed, and the inspectors are signing off the building in authorization of its listing on the market, inevitably the building inspection fails due to a certain problem. The problem, as related by the builder, has to do with the strapping that holds the piping in place under a house inevitably being broken. This occurs when the insulators climb over the pipes in the course of their task and break the strapping. If the strapping is broken, the house will not be approved, and the opportunity to list the house and sell it is delayed.

Delays are costly in the construction business, and so it is critical to avoid this problem. I asked the builder how the problem might be solved. He thought a while, and began to describe a possible product. He recalled a product used by telephone installers, a plastic strapping that ties up loose wires, lines and cables with a one-way securing device. Once the strap is secured, it cannot be loosened; the strap must be cut to free the wires it secures.

The builder considered the possibility of making such strapping larger, and therefore stronger. This would be superior to the metal strapping now in use, therefore would not break so easily, and have the added advantage of being impervious to corrosion that effects metal. Also, the strapping could be manufactured in lengths that matched the length required by the building codes, obviating the need to measure and cut the metal strap. Finally, he recalled how the pipe fitters installing the plumbing and securing it to the beams do this work with a supply of nails between their lips for convenience sake. We laughed at the calamity that might occur if, in the dusty environment of a construction site, a worker were to accidentally suck in the nails in the course of an involuntary sneeze! With this thought in mind, the builder added another feature to his "invention," and that is to have the nails required to install this strapping already manufactured into the strapping. Hence, the formerly tedious process is reduced to simply selecting the "to-code" size strapping, wrap it around the pipe, cinch it up, and drive home the already-in-place nail. This from a fellow who was first sure no changes were needed.

This is an example of the creative process the innovator must employ to "discover" a product. Note the essential steps: 1. Search in your field of expertise, or in your background. 2. Identify a problem experienced by you and others in your field. 3. Develop a product that will solve the problem you and others experience.

This process results in a product that solves problems for other people—a problem that you have discovered, or simply noted, and a product that you have developed. The "problem" is the key. As Peter

Drucker points out, it is in solving problems for others that we provide a value. And unless we provide a value to others, we will not thrive; we will provide no economic value.

Dr. Edwin Land, the inventor and founder of Polaroid-Land Camera said in 1943, "If you are able to state a problem, then the problem can be solved." A problem I see is simply seeing the problem to state. Often we simply overlook problems in our field, because we unconsciously assume the problem "comes with the territory." Part of the creative process is to stand back and see the problems to solve:

> •Warren Miller talks about the development of the ski lift and the work of legendary Howard Head of both ski and tennis fame. The process was arduous but the work rewarding in both compensation and satisfaction.[26]

> •In private conversations with Susan Obermeyer, whose father built the Obermayer winter sportswear company, she related the trials and tribulations of this successful business.

> •Mike Walker developed a means to keep expensive fishing rods afloat if they are dropped in the water.[27]

> •Patty Wetzel, a Texas physician who worked with AIDS patients that others would not touch, was pricked by a needle after drawing blood and tested HIV positive twelve weeks later. Tom Shaw designed a safety syringe that eliminates the risk.[28]

> •The California drought of the late 1980's generated enough new product ideas that the San Francisco Chronicle was able to devote an entire section to the products born of water conservation necessity.[29]

> •The Bowden Spacelander is a single speed bicycle made in Kansas and retails for $4,100 each.[30]

> •Mrs. Grossman's Paper Company has been delighting kids with paper stickers since the late 1970's.

26. Warren Miller, "Thrill of the Hill," *Alaska Airlines Magazine* (February 2000).

27 David Judson, "Inspiration, Opportunity, Invention," *The Seattle Times* (January 25, 1998): F1.

28. Jim Nesbitt, "Safer Needles Available, Rarely Used," *The Seattle Times* (June 9, 1998): A1.

29 Various contributors, "Drought Strategies," *San Francisco Chronicle* (March 24, 1991).

30. Eric Morgenthaler, "Bowden Spacelander," *Wall Street Journal* (June 17, 1994): 1.

The problems to solve can be serious or light, well-known or obscure, but always appreciated by like-minded people.

This is not limited to consumers goods, but applies to agriculture as well. Nearly every item you see in the produce section of a grocery store was designed for optimum sales: Romaine lettuce, Gala apples, Rainier cherries all started out as new designs with small sales and huge profits. Currently Ito of California is pushing "donut peaches," a delicious white-fleshed item which is flat (PLU 3113). The price is normally three times other peaches, but what is common to these new strains is the wonderful flavor. Old stand-bys, such as Red Delicious apples are generally flavorless. Indeed, the methods used to mass produce popular items such as tomatoes renders the item rather bland. The same is true in the flower business—those freesias and roses have no scent because the method used to grow them produces size and color over scent. This led a company called Colorado Paint and Dye to develop a line of aerosol cans of spray-on scents. Now florists commonly spray on rose or carnation or whatever scent on the arrangements as they head out for delivery. It is not unheard of for a mix-up to result in a delivery of roses smelling exactly like Gerber daisies.

Indeed, the introduction of new produce items gave rise to a fruit-marking industry. Check-out clerks, not knowing a Braeburn from a Fuji, would simply charge the lowest price known for apples to keep the line flowing. Thus, stores that had paid extra for special fruit were taking a loss. This led to the introduction of the PLU (price look-up) system in produce sales. Next, marking the fruit with the correct PLU number required the development of machines and their installation in the fruit packing sheds. Finally, the PLU labels themselves have to be designed to be edible since it was likely people would accidentally eat a label affixed to any produce item. And indeed, the labels are an edible vegetable material, and the inks are soy based and nontoxic.

Problem-solving becomes another mental faculty you develop, as a habit. People train their minds to do amazing things, like speak a foreign language, memorize long poems, calculate distances with precision by eye, learn some musician's secrets by watching their hands, listen for a lie, or simply do a magic trick. They all take a learned discipline, and at the small business level there is a habit you must form, and that is the habit of innovating.

You need not become an "inventor" as is commonly understood. You need only learn to spot problems, conceive of a solution, and leave the creative work of putting pen to paper to those with more specific talents, such as designers. We simple 'get in the habit" of observing and spotting problems as we go through our day. As even someone untalented may become expert at Aikido given thirty years experience, so as an innovator you'll improve as you practice constantly. And as you improve, your value in the market increases, and your compensation by the market likewise.

Specifically, as you go through your routine day, begin to challenge in your mind each and every product and process; see if you can conceive a better way. Eventually you will become fecund, and as a practical matter you must limit to your narrow field of expertise the ideas upon which you act. Sure, devise in your mind a better solution to the Mid-East crisis, but if your field is scuba diving, leave the other problems to those in their chosen field.

If getting customers is the most important, finding a product[31] is the most important step in starting your business. You alone must decide what it is that you can develop and bring to market. No one can do this for you. It is utterly creative, and although I can describe the process involved in developing a product, I cannot prescribe the content of the process. Your background, your ingenuity, your effort, your personality and your attitudes will be reflected in the product you develop. You are the content.

Don't be afraid! Everyone knows something,—it is nothing special. You know something everyone else knows, you think of solutions to problems

---

31. Product-or service for that matter. Every point made here referring to a product can be applied to a service. International trade in services, such as banking, education, software development and architectural designs is a huge business, but rarely mentioned.

everyone else thinks of, solutions they would employ if they thought about going into business. Remember the many others who have succeeded. Take neither encouragement nor discouragement from friends and relatives seriously. The customers await: Stanley Marcus, of Neiman Marcus, says, "It's a question of how you get the merchandise you're infatuated with into the hands of people you like."[32]

Sounds rather focused, narrow and personal, doesn't it? And this from one of the world's most successful retailers. You need only risk time, not money. And it's the most fun work you will ever do. Although your present field is the best place to find products, any area you can get passionate about is a good second best field.

With this challenge comes certain advantages. First, working with a problem you have solved, it is unlikely you will find many people getting involved in your product. You will enjoy a virtual monopoly to start, which will allow you to charge that premium price so helpful to the cash flow of a start-up company. As Jerry Garcia of the Grateful Dead said, "It is not enough to be considered the best at what you do, you also want to be considered the only one who does what you do."

Second, you will be excited about your product. This is critical to your success. Unless you can be excited, and have a passion for the product you are involved in, you simply will not do the work required to be successful. You will not do the research, develop the product, visit the customers, meet the service sector people, study the competition, read the trade journals, attend the trade shows, and organize the operations unless there is a very strong desire, a passion for the product driving you. Enthusiasm is contagious, and any lack of enthusiasm will be sensed by everyone with whom you come in contact, and the results will be dismal.

Our accountant called because he had a friend who had a relative who knew the owner of an epoxy glue factory in Korea. On the strength of this

---

32. *Wired* (March 1999): 116.

resource, he wanted to begin the importation and distribution of epoxy glue into the United States. I noted he knew nothing about epoxy glue and advised him of the need to have a passion for the product. He insisted he had "a passion for making money," and "wasn't this enough?" No, because in the long run, he simply would not do what was required to build a successful business.

Trying to start a business without loving the product is like trying to start a car on compression without turning the engine on; you are sure to hit the bottom of the hill but when you do, you won't keep going. No spark.

Another Certified Public Accountant and past participant in one of my seminars recently called me with a question, and in passing mentioned how she saves her client's thousands of dollars on their taxes yet they are reluctant to pay her fees. On the other hand, people gladly fork over $30 for a pair of her handmade potholders. She far more prefers the fun and satisfaction of handmade kitchen items, and she soon hopes to leave tax advising behind.

Dynamic Research and Development

Perhaps you are an avid mountaineer, and you conceive a better climber's ax. It may feature a radio beacon for climbers in distress, and is covered with teflon so ice does not stick to it. Later we will discuss how you find the best place in the world to have such an ax manufactured, but for now let us concern ourselves with product development.

The market is simply those retailers that would buy such an ax, as you have designed, from you, the wholesaler. You must first visualize by name which retailers might carry such an ax in stock. Recreational Equipment, Eddie Bauer or the North Face may come to mind. Before you put pen to paper in designing the item, visit those stores, and when the clerk approaches you and says "May I help you?", you reply, "Yes, I am looking for a climbing ax with a radio beacon and teflon covered so ice will not stick to it."

Listen carefully to the reply. You may be surprised:

"Never heard of such an item."

"We had those five years ago and they were terrible sellers."

"We had those five years ago and they were great sellers, but the company went out of business."

"Sounds like a good idea, but I haven't seen such a product."

"You know, somebody was asking yesterday for the very item."

The clerk's response will tell you how attractive the product might be in the market. Remember, you are speaking to someone who hears from the ultimate consumer all day long, and surely has a better sense of the market than you. A clerk in such a store will likely share your enthusiasm for the outdoors and take an interest in your product. In time you will have gathered a pretty good idea of the value of your product, and the store personnel will inevitably give you reason to modify your ideas based on their experience. In any event you are exercising your value as an innovator by suggesting an innovative product to the retail buyers. Learn the name of the clerk. Eventually you will ask if you can speak to the buyer about this product. Buyers are always willing to speak to customers, although they may be too busy at that given moment. Leave your name and number for the buyer to call you at the buyer's leisure. Repeat this exercise at as many stores as possible—a half-dozen should be enough.

Let me assure you that I do not advocate you mislead the retailer with untrue stories. Do not claim to be an importer, or one who plans to import such an item, during this phase. Go in strictly as a customer at this point. To ask the retailer about the product and return as your understanding and commitment grow is simply prudent. It would be presumptuous to enter a store and declare that you will be importing some advanced-design ice ax. You need to gather quite a bit of information before you can make such a claim credibly. To declare yourself an importer is the end of the process, not the beginning. In time, it will be appropriate to reveal the rest of your plans to the retailer.

A Milestone

And as you improve and clarify the idea, you will return to the stores to discuss the ideas with the buyers. You will be welcome, as long as you are acting on all the previous information the buyer has given you. Regardless of how the conversations go for your product idea, keep pushing the concept and integrating the ideas offered by the retailers, until you get to the point the retailers say, "it is a good idea, but it does not exist."

This is a milestone in your business. You have established in the marketplace, with customers, that the product for which you have a passion, is a good idea and does not exist. If some retailers say so, then all similar retailers will likely say so, all over the country. Now retailers everywhere have an interest in your innovative, problem-solving product. Suppliers overseas who want to build markets in the United States for items they make (although the items are your designs), now have a strong interest in working with you. And so far, you probably haven't spent a penny.

The method of speaking first with retailers is simple and gains you information relating directly to the viability of your product. There is nothing as important as discovering whether there is a market for your idea or product. Without the market assured, any action you take is simply a waste of time. On the other hand, once you have determined a market exists, every action required becomes quite clear and simple. Speaking with retailers is essential work that many people simply put off and instead find something else to do.

Using means I outline in the next chapter, eventually you research the best place in the world to have your product made. You will leverage the interest of the US retailers into samples from the suppliers overseas. Your business proposal to the supplier overseas will be: If you, the supplier, will make us samples of what the retailers in the US say is a good idea and does not exist, we'll take those samples back and determine if there are enough orders in the US to cover your minimum order production run, profitably. Keep in mind you are speaking to the best suppliers—whose product lines that constitute the largest share of sales are always under competitive attack, and who are always looking for newer and better to make in order to stay in business. We offer those factories what they need: designs that are a good idea and do not yet exist for the US market.

You will return to the buyer with the news that you have found a company to make the product overseas, the product those very retailers said was a good idea and did not exist. You have a sample. You will import and distribute the product.[33] Show the buyer your idea, and be ready to ask the following:

1. What are the normal retail price ranges for similar products?
2. What is the normal mark-up? Keystone (An insiders term for 100% markup)?
3. What is the optimum product mix breakdown by percent (e.g., in silver jewelry, what percent of the sales are in earrings vs. bracelets vs. necklaces vs. rings)?
4. What are the trends in motif, function, color, style etc.?
5. What is the key aspect that sells the product? Is it weight, color, price, shape, value?
6. What dollar amount are your normal opening orders (for this kind of store)?
7. What terms and conditions of order are normal?
8. Who else should you speak with?
9. Names of the independent sales representatives most favored by this retailer.
10. Names of the trade shows favored by this retailer. When do they normally place orders?
11. What are some of the common problems that plague this retailer that you could possibly solve or avoid?
12. From what countries does this kind of product seem to come?

---

33. At this point, some people wonder if the supplier and retailer will not simply go around you and work directly. This is not possible for reasons I will lay out in fuller context in chapter six.

This information will be tremendously helpful as you develop your plan to import and distribute your product. And retailers, if you sound worthwhile, are happy to share this information. But before you can find the best place in the world to have your product made, and gain samples to show to the retailers, you must get your designs down on paper to present to your ultimate supplier overseas.

Working with Designers

It is one thing to think up an idea for a product, and quite another to represent the design in some concrete form. Conservators have research and development departments to come up with designs (or appropriate innovators' ideas), or they simply hire one of the engineering and design firms that can be found in the yellow pages of any major city or online. These people are adept at providing conservative, unremarkable solutions to design problems. They know how to develop specifications that will result in simple, inexpensive manufacturing and distribution, and what size, color, capacity, and features will appeal to the broadest possible market.

Innovators have different resources. Starting with their own perceptions of what is needed in the market, and further developed by interactions with the players in the market, the innovator produces designs with one of four methods.

The most likely is just someone you know. The mountain climber who conceives of a better ice ax certainly knows other mountain climbers, and among those friends is one with a talent for design.

For simple one dimensional designs, such as graphics on a coffee mug, you may contact a local art school to gain the names of graphic artists capable of doing such work. Art schools graduate many students each quarter, all very eager to build up their portfolio with as many "professional" assignments as possible. They expect to be paid from $10 an hour and up for such freelance work. One company we know sponsored a competition with a $100 prize for the best design for a clock face. The school announced it to the students, one teacher incorporated the contest into a class assignment, and the company gained over eighty designs for the clock.

For more complicated designs, say a portable cordless telephone headset, the options become more limited. One may approach Bell Laboratories for the designs, but will find cost estimates running in the tens of thousands for the design. A friend of mine who intended to develop a cordless telephone headset came up with a novel approach: he found a master's candidate in electrical engineering at the University of Washington to design his product for him. The designer was remunerated on a royalty basis.

Collectively, University of Washington professors and their research assistants earn hundreds of thousands of dollars each year above their regular salaries. This is true at all universities. Colleges and universities are an excellent source of design talent, particularly for the more sophisticated design problem.

As a last resort, you may conduct a patent search to gain the name of a likely capable designer. Patent searches can now be done very easily on your own for free; there is no need to pay a patent attorney a $300 fee to conduct such a search. Many libraries and colleges have the patent registers on a computer database. You simply type in the name of the product you are interested in, and a list of patents issued for similar products will appear on the screen. By selecting from the information presented on the screen, you will quickly come up with a patent for something similar to your product.

A full patent report will give you information on exactly how the product performs and how to make it. Of course, the point of publishing this information is to prevent you from copying the product. If you were to do so and attempt to sell it, the patent holder might file a lawsuit against you.

If in the unlikely event there exists a patent for a product exactly like the one you thought up, then you must study the patent, do some research in the marketplace to determine how you might improve upon the patented item, and develop an item different enough from the patented item to be innocent of any patent infringement.

More likely you will find patents for items vaguely similar to your idea. Your goal is to make contact with the patent holder (whose name and location is published in the patent gazette) to inquire whether the patent holder will design your product for you. By virtue of the fact the patent holder has gained a patent for products along the lines of what you want to develop, the patent holder is a prime candidate for the job of designing your product.

Contact the patent holder with a proposal to have your design ideas developed. You will find most patent holders are talented designers with little interest in marketing their ideas themselves. They would much rather work up clever designs and leave the commercial exploitation of the idea to merchants, such as yourself.

There is a strong current of competition in this work. Competition means to "strive with" not "fight with." Indeed, there can be no art without competition. The renaissance painters closely viewed each others efforts and tried to outdo each other. Although it is widely held the Beatles and Rolling Stones were in tight competition, the fact is they were good friends. Paul McCartney always saw Brian Wilson of the Beach Boys as the man to beat. Each song introduced by one spurred the other on. The Sergeant Pepper album issued by the Beatles so upset Wilson's plans to create the best rock and roll album ever that he was confined to bed for two years afterwards in deep depression.

The music industry is an excellent one to study for business insight. The problems of costless distribution of property with the internet is naturally falling first to the music industry to solve. John Lennon and Paul McCartney had no idea one could get rich being songwriters; they loved the work and expected compensation came in the form of the parties and the girls, and if their songs were successful, they would be paid for live performances. They signed a contract giving Brian Epstein 25% of the gross, before expenses, having no idea 10%, after expenses, was standard. In any event, they ended up with a good portion when British taxes forced them into an entrepreneurial strategy of issuing stock in their songwriting business and taking untaxed capital gains as profit. Paul McCartney eventually opened a studio for any and all artists to use, and shared tapes of his work in advance with bands as far ranging as the Yardbirds in San Francisco. John and Paul often wrote tunes while thinking in terms of "What would Chuck Berry do?" or "How would Bob Dylan handle this theme?" The intensity of the competition spilled into the engineering arts where designers devised four, then eight track recording devices, and then to sixteen and so on.

Shakespeare's work was so popular new theaters were designed, which allowed for better plays to be staged. Progress goes hand in hand with competition.

Designers are far more than people who put pen to paper, they catch the scent and struggle with the changes and sensibilities. They work on a different level. But they are also in business.

As I started my company, I approached designers in Los Angeles and San Francisco to produce designs for me. In both instances, these remarkably successful designers mentioned an advance payment against royalties of $5000. This means to get the designers to provide me designs, I would pay the fee, and then as the products sold, I would deduct this advance payment against royalties earned. This is a standard practice, but I simply did not have the resources to pay this amount, or anything for that matter. I explained our start-up circumstances, and how I would like to pay, but simply could not. On the other hand, I argued, neither of these artists were designing for glassware presently, and therefore I represented a new source of income. In both instances the designers waived the advance fee requirement.

Once I needed the rights for Popeye the Sailor Man for a specific project, and the nice people at Hearst Corporation's King Features Syndicate in New York required $25,000 up front. Again I explained it was speculative, and since the rights weren't being exercised currently, they just might make money. We stipulated if we did not generate $25,000 in royalties the first year the rights would be lost. King Features agreed. I think the royalties ended up being some $300, and I never expected it to be much more, since I knew the deal was relatively small beforehand. In any event, I earned a few thousands dollars on a fun project.

I know of successful importers that are skilled designers, yet they rarely offer their own designs in the company product line. Having designs and ideas from one source leads to poor performance for a company. Creativity is something that comes and goes with people, and a company that works exclusively with one designer (or just the owner) will find their product lines accepted less and less in the market.

Part of what makes designers tick is the love of the material that constitutes their media. As a tailor might love what he can do with Egyptian cotton, and what Egyptian cotton allows him to do with a shirt idea, so it is with most designers. We do not need to get into specific materials, processes or other details. These are critical to your success, and therefore all the more important that you leave it to the experts. Calvin Klein was remarkably ignorant of how to make clothes, even after years as a designer, and had to be shown by Abe Morenstein, one of the best.[34] You solve the problem, and let the experts "execute the solution." After that, your job is to ever improve and expand.

Recall the need to sell more of the same and new product through the distribution channel you first establish for your business. This is how your company will grow. It is critical therefore to have a constant supply of new ideas. You will get many suggestions for new product from your customers and from your own experience and reflection. A company in California named Taylor & Ng had tremendous success selling woks in the United

---

34. Steven Gaines and Sharon Churcher, *Obsession, The Lives and Times of Calvin Klein* (Avon Books, 1994): 77.

States, and their growth continued as they accessorized the wok. People who bought woks came back to the store to buy wok accessories such as the rings to hold a wok steady on a stove top; drying racks for tempera; spatulas, chef's chopsticks and scouring brushes; cookbooks, sauces and spices. After accessorizing the wok, Taylor & Ng continued to build on their success by offering traditional Chinese tableware: soup bowls, plates, baskets, chopsticks, and ceramic soup spoons.

Ralph Lauren enjoys tremendous success with the thousands of products that carry his label, but he certainly does not sit at a table with pen and paper and design each shirt, coat, sheet and hand bag. Large and small, companies rely on designers for the actual design. Do you believe Pierre Cardin designs the frying pans that bear his signature?

Whether you work with an art school graduate, university faculty experts or professional designers, you will need an agreement as a basis for cooperation and equitable remuneration for the efforts of the designer.

Contracting Designers for Patentable or Copyrightable Products

There is much confusion regarding the value and purpose of patents, copyrights and trademarks. We will present these issues from the point of view of the small business, the innovator.

A patent is issued by the government to an inventor for a set period of time to assure that all rights for the use of the invention belong to the inventor. In essence, the government enforces a monopoly on the idea. Patents are for tangible products, such as a better mousetrap, a typewriter keyboard, a fog machine or some other invention. Gaining a patent is a rather long and expensive process.

From a small business international trade point of view, I object to patents because they demonstrate an error in orientation. It is an error to organize around "protecting rights to an idea" rather than organize around serving customers.

A patent is meant to restrict the market and control the benefit of an idea, by limiting rights to the patent holder. Aside from an obscure moral point regarding limiting access to material benefits unnaturally, there is a practical problem. To gain a patent you must be first to apply, generally, so you must keep your idea secret. How does one promote a secret? This is a contradiction. Would you have everyone you meet sign non-disclosure agreements? You will be laughed out of your customer's stores, and told not to return.

A patent search begins with finding out if someone else has a patent. It does not tell you if the item already exists, and if the item is selling very well right now. And when the report comes back, with assurances there is no patent (including disclaimers mentioning the report could be wrong and in time you may find there is already a patent), you then pay for a process that may gain you a patent for something that already exists. Normally if an item is already selling, this means you cannot get a patent. But some argue it does happen occasionally, so let's go with that, say you do get a patent for something already selling. Why would anyone buy your patented item? Why would any supplier work with you, or any of the other people in the international trade community necessary to get product from supplier to customer? (If you say because they would be forced to, we'll leave it to the next Dante, who did not have patent holders to describe, to wax poetic as to where in hell such people belong.)

By patenting a secret item first, you never get to "hear" from customers what might be done to ever improve you item, and gain more customers. You will never hear what changes in size, weight, shape, color, function material or whatever is necessary to make your product ever better, and ever better serve the customer. Patents suit the criminal mind, not a healthy merchant's mind.

Some six million patents have been issued in the US. Since 1971, 257 better mousetraps have been patented. About one third of the patents issued go to small businesses and individuals, the other two-thirds to the research labs of large corporations.[35] Less than five percent of patented items become products, and almost none of those are ever profitable. On the other hand, of the total sales of all merchandise and goods, almost none are patented items. One could argue the patent system is designed to limit innovation. If there is any correlation at all, it is patented items and failure in the market go hand-in-hand. The argument people make for patents is so removed from reality that I have never even tried to join the club, and the process seems generally a cruel exploitation of the hopes and dreams of people who want a better life. Indeed, there are companies making remarkable money exploiting the idea a patent is good. In a recent article in *Time* magazine, one such company is quoted as saying of the 5,324 clients in a 2 year period, only 11 had made more money than they invested. The average inventor loses $20,000 in these efforts.[36]

A copyright protects the creative work of an artist or writer from copying. You may see a copyright on a designer's dinner plate. The *plate* is not copyrighted, the *design* on the plate is copyrighted (although the plate may be patented in addition to a copyrighted design on the plate). A copyright occurs when pen hits paper, or as the artistic work is created. It is a simple process to have the government certify a copyright, and costs only about $10.00.

A trademark (or logo) is used in commerce by its owner to distinguish his or her goods from those of others. Cabbage Patch Kids and Coleco are trademarks. They are fairly inexpensive to register and can be gained only through use in the market. Trademarks have no value to the small businessperson.[37] Nobody will be looking for your trademark, because nobody knows about your product. If you think you need a trademark so your

---

35. Gannett News Service, *The Seattle Times* (January 25, 1998): F1.

36. "Inventors Beware," *Time* (December 4, 2000). I would cite the page, but apparently the magazine does not bother paging its issues anymore. The end is near.

37. And limited value to the large business, as argued in *Ogilvy On Advertising* (New York: Vintage Books, 1985): 95.

customers can find you to reorder, you are mistaken. If you do not contact your customers directly or through an independent sales representative, the customer will not reorder.

Trademarks are another one of the many diversions that in no way enhance the performance of your company. It is fun to develop a trademark, but it is a waste of time and money. Serious investors and business associates will view your trademark as evidence of a naiveté about business.

The theory behind patents, copyrights and trademarks (collectively referred to as intellectual or intangible property rights) is that an inventor or artist ought to have a certain period of monopoly and non-competition in which to exploit the fruits of the creative process. Intellectual property rights are relatively recent and very Western European in conception (William Shakespeare copyrighted none of his works; it would not occur to him to do so, because no law made such a provision). The concept is abhorrent in Asia, where Confucian ethical imperative demands that good ideas are to be freely exchanged and ought to benefit everyone. The idea of making others pay to use your idea in the Confucian milieu is rude and greedy. This is the basis for much friction in business relationships between the Occident and the Orient.

Even in the West the concept is losing some of its charm. There are some very successful software companies that will give you software free on the condition that if you like it and use it you pay some nominal fee (say $25) to the developer. The concept is called shareware. Many people copy music from the radio (the station pays for the right to play each song) for repeat airings without paying a royalty to the artists. Video piracy was a major fear on the part of movie producers who in time learned that they can make millions in the theaters as well as video rentals. Patents are losing some charm as well. Although my experience is largely with copyrights, I meet many patent holders in my classes that seem to have a jaded view about the value of patents, especially for the small businessperson. Aside from the thousands of dollars it costs to gain a patent, once awarded, the patent may actually harm your business.

For instance, if you have a patent on a very successful and popular item, no one will dare copy the item for fear of a lawsuit. Therefore, they will simply redesign the item and very likely come up with a product that is better than yours. Your item will become obsolete and there will be no more sales. If there were no patent rights held, then your competitors would have simply stolen the idea and sold theirs alongside yours. If your sales were affected, you would experience a decrease naturally, but not a complete cessation.

Nonetheless, the intellectual property laws are apparently useful and generally enforced in the United States, but for huge companies. In the mid-90's Polaroid was awarded over nine hundred million dollars in damages for patent infringement by Kodak. Kodak paid.

But this is strange, since the patent office was formed to protect the little guy; indeed, the first US Patent Examiner was Thomas Jefferson himself, the defender of the little guy. The purpose was to sort out who had first rights to an invention, to keep big powers from stealing the ideas of a little guy. The famous fight between Leibnitz and Newton as to who developed calculus first is an example of ideas developing simultaneously and independently. Darwin is famous for promoting the ideas a man named Blyth worked out first.

Regularly in the papers there are business stories about some small company suing for patent infringement. One such story[38] about a company called Sun Products, Inc. has the usual pattern: Sun invents a headrest for the beach, gets a patent, sells millions, and in 6 years gets knocked off. Instead of finding out what else customers would buy and want, and moving on to another success, Sun Products contacted an attorney. The attorney for the

---

38. Scott Williams, "Sun wins headchair patent suit," *The Seattle Times* (June 11, 1991).

Seattle company actually made it to *federal* court in both Detroit and Washington, D,C, via Denver! The outcome was typical: although Sun Products won a judgment of $4.5 million, the company is down to a handful of employees from twenty at its height, but the company against whom the judgment was won is bankrupt (as is usual). The writer of the article actually said, "But the court time, apparently, was well spent"!

If there are to be any intellectual property rights asserted, do contract designers from outside your company, but do not hold any copyrights, trademarks or patents yourself. Simply put, let the designer hold the intellectual property rights, and in turn license you to manufacture and distribute the items. The designer comes up with the designs against your ideas, and you pay a royalty (a fee) to the designer on each item you sell. If you make money on the item, the designer makes money. If you make no money on the item, the designer makes no money.

This is essentially the arrangement Charles Schultz has with Determined Productions, the San Francisco company that has worldwide license to the Peanuts characters (Snoopy, Charlie Brown, etc.). In this way, any copyright infringement will be dealt with by the designer at his time and expense, and you can avoid the legal problems. Not only multi-million dollar companies operate in this manner, but also start-up companies.

The royalties are anywhere from a few cents an item to ten percent of the gross sales, depending on the industry standards. In the research phase we will see how we can find out about the royalty rates paid for a given industry.

An alternative to paying royalties is to buy the design outright. That is to say you pay the designer some fee up front and the designer has no claim to the intellectual property rights. You have purchased all the rights. Usually you must pay thousands of dollars for the rights, the value of which is unknown until you begin to sell the item, or more accurately, the value is unknown until the item *stops* selling. In effect, whatever you pay up front is the amount you are gambling on the bet that the item is commercially successful. This is an unnecessary risk.

Many people are convinced before they go into the market with an idea that their product is worth millions; therefore, to maximize profit they want to buy the product design rights outright. Why pay a designer tens of thousands of dollars in royalties over time when we can have all the rights for a few thousand now? This is precisely the thinking of people who become overconfident in their products. I believe the risk is not worth the investment; it is not the standard operating procedure for small businesses. Furthermore, it is very beneficial to have your designers get rich designing for you.

If your designer produces an item that is a hit in the marketplace, you and the designer will do very well. As more and more designers become aware of the profit potential of working with your company, you will have more and better designers contacting you with their ideas. A flow of good designs is critical to your success.

And as your renown grows, you can charge the product development costs, cost of samples to the sales representatives, and other direct costs to the designers as an advance against royalties.

Contracting designers need not involve lawyers at the small business level to enjoy the full protection of the law. You and the designer simply write up an agreement between you (the distributor) and the designer covering the following points:

1. The items being licensed (attach pictures or designs to the agreement as "Exhibit A").

2. The amount of the royalty, e.g., 2 cents per item sold, or six percent of the net revenue generated from sales at the wholesale level.

3. When the royalties will be paid. A standard formula is to pay royalties quarterly based on orders invoiced during the respective quarter. Payment is made no later than fifteen days following the end of each quarter.

4. Sales by item are recorded in a computerized bookkeeping system. The designer may inspect the records at any time during normal working hours. Any auditing will be at the designer's expense. Any discrepancies beyond two

percent of what is due the designer will warrant a full and complete audit at the distributor's expense.

5. The designer is licensing the distributor to commercially exploit the designer's creation. Any and all intellectual property rights for items covered in this agreement are retained and protected by the designer.

6. The term of the agreement. The agreement shall continue until canceled by either party giving the other party 180 days notice in writing of the cancellation. In any event of cancellation, the distributor has the right to continue distributing all product for which he has made commitments, until all commitments are fulfilled, including products on order to be manufactured but not yet sold.

7. The effective dates of the agreement.

8. Signatures of both parties.

Item six can also be handled by naming a certain amount of sales. Say it is not worth your while to handle a product that generates less than $20,000 a year in sales. You can then put in an alternative provision for item six keeping the agreement in force as long as the item generates at least $20,000 a year in sales.

As a final note of caution, don't worry too much as to how well the samples turn out. Perfectionism will keep some people from the market. They work on the design hoping to some day have it perfect. Ralph Lauren is known as a clothing designer, but he is a major manufacturer, importer and distributor of clothing and accessories. After changing his name from Ralph Lifshitz (a name with fine connotations in Eastern Europe) to Ralph Lauren, he began his career by fashioning neckties out of upholstery material. The ties were objectively ugly, even by 1967 "everything is beautiful" standards. They did not sell well, but by getting product on the market, and having the market respond, Lauren could come back with ever-improving designs and styles, until he reached the point he is at today—one of the best in the world. Another forgotten aspect of Ralph Lauren is at that time when $25 neckties were the limit, Lauren charged $50 for his.

People tell me in my seminars, "You make it sound easy." My first job is to make it sound clear, and that often means simplifications or exaggerations, like an artist who distorts an image to make the subject clear, or shadows an image in a certain way to the same end.

Also, some instructions are plain enough to state, but if you ever try it yourself you know it is exceptionally hard. "Love your neighbor" is such an example, or better yet, "love your enemy." People expect international trade rules, regulations and compliance, and logistics to be the hardest part, but these are rather easy. The most important thing is the customer in this business, and in any business, and this is theme in this book. Of course, no product (or service), then no customer. So coming up with the right product is critical.

What I teach is to grow a business from a problem you experience, and offer a solution that will please your customers. This is sound in theory and in experience, and in what we see historically in businesses we see that thrive. So far so good.

Here is the rub: those who come to the field with a product in mind, or a resource like a contact overseas, or a desire that focuses on a resource rather than on a customer, tend to run into problems—not in finding a product, which is rather simple in such instances, but finding a customer.

The easier it is to find your product, the harder it is to find a customer. Let me elucidate with an exaggeration. Toblerone chocolate is a brand familiar world-wide. Surely you can find a customer anytime and any-where. And you can get it easy enough, if not directly from the factory, then certainly from one of the multitudinous distributors. Now comes time to find a customer in the USA. Since Toblerone is so easy to come by, competing on price is required, in other words you'll have narrow profit margins. And with narrow margins, volume is required. Now the product was easy to find, but we have to find a customer who will trust us to handle a very big load of chocolate. Proper finance, logistics, handling, etc. must be organized and the product delivered on time, normally within a 24 hour "delivery window." Who will trust us with such a deal? And as we have seen, forget Wal-Mart.

Or, how about the business that proposes to sell native handicrafts—the idea that one might visit a country, buy up samples of various items, bring them back to sell at a trade show. Will this work? Sadly no, even if you try to charge a nice premium price on your items. The reason is that the items are rather easy to find, and therefore you are probably the 10,000th person in the last twenty-five years to bring those exact items to a trade show; and, becoming disenchanted as nothing sells, or sell so little as to never cover the costs of the trade show booth, etc., you quit.

Now, I don't expect people who are excited about the idea they presently have in mind to be persuaded by me. Indeed, I think I am a terrible judge of what sells, hence my complete dependence on the retailers themselves. And since none of the retailers claim to have any idea of what sells either, we all depend on their ability to take small test orders to get us precise feedback from the ultimate consumer.

No matter what your plan, idea, hopes or prayers, at some point you must speak to a customer. You are free to do this first, instead of last. Certainly, the earlier you speak to a customer the better. The customer will dispel all nonsense instantly. They will tell you the truth. No charge. If your product solves a problem and provides a benefit not otherwise available, then the conversation with the retailer will be easy. If it has been done before, or serves no particular purpose, you may find the conversation harder.

Having come up with the idea and gained an initial reaction from the marketplace, as represented by the retailers, to an attractive product, and with that product designed either on paper or in a mock-up stage, you must now begin the intensive process of research and immersion into the culture of the market (or industry) you intend to enter.

CHAPTER FOUR:

▼

THE BEST PLACE IN THE WORLD TO HAVE YOUR PRODUCT MADE

Of the last thousand years of Chinese history, just over half the time China has been ruled by Chinese.[39] The Manchus ruled China from 1644 through 1911 with a remarkable series of long-lived and talented emperors, but in general the Chinese themselves esteemed the arts of poetry, painting and calligraphy, de-emphasizing their historical creativity, since it would merely benefit foreign conquerors. Chinese innovation seemed to cease. The Manchus welcomed foreign arts.

In the 1700s Jesuit missionaries were sent to evangelize China. While the Franciscans are known to serve the poor and down-trodden, the Jesuits tend to minister to the rich and up-trodden. Indeed, starting with Matteo Ricci, Jesuit priests became subjects to the Qing emperors, serving them directly in the imperial courts. In particular, these extremely talented men

---

39. Yuan, 1280–1368; Qing, 1644–1911; Mongolians and Manchurians, respectively.

provided China's elite with access to the best in European science and art, both theoretical, like perspective and tromp l'oeil painting, and the practical such as how to cast cannon.

The Emperor Qianlong wanted the news of a series of battles he won to be broadcast and immortalized and the Jesuits had shown him that great expression of European Art, the engraving. On July 13,1765 the emperor issued a decree that directed paintings of his victories be rendered onto plates of copper. This meant the French would have to execute the work, they being the best in the world, but the copper raw materials would have to come from England, the best source in the world for that. The Kings of both nations would have to give approval to have their artisans put other projects on hold, but the idea of promoting good relations with a Chinese emperor proved irresistible. A purchase order, of sorts, was drawn up by Guiseppe Castiglione, a Jesuit painter, with explicit instructions on how to execute the work. The Chinese in Guangzhou (Canton) who were allowed to trade with the outside world had a complex and strict system which prescribed what Chinese company was allowed to trade with what country. This importation carried serious consequences if it failed. The logistics had to be worked out; to reduce risk of total loss, a system of splitting up the original art for the copper plates onto various vessels was devised, both for the outbound designs and the inbound merchandise.

Recall how it is not so important that we all get rich, as it is that the price of material benefits continues to drop. What once only an emperor could afford to have done, now kids out of college flush with business success have such power—thousands of mini-emperors, so to speak.

Curiously, the French received the order written by Castiglione six months after he had died; nonetheless, the order was executed and the result is still a part of Chinese imperial treasures.[40] Then as now, the financing was the

---

40. *Giuseppe Castiglione, A Jesuit Painter at the Court of Chinese Emperors*, by Cecile and Michel Beurdeley, Chas. Tuttle, 1971.

easiest and last thing to consider. A buyer finds a particular need, sources the best place in the world to have it made, the details are worked out, and the product is delivered. Much has changed in the world of manufacturing and distribution in the last 200 years, but the process is the same: conceive a product, verify a market, find the best source in the world, work out the details. Everything is the same, except far, far more people can do it now, for far, far more customers.

Before we get on track to finding the best place in the world to have your product made, let me explain a very common error in selecting suppliers. Since 1984 people have approached me at my seminars and said, "I have a cousin in Germany," or, "I've been to China a dozen times" or "I speak Portuguese and want to trade with Brazil," or some variation thereof. The common thread is the person has a resource in international trade, and he wants to organize around it. This is contrary to what is required—namely, that you organize around the opportunity, not a resource. To organize around resources is to shift your focus from the needs of the customer to the needs of the factory. That shift in focus will cost you time and money and get you nowhere. It is essential to focus only on the market (the opportunity), and work back from there. Let me give you an example.

A friend of mine imports exotic fruit juice concentrates from Brazil. He does so because he speaks Portuguese (a resource). His business is doing well and he is breaking out beyond the Pacific Northwest market. As his products gain wider and wider market acceptance, of course, he will gain what every entrepreneur fears: competition. The competition won't care where they get the products, so they will do the research to find the best place in the world to have the products made. This research is free and easy, and is the core information in this chapter, but on with the scenario.

Say the research shows Thailand is the best place in the world to have exotic fruit juices made, and the competitors source the product there. What happens when they come into his markets? Of course, with the sourcing advantage they pull the rug out from under his business.

A fundamental step in building your business is to research the best place in the world to have your product made, regardless of where you want to have the product made. If you don't do the research first to find the best place in the world to have your product made, then you cannot get the best made product . If you don't have the best made product, even if it is your design, someone else will do it. If he found Thailand to be the best place in the world, but wanted to trade with Brazil, then he has two options: either import from Thailand, get rich and visit Brazil as often as he likes; or find out why Thailand is the best place in the world for the product and develop a plan to make Brazilian suppliers as good as Thai.

You will need samples to inexpensively prove that the market not only likes your idea, but an example of the idea executed as a sample. This too comes from the best supplier in the world. You are not just seeking a sample, you are seeking a partner, who among other things will be supplying you with samples.

I understand why people want to organize around resources. They want something solid upon which to start. To say you are going to import and you have this great resource (or contact) overseas sounds assuring. But the fact is it generally goes nowhere.

I often meet people who want to import something from a particular place simply because they have relatives there. With research you may discover your friends or relatives overseas are not the best source in the world for your product. Do not worry—as you build markets in the United States you will make very good friends with your overseas suppliers. And you will no doubt find them less troublesome than relatives.

When trade with Viet Nam was opened, I spoke with a Viet Namese restaurateur friend of mine who also imported from China. I expected her to be eager to trade with her home country. "No," she said, "too much work, and they don't really have anything I want to trade." What she wants comes from China, and that is where she will do business.

Speaking of China, I had the pleasure to meet in the early 1980s a college student who had met someone related to a worker in an anchor chain factory in China. This college student was quite convinced with this connection he would be a titan in the anchor chain industry before he graduated. I asked him what he knew about anchor chain. He said he knew nothing. I asked him if he knew who was the biggest distributor of anchor chain in the United States; he did not know. I asked him if he knew who was the largest user of anchor chains in the United States. He did not know. I asked why the largest anchor chain factory in the world was asking him to distribute their products; he said because of his connection. I asked him if he knew that not all anchor chains are equal, that there are some chains not as good as others. He assumed so. I asked him how they got rid of defective anchor chains nobody would buy. He did not know. I believe he found out in good time. He ended up with defective goods.

Another student wanted to import leather garments she designed, but a friend knew someone who had a source in Hong Kong for dirt cheap blank video cassette recorder tapes. The plan was to get rich on VCR tapes, and then invest the money in starting the leather garment business. Again, what do manufacturers do with rejected VCR tapes? Better to just start your leather garment business and get on with it.

Why not just search the new online databases and matching services like www.alibaba.com for potential suppliers? These have always existed, and have always been a waste of time. Putting such services on the web simply allows you to waste time at a higher rate. The problem is serious businesses trade, they do not leave their success to chance. Almost every posting to such matchmaking services is some exporter with no factory talking to some importer with no customer. Nothing happens. And in any case, such muddling about is wasting time when you can gain a laser focus on the best supplier and know the going prices before you even begin.

I mean these as cautionary tales. If you expect to get rich quick, there are people all over the world willing to give you the impression you will, but they charge an awful lot for that impression. And this is not to denigrate traders overseas. There are millions of transactions worldwide, almost all satisfactory, without the protection of law as mentioned before, yet trade just keeps growing. These people in Germany, Taiwan and Korea and so on who are thriving are not getting rich ripping people off. They are getting rich delivering product to specification, on time and at a fair price.

Having pointed out what not to do, let's look at the steps in finding the best place in the world to have your products made.

The National Trade Data Bank (NTDB)

Each and every item imported into the United States is tracked by United States Customs Service. The importer fills out an import declaration, whether the "importer" is a traveler coming back from vacation, someone at the airport to pick up some samples, or someone clearing a container-load of goods at the docks. Imported items fall into categories described in a reference book called the Harmonized Tariff System of the United States. This book also lists any taxes and restrictions on goods, and states how much information must be declared for a given item (weight, quantity, in addition to price). From this book you may learn the Harmonized Tariff System (HTS) classification number for your item. Everything imported is declared to Customs, and the HTS is a guide to proper declarations.

The HTS book is available in many libraries and online, but it can be confusing. Another approach is to look up a listing in the yellow pages for "customs brokers." These are private companies licensed by the government to assist importers. I will tell you more about how Customs brokers help you later, but for now know they will gladly tell you what the HTS number is for your product. If your phone book does not list Customs brokers, then go to the library and get a phone book for the nearest port city, or search the internet for US Customs Service and the HTS.

Call the Customs broker, tell him you are starting a business, and you plan to import (describe your product). Explain for research purposes you need the HTS number for the product. If any Customs broker is not helpful, go on to another.

The import declarations are tallied by the Bureau of the Census, and the information is published in the National Trade Data Bank (NTDB). The NTDB is available online in most city and college libraries free of charge.[41] It is available over the internet as well, for a fee, from the Department of Commerce website.

Wherever you access a copy, by reviewing the importations for your HTS item number, you can learn what country, collectively, all of the US importers of items similar to yours go to buy their products. The best place in the world to buy your products will become clear, regardless of where you would like to buy in your fantasies.

The process of extracting the data from the NTDB is complicated, but they have some easy to follow tutorials that explain it well. You may review these at no cost online at the www.stat-usa.gov website. Expect to spend about two hours reviewing these tutorials to learn how to use this research resource. Once you have extracted the relevant data, you can analyze it with a view to putting your business strategy on solid premises.

Let me start with the finished product, a spreadsheet outlining the best place in the world to have your product made. This is the goal, to learn this fact, so let us start with the goal and later I'll show how we got from the raw data in the NTDB to the goal below. Let us assume that your passion extends to sailboards, and you have come up with a design for a better sailboard.

The first thing we want to determine is if importing sailboards is a growth industry. If more and more is coming in, fine, but if less is coming in each year, then the item may be dying out.

The spreadsheet in Fig. 4 shows in line 5 the last full years reported, columns B through D, and in line 6, dollar amounts for all countries:

---

41. Contact Stat-USA, US Department of Commerce at www.stat-usa.gov

Ranking/ $value	1999	1998	1997	1996
World	$8,024,138	$6,366,494	$5,178,331	$5,558,752

After reviewing the total for the whole world, I break down an analysis by the top six countries and note important trends. Note that not only are dollar amounts of sailboards shown, but units (each) as well. For other items, such as beer, it may report liters imported; for steel, kilos, etc. This is terribly useful information, because it tells you what US importers are paying, collectively, for the item in question. As you begin getting prices from vendors, you will already know, before anyone quotes you a price, what the going price is presently. You will not be in the dark. Not all items have a quantity reported, so getting the price paid from here in those cases will not work. You'll have to discern that from other research we'll do later.

Knowing the price usually paid is always a good idea when entering negotiations. In any event, knowing the price, at the small business level, is not to get a lower price than normal. Expect to pay a premium, maybe ten percent higher than normal for your product. At the small business level, there are extra costs for the supplier. You are not competing on price, and you will be able to build in some extra room in the price of your "price-blind" item.

Now back to our spreadsheet, as it may appear on your computer:

sailboards-Fig.4 (SS)

		FAS Value			Rank/	Units/Number			
Ranking/$ value	1999	1998	1997	1996	QTY	1999	1998	1997	1996
World	$8024138	$6366494	$5178331	$5558752		54114	32520	19777	25115
Increase over 1996	44.35%	14.53%	-6.84%			115.46%	29.48%	-21.25%	
Average Price Paid	$148.28	$195.77	$261.84	$221.33					
Thailand #1	$2851576	$703157	$457799	$222063	#1	5829	1306	681	435
Increase over 1996	1184.13%	216.65%	106.16%			1240.00%	200.23%	56.55%	
% of World Total	35.54%	11.04%	8.84%	3.99%		10.77%	4.02%	3.44%	1.73%
Average Price Paid	$489.21	$538.41	$672.25	$510.49					
France #2	$1171766	$1647890	$828592	$1241204	#3	6598	9688	3405	7955
Increase over 1996	-5.59%	32.77%	-33.24%			82.94%	21.79%	-57.20%	
% of World Total	14.60%	25.88%	16.00%	22.33%		12.19%	29.79%	17.22%	31.67%
Average Price Paid	$177.59	$170.10	$243.35	$156.03					
Germany #3	$971443	$1090601	$1798342	$2317886	#2	3210	4024	8424	8336
Increase over 1996	-58.09%	-52.95%	-22.41%			-61.49%	-51.73%	1.06%	
% of World Total	12.11%	17.13%	34.73%	41.70%		5.93%	12.37%	42.59%	33.19%
Average Price Paid	$302.63	$271.02	$213.48	$278.06					
Austria #4	$852628	$1155335	$1087543	$1109660	#4	1853	2669	4481	4290
Increase over 1996	-23.16%	4.12%	-1.99%			-56.81%	-37.79%	4.45%	
% of World Total	10.63%	18.15%	21.00%	19.96%		3.42%	8.21%	22.66%	17.08%
Average Price Paid	$460.13	$432.87	$242.70	$258.66					
China #5	$815995	$197000	$4563	$20422	#5	7996	3209	83	2099
Increase over 1996	3895.67%	864.65%	-77.66%			280.94%	52.88%	-96.05%	
% of World Total	10.17%	3.09%	0.09%	0.37%		14.78%	9.87%	0.42%	8.36%
Average Price Paid	$102.05	$61.39	$54.98	$9.73					
Taiwan #6	$439495	$359989	$91412	$76559	#6	25231	7162	803	157
Increase over 1996	474.06%	370.21%	19.40%			15970.70%	4461.78%	411.46%	
% of World Total	5.48%	5.65%	1.77%	1.38%		46.63%	22.02%	4.06%	0.63%
Average Price Paid	$17.42	$50.26	$113.84	$487.64					
% Total Represented	89%	81%	82%	90%		94%	86%	90%	93%

Imports, Sailboards, in dollars and units, 1996-99; "Top 6 out of 17" Analysis ©John Wiley Spiers 2000
Source Data: NTDB; USDOC, Census; Trade; Imports

100 Page 1

Fig. 4. NTDB data on sailboards

Notes on analyzing NTDB data

1. If my passion is with sailboards, I will return each year to fill in the new years such as 2000, and 2001.

2. I first consider the world total amounts: is this a growth industry? Are more and more sailboards being imported? In line 6, columns C and B we see indeed importation in dollar amounts are increasing. The dip in column D, for 1997, will be an item for us to research, to learn why. Also, in columns H and G we see importation by unit is increasing as well, with the same dip in quantity in 1997.

3. In line 7, we see the increase expressed as a percentage, each year over the base year of 1996. For the first 18 years in this business, I worked out such analysis with paper and pencil and calculator. (The spreadsheet formulas will be given to you later in the chapter.) If you are not using a spreadsheet, then subtract the ending year total for a country by the beginning year total, then divide that by the beginning year total to arrive at a percentage of increase or decrease. In a spreadsheet this formula is expressed in the cell as "=(B6-E6)/E6." A 44% increase is very healthy business, and in this instance the units imported is growing at a faster pace than the dollar amount imported, so we can conclude the average cost of sailboards imported is decreasing.

4. Indeed, in line 8 we see the average price paid for sailboards collectively by importers, the price has dropped roughly a third over the base year of 1996. Now we know roughly what other importers pay for the product for which we have a passion.

5. The NTDB raw data reports sailboards coming from 17 different countries, but most of them with negligible amounts of exportation to the United States. Therefore, I analyze only the top exporting countries, and in this instance Thailand is number one. This is surprising to me, but very often the raw trade data surprises. From a base of $222,000 in 1996 (cell D10), they make a 1100% increase to $2.8 million in 1999 (cell B10).

Although Germany, France and Austria were the largest suppliers in the world in 1996 in exports of sailboards to the United States, note the data shows they have been losing market share (compare lines 12, 17, 22, 27 and cells B,C, and D).

6. Is Thailand gaining market share of sailboard sales to the United States because theirs are cheaper? Line 13 shows the average price paid by US importers for Thai sailboards is dropping, but they are consistently more expensive than any European sailboard. So much for cheaper prices making a difference! France has cheap sailboards and a steady price; Germany's prices have gone up a little, but are still cheaper than Thai; Austria's prices have gone up considerably, yet they are still cheaper too. Price isn't everything.

7. The United States' #2 source of sailboards is France, where the market share has been something of a roller coaster ride, up and down.

8. Germany and Austria are losing market share as mentioned, and this just may mean that they have sourced their production in Thailand as well, and are slowly getting out of the business. European laws make it difficult to fire workers, so these figures may reflect rules which forbid an otherwise productive employee from being fired. In any event, the research phase later will no doubt shed light on the events causing these changes.

9. China and Taiwan present a bit of a problem. China is enjoying a 3,900% growth with prices rising ten times. The problem is the sailboards from China start at about ten bucks! We may be comparing apples and oranges, because perhaps China sells sailboards that are of poor quality given away as promotional items, or they are actually some sort of toy that is still required to be classified as a sailboard. Another possibility is an importer and exporter are related and the exporter is falsely declaring the value low so the related US importer can bring the goods in and avoid much duty. In this case the importer would pay the full amount directly to the exporter later. Customs has ways of spotting this which is why we may be seeing prices rise, due to enforcement. On the other hand, Taiwan started with $500 boards and are now down to $17 boards! You may also

call a commodity specialist at US Customs and ask them what they think the problem may be. It is possible that the strange numbers are simply the result of data processing keystroke errors.

10. If your research indicates that very little of your product is imported into the United States, compare the amount imported to the amount sold in the US (US Census compiles data on sales by product category). You may discover the product in question is not generally imported because the best place in the world to have the product made is right here in the US. If so, then have it made here and study the possibility of exporting the item!

Research generally yields the answers to questions, but the process usually raises a few more questions. Nonetheless, we now know which country to contact for the names of the best possible suppliers. Before we get to that, let me explain how how we arrive at the spreadsheet we just reviewed.

The spreadsheet is based on information from the NTDB. The raw data upon which the Fig. 4 spreadsheet is based follows, as it appears directly from the NTDB:

Title: Imports-Annual Data for 1999, 1998, 1997 and 1996
ITEM: Value
HS Commodity: 9506214000 Sailboards (No)

TIME	1999	1998	1997	1996
COUNTRY				
World Total	8,024,138	6,366,494	5,178,331	5,558,752
Thailand	2,851,576	703,157	457,799	222,063
France	1,171,766	1,647,890	828,592	1,241,204
Germany	971,443	1,090,601	1,798,342	2,317,886
Austria	852,628	1,155,335	1,087,543	1,109,660
China	815,995	197,000	4,563	20,422
Taiwan	439,495	359,989	91,412	76,559
Switzerland	222,286	339,715	430,389	17,428
Hong Kong	215,611	0	0	16,349
Malaysia	213,170	161,858	0	0

Fig. 5. NTDB Raw data sample: value

Title: Imports-Annual Data for 1999, 1998, 1997 and 1996				
ITEM: Quantity				
HS Commodity: 9506214000 Sailboards (No)				
TIME	1999	1998	1997	1996
COUNTRY				
World Total	54,114	32,520	19,777	25,115
Thailand	5,829	1,306	681	435
France	6,598	9,688	3,405	7,955
Germany	3,210	4,024	8,424	8,336
Austria	1,853	2,669	4,481	4,290
China	7,996	3,209	83	2,099
Taiwan	25,231	7,162	803	157
Switzerland	459	540	605	26
Hong Kong	1,500	0	0	432
Malaysia	606	483	0	0

Fig. 6. NTDB Raw data sample: quantity

There are more countries tracked than I bothered to analyze. The NTDB allows you to reformat the reports to tables useful to you. There are many options. From this document, we will build the spreadsheet. I will show you the formulas so you can work out your figures with paper and pencil, as well as what formula to put in your spreadsheet.

In essence there are just four formulas: three used over and over, and one summary at the end to figure the percent of increase or decrease of importations over the base year I covered above.

We can compute the percent of the world totals of importation into the United States of this item for each country each year, and determine who are the winners and losers in "market share." For this, simply divide the country total by the world total and that will yield the country's percent of the world total, or market share.

Country by country, we can determine the average prices paid for the commodity. (This can be computed only if quantity is reported along with dollar value.) We divide any given year total by the same year's quantity total to yield the average price paid for the item.

Here in Fig. 7 we have what the same formulas look like in a spreadsheet program on the screen of a computer.

Cell D6 shows highlighted how we enter the raw data from the NTDB data, after setting up the headers.

	sailboards import data (SS)					
D6		fx × √	5178331			
	A	B	C	D	E	F
1	Imports, Sailboards, in dollars and units, 1996-99					
2	Top 6 out of 17 — Source Data: NTDB; USDOC, Census; Trade; Imports					
3						
4			FAS Value			Rank/
5	Ranking/$ value	1999	1998	1997	1996	QTY
6	World	$8024138	$6366494	$5178331	$5558752	
7	Increase over 1996	44.35%	14.53%	-6.84%		
8	Average Price Paid	$148.28	$195.77	$261.84	$221.33	
9						
10	Thailand #1	$2851576	$703157	$457799	$222063	#1
11	Increase over 1996	1184.13%	216.65%	106.16%		
12	% of World Total	35.54%	11.04%	8.84%	3.99%	
13	Average Price Paid	$489.21	$538.41	$672.25	$510.49	
14						
15	France #2	$1171766	$1647890	$828592	$1241204	#3
16	Increase over 1996	-5.59%	32.77%	-33.24%		
17	% of World Total	14.60%	25.88%	16.00%	22.33%	
18	Average Price Paid	$177.59	$170.10	$243.35	$156.03	
19						
20	Germany #3	$971443	$1090601	$1798342	$2317886	#2
21	Increase over 1996	-58.09%	-52.95%	-22.41%		

Fig. 7. NTDB Spreadsheet: entering raw data

Then in cell D7 (fig. 8) the formula is entered, as you can see at the top of the window: D7=(D6-E6)/E6. This formula would be in all line 7 cells, and most spreadsheets allow you to write it in one cell and "fill-in" to all other cells.

	A	B	C	D	E	F
	sailboards import data (SS)					
	D7	fx ✕ ✓	=(D6-E6)/E6			
	A	B	C	D	E	F
1	Imports, Sailboards, in dollars and units, 1996-99					
2	Top 6 out of 17 — Source Data: NTDB; USDOC, Census; Trade; Imports					
3						
4			**FAS Value**			Rank/
5	**Ranking/$ value**	**1999**	**1998**	**1997**	**1996**	QTY
6	World	$8024138	$6366494	$5178331	$5558752	
7	Increase over 1996	44.35%	14.53%	-6.84%		
8	Average Price Paid	$148.28	$195.77	$261.84	$221.33	
9						
10	Thailand #1	$2851576	$703157	$457799	$222063	#1
11	Increase over 1996	1184.13%	216.65%	106.16%		
12	% of World Total	35.54%	11.04%	8.84%	3.99%	
13	Average Price Paid	$489.21	$538.41	$672.25	$510.49	
14						
15	France #2	$1171766	$1647890	$828592	$1241204	#3
16	Increase over 1996	-5.59%	32.77%	-33.24%		
17	% of World Total	14.60%	25.88%	16.00%	22.33%	
18	Average Price Paid	$177.59	$170.10	$243.35	$156.03	
19						
20	Germany #3	$971443	$1090601	$1798342	$2317886	#2
21	Increase over 1996	-58.09%	-52.95%	-22.41%		

Fig. 8. NTDB spreadsheet: growth % calculation

In cell D12 (fig. 9) we have the formula for arriving at market share: D12=D10/D6.

	sailboards import data (SS)				
D12	▼ fx ✕ ✓	=D10/D6			
	A	**B**	**C**	**D**	**E**	**F**

	A	B	C	D	E	F
1	Imports, Sailboards, in dollars and units, 1996-99					
2	Top 6 out of 17 — Source Data: NTDB; USDOC, Census; Trade; Imports					
3						
4			**FAS Value**			**Rank/**
5	Ranking/$ value	1999	1998	1997	1996	QTY
6	World	$8024138	$6366494	$5178331	$5558752	
7	Increase over 1996	44.35%	14.53%	-6.84%		
8	Average Price Paid	$148.28	$195.77	$261.84	$221.33	
9						
10	Thailand #1	$285 1576	$703157	$457799	$222063	#1
11	Increase over 1996	1184.13%	216.65%	106.16%		
12	% of World Total	35.54%	11.04%	8.84%	3.99%	
13	Average Price Paid	$489.21	$538.41	$672.25	$510.49	
14						
15	France #2	$1171766	$1647890	$828592	$1241204	#3
16	Increase over 1996	-5.59%	32.77%	-33.24%		
17	% of World Total	14.60%	25.88%	16.00%	22.33%	
18	Average Price Paid	$177.59	$170.10	$243.35	$156.03	
19						
20	Germany #3	$971443	$1090601	$1798342	$2317886	#2
21	Increase over 1996	-58.09%	-52.95%	-22.41%		

| 100 | Page 1 | | |

Fig. 9. NTDB spreadsheet: market share calculation

Having these calculations available also gives you a more professional, serious aspect as you discuss this information with your suppliers overseas. I find them fascinated with the scope and availability of US trade research data.

The average price paid by US importers for a commodity can be figured as we have in cell D13 (fig. 10). To get to the average price paid, just insert the formula D13=D10/I10.

		D	E	F	G	H	I
				=D10/I10			
	A	**D**	**E**	**F**	**G**	**H**	**I**
1	Imports, Sailboards	-99					
2	Top 6 out of 17 — S	C, Census; Trade; Imports					
3							
4		e		**Rank**	**Units/Number**		
5	**Ranking/$ value**	**1997**	**1996**	**QTY**	**1999**	**1998**	**1997**
6	World	$5178331	$5558752		54114	32520	19777
7	Increase over 1996	-6.84%			115.46%	29.48%	-21.25%
8	Average Price Paid	$261.84	$221.33				
9							
10	Thailand #1	$457799	$222063	#1	5829	1306	681
11	Increase over 1996	106.16%			1240.00%	200.23%	56.55%
12	% of World Total	8.84%	3.99%		10.77%	4.02%	3.44%
13	Average Price Paid	$672.25	$510.49				
14							
15	France #2	$828592	$1241204	#3	6598	9688	3405
16	Increase over 1996	-33.24%			82.94%	21.79%	-57.20%
17	% of World Total	16.00%	22.33%		12.19%	29.79%	17.22%
18	Average Price Paid	$243.35	$156.03				
19							
20	Germany #3	$1798342	$2317886	#2	3210	4024	8424
21	Increase over 1996	-22.41%			-61.49%	-51.73%	1.06%

sailboards import data (SS) — D13

Fig. 10. NTDB spreadsheet: average price calculation

And then finally in row 40 (fig. 11), we add up all the percents of world total (market share) from the top countries so we can see what percent of the total are for the few countries we actually review. This formula can be quickly set in place with the "sum" function in you spreadsheet for the first cell, and then filled right to cover the cells in the row.

	sailboards import data (SS)				
D40 ▼ fx × ✓	=SUM(D12+D17+D22+D27+D32+D37)				

	A	B	C	D	E	F
1	Imports, Sailboards, in dollars and units, 1996-99					
2	Top 6 out of 17 — Source Data: NTDB; USDOC, Census; Trade; Imports					
3						
4			FAS Value			Rank/
5	Ranking/$ value	1999	1998	1997	1996	QTY
6	World	$8024138	$6366494	$5178331	$5558752	
7	Increase over 1996	44.35%	14.53%	-6.84%		
8	Average Price Paid	$148.28	$195.77	$261.84	$221.33	
9						
10	Thailand #1	$2851576	$703157	$457799	$222063	#1
11	Increase over 1996	1184.13%	216.65%	106.16%		
12	% of World Total	35.54%	11.04%	8.84%	3.99%	
13	Average Price Paid	$489.21	$538.41	$672.25	$510.49	
35	Taiwan #6	$439495	$359989	$91412	$76559	#6
36	Increase over 1996	474.06%	370.21%	19.40%		
37	% of World Total	5.48%	5.65%	1.77%	1.38%	
38	Average Price Paid	$17.42	$50.26	$113.84	$487.64	
39						
40	% Total Represented	89%	81%	82%	90%	

| 100 | ▄▄✔▥ Page 1 | | ▥ | | ◀ ▶ |

Fig. 11. NTDB spreadsheet: total % of sales calculation

Closing in on the Best Supplier

Earlier in this chapter we left off with having found Thailand to be the best country in the world to have the product made. From here we must work down to the very best supplier in that country. There is no entity in the US, technically, willing and able to give us the name of the best supplier. We must arrive at that through a process of elimination.

Having identified the best country, we now contact representatives of that country. Every country with which the United States does business has an embassy—usually in Washington, D.C., though sometimes in New York. At the embassy there is a commercial attaché whose sole reason for being is to promote the products of that country into the United States. They will welcome your inquiry for products from their country and for the names of suppliers. Most libraries have a directory of embassies, and often you can call the library to get the address for the embassy of the country you have targeted.[42] In other words, a commercial attaché at a foreign embassy helps US importers track down likely suppliers.

The best way to start this process is to write a letter with wording along these lines:

> September 14, 2000
>
> The Commercial Attaché
> Embassy of the Federal Republic of Germany
> 4645 Reservoir Road NW
> Washington, DC 20008
>
> RE: PAPER MODELS
>
> Dear Commercial Attaché,
>
> Our research indicates the demand for paper models of castles, animals, aircraft, etc., is growing rapidly in the United States. According to the United States Commerce Department, Germany is one of the top three suppliers of this product to the United States. The HTS number is 4601 and I've included some sketches to assist in identifying a proper supplier.
>
> Please forward a list of suitable manufacturers of these products so we may contact them directly. Feel free to list our company as an interested party in any trade notices you publish and distribute in Germany.
>
> We look forward to your kind reply.
>
> Sincerely,

Two events will occur when you send out one of these letters. First, the commercial attaché will refer to current trade directories or a computer

---

42. Instead of filling this book with lists of names and addresses that go out of date, I maintain a website (www.johnspiers.com) where you can access links to useful resources.

data base to find the names of the most likely suppliers. These companies are the more famous and more established companies in the country from which you hope to import. The commercial attaché will send you a list of perhaps a dozen or so companies listed as the most likely suppliers.

Second, your inquiry will be distributed in the target country by means of internal trade bulletins which are read by many other manufacturers and agents. These might be companies too small or too new to be listed in trade directories or data bases. You will begin to receive unsolicited offers of product, some of which may be useful. Nonetheless, you will gain the names and addresses of a variety of suppliers, and now you must decide which is the best supplier in the world for you.

But first a technical note: depending on the product and country, a commercial attaché at the embassy may refer you either to a consulate or a trade association instead of helping you directly. A consulate is simply a branch office of an embassy. There is the Italian Embassy in Washington, D.C., and an Italian consulate in San Francisco. The Italians have decentralized the commercial work, so people making inquiries on the West Coast will work with the Italian consulate in San Francisco instead of the Embassy in Washington, D.C. A trade association has no formal ties to a country, but may be handling a portion of the commercial attaché's work. For instance, the German Embassy will refer most inquiries to the German American Chamber of Commerce, which maintains offices in about a dozen cities. If you live in a major city, simply check the white pages for "Consulate of…" to determine if there is a consulate with a commercial section where you live. If not, then contact the embassy. If the embassy refers you to another source for the information you seek, do not be surprised, just write another letter similar to the letter you wrote to the commercial attaché. In any event, whether or not the embassy helps you directly, the embassy is a sure starting point for any search for the names of likely suppliers.

It is useful to keep in contact with whomever ultimately provides you with the information. When you identify a good supplier, write the party who gave you the lead and thank him for the assistance. At least every year or so drop the helper a line, maybe put him on your Christmas card list. Aside from the good manners, memory of you might be useful when your supply country is looking for US partners in trade promotion.

I know of wholesale florists who were provided with thousands of dollars in advertising and prizes, including a luxury free round trip flight to a European capital, to promote a certain country's flowers. This type of cooperation is not uncommon, and you, too, may be able to eventually participate in (or even suggest) such a plan.

So far we have the names of likely suppliers. But before we contact them to see which is the very best, we must do a bit more research.

The Research Interlude

The success of the Harley-Davidson in rebuilding its US markets teaches many lessons (as well as helping make America competitive in the world market). After years of decline, the motorcycle manufacturer was purchased by its employees, who in turn required their management to work up a business plan for revitalizing the company. Having no money to do a market study, the managers simply joined motorcycle clubs to find out why people were buying foreign motorcycles, and not buying American. They discovered motorcyclists were most interested in reliability and styling.

Taking this to heart, Harley-Davidson redesigned their motorcycles to meet these requirements, and are well on the road to recapturing the lion's share of the US motorcycle market for machines over 500 cc in size. Indeed, company officials lobbied Congress to rescind the restrictions and taxes on motorcycles imported from overseas, so Harley-Davidson could "play on a level playing field," that is, give the foreigners the best chance to compete. Harley-Davidson's success has been so good that Indian

Motorcycle Company is scheduled to re-start to match the success of Harley-Davidson.

This story illustrates that simple steps can be taken to learn about your market. To use the phrase borrowed from the Harley-Davidson executives, you must "immerse yourself in the culture of your market." You must begin to gather information to learn what your competitors know. Even though your product is unique, you are still competing for buyer's dollars, hence you have competitors. (Who is a florist's most fearsome competitor? Another florist? No, a chocolate manufacturer, because flowers and chocolates serve the same purpose.)

To immerse yourself is to learn everything the others in the industry know and are aware of. In this way, you are able to discuss intelligently the problems and opportunities available in the industry, and clearly communicate the value you provide to both the buyers and the sellers.

Let us look at a list of points to keep in mind while doing research and immersing yourself in the culture of the market. If these points look suspiciously like points to cover in a business plan, you are right. Eventually you will use this information to write a business plan. Make separate file folders for each of these ten areas; everything you learn can be dropped into one of these folders. The folder contents then become the raw data you will use to write your business plan. Then, when it comes to financing when the banks will not (as a later chapter is titled), it will be easy to write your business plan.

1. Discover what problems exist in the market, or field. Problems are opportunities.

2. Design the product to solve the problem.

3. Define the market. Gift and housewares? Auto parts?

4. Learn the buying process in your market. How do customers order the items?

5. Identify major competitors for your product.

6. Outline your strategy for marketing.

7. Articulate why your product will appeal to the market. Here you will write a

focus statement that spells out the mission of your company, consisting of a brief paragraph or two on your company describing the essence of your value in the marketplace. With this focus statement you can:

    A. Explain the reason consumers will purchase your product.

    B. Convince the retailers to carry your product.

    C. Persuade the independent sales rep of the value of your company.

    D. Demonstrate your knowledge of the market to the suppliers overseas.

    E. Present a position in advocacy of gaining financing from the suppliers overseas.

    F. Write effective, order-generating press releases and ads.

    G. Begin to build your value with the suppliers and the customers.

8. Audit the strengths and weaknesses of your approach.

9. Forecast your potential and detail this in operating plan forecasts and cash-flow projections.

10. Learn the process of buying from overseas.

With these goals in mind, let us begin the process of gathering the information required to immerse ourselves in the culture of the market.

Minimum Research Steps

The importers you observe doing well enjoy a knowledge of the industry in which they operate: the markets, the products and the sources. They are also tied into the information flow regarding their industry, information which contributes to the importer's growth and prosperity. Taking the following fifteen steps will allow you to gather the information outlined above necessary for a reasonable business plan, and educate yourself so that you may carry on useful discussions with customers, suppliers, sales organizations, service sector experts, government agents and competitors.

The best place to conduct this research is in a public library in the business section. Most colleges and universities keep these resources in the library as do most city libraries; if not, the librarians are always willing to advise you on alternative sources. The last step can be performed at most university engineering libraries.

1. *HTS Harmonized Tariff Schedules of the United States*, United States International Trade Commission. This book has the US Customs Service classification for every product imported into the United States along with any tax rates and quota restrictions. You may find it easier to get your product's HTS number from a customs broker as advised earlier, but it might be enlightening for you to review this document while at the library. It is also available online.

2. INFOTRAC. Almost every library in the country is connected to a database information service called INFOTRAC. The service is free, and is simply a computer to which you can walk up and type in a word like "glassware." The computer will scan the database of the hundreds of magazines, newspapers, trade journals and periodicals for the last ten years to find any articles referring to glassware. For some topics like glassware, the computer will reply there are too many articles on glassware. You may then want to type in glassware design, or glassware imports, or glassware pricing, and the computer will display citations for matching articles from the database. Web search engines (such as www.google.com and www.dogpile.com) can also be helpful.

The citations in INFOTRAC note the title, the author, the date, the publication, and a very brief description of the content of the article. From the citation, you can quickly decide if the article serves the purpose of gathering information relating to the ten points outlined above for enhancing your effectiveness in the market.

When you read a citation that interests you, simply push the "print button" on the computer keyboard and the citation will be printed for you.

You may also check through the databases to find out who is writing what about your products, markets and industry. Eventually these experts may be sources of information specific to your project.

3. *Predicasts* (Quarterly): this book lists predictions made about a variety of industries, and is good indicator of how the experts assess the potential for your industry. This is very general information, but it describes well how the whole industry is faring. You look up your product by SIC number (Standardized Industrial Code, Census numbering system). Citations similar to that found in the INFOTRAC are listed.

4. Inter-library Loan: the previous two steps probably yielded you plenty of article citations of interest, but the journal cited may not be readily accessible. In that case, you may ask the librarian to find out which libraries in the country carry the periodical and borrow it from that library for you. There is no charge to you, and every library has a budget for this, especially if the information is to be used starting a business. I have had good luck corresponding directly with the "experts" who wrote the article for more information and clarifications.

If in your research you determine that many of the articles of interest come from one publication, then you certainly ought to subscribe to that publication. This is an effective way of determining the most important periodicals or trade journals for you to be reading.

5. *Business Organizations and Agencies Directory*: look up your industry and review the services provided by the trade associations listed. If the organizations listed appear to be helpful to you, contact them about membership. These organizations are generally repositories of information about your industry. *Encyclopedia of Associations* is another excellent source of information on industry associations. You may wish to join an international association as listed in *World Guide to Trade Associations*.

6.*Directory of U.S. Importers*: listed in this volume by HTS number and alphabetically by state are your competitors, whether you know them or not. Names, addresses, phone numbers, product lines, countries they are dealing with, dollar volume of imports and other useful information are listed in this book, published every year by the *Journal of Commerce*. Write and ask those listed under your HTS number for their catalogs, price lists, and the names of their sales representatives. Although competitors share information readily, this might be too much to ask up front. Therefore, simply write the request on a plain piece of paper stating that you are starting a company, you are interested in their products, and please send the catalog. All of this is true, and from this activity I am on the catalog mailing list of all of my competitors.

After you review the replies of your competitors, call their sales representatives and get any questions regarding size of the company, strengths and weaknesses in the company itself and its product lines, etc., answered. Independent sales representatives are paid by the importers but they work for the retailers. Representatives are constantly on the lookout for new products. Bring your idea to them at this point, and share your ideas. The representative will respond based on their experience with the company upon which you are, in effect, spying. This will be preliminary research; later we will discuss how to find the best representative for your product. Although his information may be valuable, your competitors's representative may not be the best for you.

Your competitors may very likely have websites. Do a Web search to find your competitors online and study their online offerings closely.

Although I developed the technique to scour for more ideas, ironically over time I found myself using the technique to decide what product lines to avoid, rather than what new ideas to exploit. For instance, a few years ago just before iridescent glassware became popular, I began working up a line of such glassware for my company. Before I finished developing this new line, however, I saw in the catalogs of many of my competitors iridescent glassware similar to what I was developing. Obviously I do not want to enter such a crowded field; since then I have been using my competitors' catalogs more to eliminate ideas rather than find inspiration.

7. *Research Centers Directory*: this is a listing of centers for research in every field. People innovating and applying new knowledge in products and markets can be found here. These centers are usually associated

with universities, and although the staffers may be busy, they usually are very helpful.

8. *Thomas Register*: this is a listing of domestic manufacturers and sales representatives of your kind of products in the United States. It is useful to gather as much information as possible on both domestic and import competition. I have found certain categories of glass are best made in the United States, particularly barware. This has led me to exporting US glass, in particular some very good business air freighting drink ware to Switzerland! *Thomas Register* is also available at www.thomasregister.com.

9. *Trade Shows and Professional Exhibits Directory*: in addition to this publication, your earlier journal research will generally refer you to trade shows. Just about every important event in an industry is announced at a trade show. As you read journal articles, you will begin to see a pattern of which trade shows are the major news announcement sources.

10. *Sales and Marketing Management Magazine* publishes a yearly buying power index for the United States, breaking down the relative market strengths around the U.S. This information is critical when preparing credible business plans, and plotting your sales plan in dollars, as we will do later.

11. City and university libraries have a wealth of books written on your industry and products. Read some of the technical works on your products and materials. Librarians will gladly assist you in locating books.

12. At most university engineering libraries you can do a patent search on your own, free of charge. The librarians will instruct you in the correct methods, and usually you need not be a student to use university libraries. By attempting to determine if there is a patent on your idea, you will quickly identify talented designers for your kind of product, as discussed in "Working with Designers" in Chapter 3.

All of these steps require enormous time and effort initially, and then require a few hours a week in order to keep up with the changes in your field. Assuming you are working with a product you enjoy, the research will be enjoyable.

Researching Suppliers

Now that we have a better understanding of the milieu into which we will introduce our product, it is time to directly contact the suppliers within the best country to determine who is the best. Our research has been extensive. Our letterhead looks proper, and retailers say our idea is a good one and it does not exist. A letter similar to the following example is a good opening move:

September 30, 2000

Export Sales Manager
VERLAG J.F. SCHREIBER
Postfach 285
D-7300 Esslingen
Germany

RE: PAPER MODELS OF CASTLES, AIRCRAFT, SHIPS, ANIMALS, ETC.

Dear Sir,

The Commercial Attaché at your Embassy in Washington, D.C. has identified your good company as a leading supplier of paper models to the United States. We have presented our designs to leading retailers (name names) in the United States, and they have affirmed these products will be popular and do not otherwise exist.

Our research indicates the demand for paper models in the United States market is growing rather rapidly. According to the United States Commerce Department, importations of these products have grown over 25% from 1995 through 1999. Germany's share of these importations have grown over 400% in the same period.

We have identified potential markets for paper models, and would like to specialize in products of our own design. Please send us your current catalog and price list, and full information regarding the conditions under which you will produce our special designs.

For our part, we would like to discuss in-depth our strategies, markets, policies, and competition with representatives of your company. Presently we have no plans to visit Germany. Please let us know if you plan to be in the Seattle area. We would be delighted to have a face-to-face meeting with you.

If you feel it would be appropriate, we would be pleased to arrange a showing of your products to leading retailers in the area for their reaction and comments. If we plan carefully, perhaps such a showing could be arranged at one of the regularly scheduled trade shows.

We look forward to your kind reply.

Sincerely,

The letter is in English. It is acceptable to write the letter in the language spoken in the country you are writing to, but only if you are fluent (two years of college language study is not fluent, it is conversational; fluent is when a native speaker does not notice hesitation in the person claiming to be fluent). English is the language of international trade and transportation, so feel free to communicate in English.

The first paragraph of the letter informs the reader where you obtained their name, and they will want to know. It then hits the point they care about: in the US your product design is a good idea and does not exist. Although this sample letter does not do so, you should be specific about listing names of stores that affirmed your product.

In the second paragraph, hit them with numbers, the fruit of your earlier research. None of what you learned will be news to them, but you will establish that you know what they know and you care. This paragraph will distinguish you from the hundreds of letters overseas suppliers receive weekly which have no substance.

The third paragraph explains why you are contacting them. In this introductory letter make clear you want them to produce your designs. There are some companies overseas not interested in this kind of work, and so they will not reply and waste your time.

In the fourth paragraph preempt their offer to have you visit them. Every supplier in the world would love to have you visit them. If you can, certainly do so. But it is not necessary, and if you are financially strapped, save your money for visiting independent sales representatives in this country; don't spend it on a trip to Timbuktu.

It is good to meet with the suppliers. Just as you look forward to regular trips overseas as part of the excitement of the work of international trade, your suppliers look forward to visiting the United States at least once a year, so it is likely they will come here.

I spoke at length once with a tailor with a thriving street-level business in Seattle a few years ago. I understood how he operated: he took measurements of customers, telexed these to Hong Kong tailors with the fabric item numbers, who in turn pretty much completed the suit. The Seattle customer would return a week later for final fitting of the airmail-imported suit and the tailor would have local seamstresses make final adjustments. The tailor surprised me by asking how to find the best source in Hong Kong. Knowing he had been thriving for twenty five years importing suits, I asked how he found his first supplier. His reply, "They found me. I was tailoring when these people from Hong Kong showed me how to make a lot more money with less work. But now, my business partner in Hong Kong is retiring, and his son is an idiot. I won't do business with the boy." I said surely on his travels to Hong Kong he must have met other tailors, and he replied he had never been to Hong Kong. If he traveled, he preferred Europe. Here we have the extreme example of an importer who never visited his suppliers, they always visited him. Customers will come to you.

Although a supplier's itinerary is likely to be New York, Chicago and Los Angeles, they are more than happy to make side trips to visit potential customers. Once I met with a exporter from Thailand in Seattle who mentioned her visit to the United States included business in Los Angeles, Dallas and Spokane. I tried to explain that there were more interesting places in the United States to visit than Spokane, Washington—many, in fact. The Thai explained she had a potential customer to see and naturally visited the town. Upon her return she had nothing but praise for Spokane, which reminded me that people overseas are amazed at what we find interesting in their country, as we are of them in ours.

So preempt their offer for you to visit them if that is appropriate, but certainly offer to them the possibility of visiting you. If they do accept your offer to visit and you are working out of your home, will you hold a world trade power meeting on your dinette in the kitchen? We will consider that in a moment.

In the last paragraph, suggest your strength in the market. Certainly never misrepresent your ability or strength. It should be a simple matter to "arrange a showing to leading retailers in the area." Remember we spoke with the retailer and established an interest and a relationship. If the supplier is coming to town, make an appointment with the retailer for you to host a meeting (preferably in the store) to discuss the product and its US marketability.

Do not concern yourself with the possibility that the retailer will work directly with the supplier and cut you out of the deal. Remember, the retailer is too busy to pursue this project alone and cannot tie up the money necessary to make a minimum purchase from the supplier. The retailer has only one store, or a few stores. Even if the buyer is for a store like Nordstrom, he wants only a few items to test. You are offering a potential market of hundreds of stores to the supplier, because you will develop sales representation eventually covering the entire United States. If the improbable happens and the retailer does go around you, before you finish this chapter you will see how you will make money off that event anyway.

And finally, if a trade show is going on, independent sales representatives (reps) love the extra excitement of a foreign manufacturer in their showroom. This will add to the prestige of the rep, and enhance his image in the eyes of the customers.

Notice that the letter to the potential supplier is rather short. It is important to keep letters to suppliers overseas short. Give them only one or two tasks to do with each piece of correspondence. Overseas suppliers are very busy, and if they receive a letter with many tasks to perform, they will set the letter aside until they have time, which is never. The letter outlined above requires only a catalog and a price list, and standard terms for special design production.

Corresponding By Fax and E-mail

When I began teaching seminars in 1984, I did not mention fax machines because few companies used them and few people had heard of them. By 1986, students were telling me of the newest features and capabilities of fax machines. Rarely does an innovation become so widespread so quickly (although the technology has been available since the late 1800s)!

With the quick expansion of fax use, there has been no definitive etiquette established for communicating by fax. Some protocols have emerged. For instance, many companies use fax "cover sheets." This is the first page of a fax and explains its provenance, the addressee, and the number of pages . The cover sheet evolved because the first fax machines were often unreliable. A sender could be pretty much assured the first page would get through, but after that transmission was rather dicey. Nowadays fax machines are much more reliable so cover sheets are usually unnecessary. If you do send a multi-page document by fax, you may want to mark each page 1/6, 2/6, 3/6…6/6, so the receiver knows what to expect.

Fax machine users all despise receiving sale pitches by fax. Some companies use fax directories to make contact to sell products. These incoming faxes are a waste of sometimes-expensive fax paper, can overload the memory, or block out important faxes because the "junk faxes" use up the fax paper in the machine. (These companies usually transmit at night because long distance charges are cheaper at that time.) For this reason many companies keep their fax numbers secret, and reveal the number only to people with whom they actually do business. All of this is true of e-mail as well.

Therefore, never send an initial inquiry letter by fax or e-mail. It is generally considered rude to communicate by fax if you have not been introduced. Your first letter must be by regular airmail, on standard letterhead.

The methods laid out in this book are very precise in identifying likely suppliers of product. Perhaps only the ten or fifteen most likely suppliers in the world will be contacted. I know of an entrepreneur who "shotgunned" inquiry letters to some 220 companies overseas. This entrepreneur hired a telex and fax service to use instead of buying a fax, and agreed to pay a fee of $2.50 per incoming fax. Approximately 175 companies responded to his inquiry letters by fax, costing him over $400 in fees to the fax service. And not one of the replies was helpful.

Following Up

You will send the letter outlined above to all of the addresses you gain from the commercial attaché, plus addresses from any unsolicited letters generated by the circulation of your inquiry to companies in the target country.

Of the two dozen or so letters you send out, you will be lucky if ten reply. Out of these ten, at least two will be utterly incomprehensible. Out of the remaining eight, a few will be so far removed from what you are doing you will eliminate them. What you are left with is companies that appear to be likely suppliers.

In each of these replies from potential suppliers you will be asked questions that will help the supplier clarify or qualify your interest. The quality of these questions helps you get closer to who is the best supplier. Potential suppliers who ask you technical questions you had not thought of, or offer suggestions on function or material, will impress you favorably. In the few weeks it took your letter to be received and replied to, you too will have come up with more questions and ideas. At this point you continue the correspondence getting deeper and deeper into a relationship with the supplier. Invite them to reply by fax if time becomes a factor for you, and inquire if you may contact them by fax as well.

Eventually you will find that one of the suppliers you are corresponding with is head and shoulders above the others. The interest level, as demonstrated by the quality of the questions and speed with which they reply, and technical capability, as evidenced by the quality of their replies, will recommend the supplier to you.

Please keep in mind, as explained earlier, often importers do not deal with actual factories overseas, but agents that represent those factories. The process we are explaining now may result in the name of a factory, but it is more likely the process will result in the name of an agent representing a factory. It is imperative that this agent be a resident of the country of origin of your goods, otherwise none of the benefits mentioned in the introduction can apply.

It really is no concern to you whether you are working with an agent or dealing directly with the factory. Your only concern is whether or not this entity with which you are corresponding can supply you with samples and eventually product. If that is possible, that is enough.

This correspondence process will naturally take a few months. The initial goal is to gain samples of your product to test market.

A dynamic process of bouncing back and forth between suppliers and retailer, sharing the information each gives you, building your own knowledge and experience, will occur. This improvement in your knowledge and experience allows you to perfect your product idea. When the major points of concern about your products are ironed out, it is time to get samples.

Ask each of the suppliers you are happy with to prepare samples for you (by this time you may be down to one supplier, which is not unusual). By now they will have informed you under what conditions they will produce samples.

It is quite usual to gain samples absolutely free. Even a few hundred dollars in expense to the supplier overseas is a very good gamble when the stakes are breaking into more United States market. Some suppliers will give you three samples free, but charge you for any more than that. Some will give you samples free, but require you to pay the transportation charges. And of course, it is reasonable for the supplier to ask you to pay for the samples and transportation charges, although in my experience this is rare.

Some suppliers will offer hundreds of free samples of your item, if it is a simple plastic gadget you have designed. But they will require $40,000 up front to create the mold for the little plastic gadget. Naturally you do not want to expend that kind of money without first testing the product. In such an event, simply carve the gadget in wood and lacquer it to appear to be plastic for purposes of test marketing.

This is precisely how a very old and successful importing company started. The company was selling boxed matches, and the distinction this company offered was simply the designs on the boxes. The designs were drawn on paper, and then wrapped around a block of wood to look like a set of boxed matches. This was then wrapped in cellophane and put on display at a trade show, where it enjoyed huge success. The admiring customers were discouraged from picking the item up, for fear the ruse would disinterest them in the product.

Technically speaking, samples come in three stages: the mock-up, prototype and production sample. The mock-up, which can be something fashioned by you, gives the general idea. A prototype is produced to exact specification, usually by the factory, although it is probably hand-made and certainly the only sample (also called "one-off"). The production sample is an example taken from a production run of the item. The most likely sample to use to test the market would be a prototype.

About this time you may meet your supplier face to face. If you meet the overseas suppliers in your hometown then you may naturally be concerned about protocol, especially working out of your home. When your suppliers (or potential suppliers) notify you they will be visiting your town, the standard procedure is ask what hotel they are staying at, and then invite them to dinner. You pick them up at the hotel, take them to dinner and pick up the tab.

Over dinner, spend the time getting to know each other: interests, hobbies, sports, theater, politics, whatever you can learn. Dinner is a terrible place to discuss business, because your mouth is full of food. If "the feel" is right, move into the bar after dinner to discuss the business, and if appropriate, hammer out agreements on the ten points mentioned next.

As the waitroid is seating you and your guest(s) at a table in the bar excuse yourself and say you will join them in a minute. When your guests are out of earshot, instruct the bartender that whenever you order a gin and tonic, the bartender is to pour you only the tonic. And whatever your guests order, the bartender is to make them doubles. Then return to your guests, order drinks, and get down to the serious business of hammering out some solid business agreements. (This is precisely what they will do to you overseas).

The following are a few basic elements to discuss with your potential suppliers:

1. The supplier's willingness and ability to produce mock-ups or prototypes of your designs. If they won't do special designs, there is no future with them.

2. The price basis of each order: FOB vs. C&F, and what currency will be used. FOB vs. C&F are technical terms I will cover in detail in the chapter on costings. As to the currency used, the heart of this question is, "Who runs the risk of currency fluctuations?" The answer is the importer. It is always the importer who runs the exchange rate risk, and whether you pay in US Dollars or Lira will be up to the changing needs and strategies of the exporter, your supplier.

Although banks and financial institutions offer many ways of protecting yourself against currency fluctuations, none of their methods are appropriate to the small business. The height of sophistication in this area for the small business is to look at the trends in the currency rates and make a decision based on the best guess as to where the currency is going. For instance, if it is January, you are flush with receipts from Christmas sales, and you are buying products from Spain, then you read the Wall Street Journal and talk to your banker about "where the peseta is going." If the peseta is getting more expensive, buy it now so when you are ready to buy more Spanish products in June you can pay for them with old, cheaper pesetas. If the peseta is getting cheaper, hang on to your dollars until the last minute. Any larger bank can accommodate your requirement for a peseta bank account, as well as most other currencies.

3. The minimum order your supplier will sell to you. How few will they sell? You need to know the minimum because you must forecast how long it will take you to gain enough orders to warrant a minimum order from the supplier. If the minimum is two thousand pieces of an item, and you feel you will gain orders for one hundred per week, then you will be taking orders for twenty weeks (five months before you will place your order). This kind of delay will have to be mentioned to your potential customers. While it may lead to customers declining to order, retailers are generally willing to wait longer for new products. The retailers rarely place significant opening orders for new products anyway; the order to you may be for only a few hundred dollars. These orders, when gained from many retailers add up to the minimum required by the supplier, so they are very important to you, but to each retailer they are not important orders.

Also, minimums are flexible. Often a minimum order reflects minimum materials purchases the supplier overseas is facing. Therefore, on a coffee mug with a decal design, the minimum might be 1,200 mugs. Initially, you may only need 300 mugs. Discussions with your supplier might reveal that the mug is a stock item without any real minimum required, but the decals of your design that are to be applied to the mug have a minimum of 1,200 pieces.

Then you note that the mugs cost $1 each, and the decals are 4¢ each. A solution presents itself: make up the minimum 1,200 decals (1,200 x 4¢ = $48) and apply only 300 of them to the mugs, which in turn are shipped to you. If you get new and reorders from your customers to warrant your buying more mugs from overseas, then the decals are ready to go, up to 900 more. If there are no more new or reorders, then you have lost only the (900 x 4¢ = $36) value of the balance of the decals. (Unused decals have a shelf life of about a year, so this might be a consideration also).

4. The production capacity of the supplier for the product. Production capacity refers to the maximum the supplier can produce. If the maximum is 5,000 units every month, and you are gaining orders for twenty thousand a month, then you must notify customers of the inevitable delays. It would be wise to simply place a sign near the samples in the showroom that states "due to popular demand, delivery of this item will be in June of 2002 (or some estimated future date)."

5. The delivery schedule anticipated for the merchandise. Would that be 30 days after order, 60 days, 90 days? You must work this into your plans.

6. The merchandise packaging details and the weights and measures of the export packaging. This information will be necessary when you are developing your costings.

7. Copyright, patent and trademark rights and responsibilities. This I have covered, but before this chapter ends you will understand another aspect of this peculiar to international trade.

8. When samples will be delivered (to coincide with trade shows).

9. Under what conditions the supplier will provide financing. This I will cover in detail in the chapter on financing.

10. Price of the item to be produced, and any relationship to volume. Never negotiate prices with suppliers overseas. The supplier, whether it is

a factory or an agent, will quote you a price for the item which will reflect the supplier's cost, overhead and reasonable profit. If you demand a price reduction or a discount, we can guarantee if you threaten to cancel your order or take your business elsewhere, they will cut the price for you. Some importers are proud of their ability to "squeeze" their suppliers on price. However, this victory is always pyrrhic.

The price the supplier quotes is just compensation for the services and products rendered. If you ask an agent what they are charging, they will swear that for you they are working for free. That is a joke, but they are typically charging only a 7–10% fee for their services. If you squeeze the price down three percent, the arithmetic will result in tremendous cut into the profits of the supplier. For example, if an item costs an agent $1.00, and the agent adds an 8% markup, then the price to you is a $1.08. If you demand a 3% discount, then the price drops to $1.0476, which is a 41.5% reduction in revenues to the agent.

Whether a factory or an agent is involved, there is a finite amount of production capability. Suppliers are collecting as many orders as they can, and scheduling the production. It might take about 60 days to produce goods overseas, so if you negotiate a contract on June 1 you can expect to have it produced by August 1. If you squeeze the supplier on price, you may find on August 1 they have not yet begun to produce your item. Why? Because they have many other orders that generate full revenue that they will produce first, before yours, to assure the best profits for their company. Why do they not just tell you lower prices mean later delivery? Because you are difficult and unreasonable. If you had asked if you can get lower prices if you take the merchandise in an off season, then they may have discussed that with you. But if you simply demand lower prices, they will treat you as they do other unreasonable importers.

Another way suppliers can cut corners to make up the loss of revenue is to ship you defective goods. Normally, if your order is for, say, 2,000 pieces, they would make 2,200 pieces, sort out the defectives, and ship you 2,000 excellent items. (The other 200 pieces they can sell to some poor fool who comes from the United States and says, "do you have something cool I can sell and make a killing?") But if you squeeze the supplier on price, they might make you 2,000 pieces, ship you 2,000 pieces, and you can pay the freight, taxes (duty) on the defectives and have to sort them out yourself.

The bottom line is that you must never deny the supplier just compensation for his efforts. Your products will help you get rich, so let the supplier get rich with you. You have a ball-park idea of what the price ought to be, because various other potential suppliers have also quoted prices. You live with the price the supplier quotes. As I said before, these people overseas are not getting rich ripping people off, they are getting rich delivering product to specification, on time, at a fair price—but the fairness must be mutual.

It may occur that the price the supplier quotes is far too high, price-blind item or not. A child's doll in the $400 price range may be unreasonable if it is a simple plastic doll featuring more attractive doll clothing. If you encounter this sort of pricing, ask to have the price "broken down." The supplier then provides you with information on the cost of each part of the item, in this case the doll, and the labor to manufacture, the packaging costs and business overhead. Such requests are not unusual, and for certain products like footwear the US Government requires the report.

By examining a item price breakdown you may discover a problem like, perhaps, the plastic you specified is a high tech space-age plastic that costs hundreds of dollars per pound. You heard about this plastic and specified it without knowing the cost. You find a very cheap substitute that in no way effects the attractiveness of the doll. By specifying this substitute, you are able to bring the doll's price in line. In this instance you have not negotiated the price; you have changed the product and used lower cost materials.

For the conservator, price is the first issue discussed. The conservators know exactly what they want (what happens to be selling very well right now), they are concerned only with how cheaply they can get it. For the innovator, price is the last issue discussed. Since the innovator's idea evolves, the changes mean the price cannot be determined until all the details are agreed upon.

As promised earlier, we will now explain how small business international traders protect their products and "intellectual property" when such provisions either do not exist or are beyond the resources of the entrepreneur.

Protecting Your Ideas

The factory you work with will also have buyers from all over the world visiting all year round. If you deal in lawn furniture, naturally your factory produces lawn furniture. The buyers from around the world come to this factory, too, for lawn furniture. When these other business people visit and see your superior design either in production, or the samples laid casually around, they will no doubt be attracted and want to place orders for your product as well.

It is not uncommon for a supplier to fill your order and continue production for a few hundred more to fill other orders from third countries. If your product is worthwhile, it will begin to sell worldwide. (Another source of these orders is foreign buyers who attend trade shows in the United States and see your product. These orders for merchandise to export to the foreign countries are easy to control since they come to you). The orders the supplier gains from other countries around the world are completely out of your control. How does the small company gain remuneration when its designs are used to sell product around then world? The solution is simple: The supplier pays you a royalty on each one of your designs produced by him and sold anywhere else in the world.

For instance, if the supplier quotes you a price of $1.00 for the item, then that is your price. You instruct the supplier to make your product available to anyone else in the world for $1.05 (or any price you think fair; don't make it too high, because your "customers" will simply redesign or decline. But do make the royalty worth your while).

The supplier takes $.05 of that $1.05 and deposits it into an account for you. Remember that the supplier originally quoted $1.00, and is making a fair profit at this price, and you enjoy a reasonable royalty on your product with the five cents premium.

Two questions come to mind: why would a supplier do this and how does the importer keep tabs on the supplier?

The answer to both questions are essentially the same: the suppliers overseas do well and are getting rich by being honest, reliable suppliers of good products made to specification at the right price and on time. Because you ask them they will agree to the plan. The practice is fairly common and your supplier will be pleased with your acumen when you request this program.

And let me nuance the argument regarding your role and value: it is far more important to *know* what people want to buy than to *make* what people want to buy. What people want to buy changes often; if today you own a factory making what people want to buy, what about tomorrow when people's tastes change? The factory owner is saddled with a useless factory, but the importer/distributor is free to work with other factories, who now make what people want to buy. To keep the factory viable, owners work closely with those who know what people want to buy. Suppliers want to keep your business, especially if you bring them hot ideas to produce. And the more orders from around the world, the hotter the idea. They will go along with your plan because they want you to continuously bring in newer and better products. And if they fail to cooperate you will go somewhere else next time.

As a side note, if you leave the five cent each royalty overseas in a bank account, you are legally obliged to report it to the IRS as income.

Now that you understand the practice of gaining royalties for your ideas when they are distributed worldwide, let me ask a related question: would you be willing to let competitors in the United States buy your products? It is one thing to allow foreigners to buy your product directly from the factory; this practice generates extra income for you with out any effort on your part. It is another thing to see other US companies offering your products for sale.

I believe it is good business to allow other US companies to buy your products from your suppliers overseas, as long as they are paying the higher price (the $1.05). There are two scenarios in which a US company would buy your product. Either the company is presently in your market, or intends to sell your product in another market (for instance you are selling a special blend venison sausage as a gift pack item, and the other US company is selling it to hospital kitchens). If the company intends to sell in a market you do not cover, then you will be making a risk-free $.05 per unit on a market you never even considered. This is good business.

If the US company intends to compete directly with you, then what? I still advise you to let them buy. Either they will succeed and do better than you, in which event you earn money while they teach you more about the business and show you a better way, or they fail at which point you have made extra money with no adverse effect on your markets. And if they do fail, you can buy your own product from them out of their garage at liquidation prices, lower than you could get direct from the factory.

Although rare, you may find a customer going around you to buy your product. This too is acceptable when you realize you are earning a profit without any risk on your part in this instance.

These concepts are not new, and certainly not peculiar to small business. Sears Kenmore appliances are in direct competition with Whirlpool appliances. But Whirlpool manufactures both Whirlpool and Kenmore brands. There are dozens of brands of VCR's on the market, yet there are only two VCR factories in the world.

As you discuss the ten points mentioned earlier in this chapter in a face to face meeting with a supplier, all of this would be under number seven, patents, copyrights and trademark rights and responsibilities. But keep in mind what was said above about "intellectual property rights." The customer is the thing, not the competition. Ultimately the only defense against competition is the customer's good will, and every trace of effort ought to be directed to the customer, and none to any malinvestment in the form of "barriers to entry" or "intellectual property rights protection." Unpatented Tylenol is the world's most popular medicine, hugely profitable, safe, cheap, plentiful, accessible with endless versions, and much competition. The chemical that makes up Viagra costs as little as acetomenaphin, yet Viagra is expensive, severely limited, dangerous inasmuch there are only two doses available, expensive, and hugely profitable for only one company.

Exclusives

Many entrepreneurs desire exclusive relationships with overseas suppliers to enhance their position in the marketplace. Under no circumstances should you ever seek an exclusive distribution arrangement with a supplier overseas. Exclusive arrangements harm your economic position and in no way enhance your competitiveness.

Every exclusive contract has two essential features: first, the company granted the exclusive distribution rights must pay a premium price for the product to gain the exclusive; second, the company granted exclusive rights must agree to buy a certain fixed amount of product each year. For these reasons alone, exclusives are poor business strategy at the small business level. It makes no sense to pay more than you have to, and it makes no sense to buy what the supplier demands, rather than what the market demands. The second point bears repeating; by agreeing to accept a predetermined amount of merchandise, there is a subtle shift in focus from the needs of the customers to the needs of the supplier. This is a shift in focus that threatens any possibility of accomplishment.

And, more fundamentally, an exclusive arrangement is worthless because exclusives cannot, under any circumstances, be maintained in international trade. A supplier overseas in city "A" refused to sell some product to me once because he had an exclusive arrangement with an established importer in New York. I wanted the product, so I contacted an independent agent in city "B" in the country overseas. The agent in city "B" bought the product from the supplier in city "A." The supplier presumed this was a domestic German sale. The agent in city "B" actually shipped the product to me. I displayed the product and enjoyed good sales. I charged the same price as the exclusive holder, but because even with a commission paid by me to the independent agent our prices were lower so our profits were better.

The exclusive rights holder in New York complained to the factory but the factory could not figure out how we got the product, let alone do anything about it. The only way the factory could stop the process was to cut off all domestic sales in the country overseas. This solution was impractical for the factory.

In another instance, a factory in China had wonderful new baskets in attractive materials for sale, but an exclusive agreement with a Los Angeles importer. Therefore they would not sell to me. I simply had my Hong Kong agent buy the baskets and transship to me in Seattle. At the next trade show I had a better display, wider selection, lower prices and all items in stock, as opposed to the company with exclusive rights.

Gaining delivery before the exclusive holder gained delivery surprised me; how did that happen? My agent explained that the exclusive holder, the Los Angeles importer, is obligated to buy. My agent had no exclusive agreement, so my agent got higher priority in shipping because my agent might cancel the order if it was not shipped promptly.

Would anyone dare tangle with Mercedes-Benz, a huge company with fearsome lawyers and exclusive distribution contracts with dealerships all over the United States? Again, anyone can buy a Mercedes overseas and sell it in the United States, under precisely the same conditions as Mercedes-Benz operates. If you are familiar with the term gray market, then you know that it is precisely this kind of business, not official, but not illegal, that constitutes the gray market. The most difficult part of gray market business is not the fearsome lawyers at Mercedes-Benz, but the simple fact that anyone that can afford even a discounted Mercedes-Benz wants to have the security and service that only a factory-authorized dealership can provide.[43]

An entrepreneur retained me to consult and advise him on the purchase of exclusive US distribution rights to a versatile home lathe and tool shop manufactured in China. The man was about to mortgage his home to obtain the $75,000 to buy the rights. Knowing the "rights" to be worthless, I met with the buyer and seller. During the course of the conversation I asked the seller what was to keep a third party in the United States from buying the home lathe tool shop from a Hong Kong agent and importing it into the United States, effectively going around the "exclusive holder"? In time the seller not only admitted this was possible, he announced it was already occurring! Hence his eagerness to sell the "rights." Our client himself joined the ranks of those buying the machine through Hong Kong and saved $75,000 in fees for "sole distribution rights."

We must make clear that we are speaking about products of foreign manufacture that have no copyright, patent or trademarks registered in the United States. Without permission from Disney, no one can bring Mickey Mouse items into the United States under any circumstances, because Mickey Mouse items are copyrighted in the US, and Customs will seize the products. But this is in compliance with domestic laws. International laws, beyond the strength of relationships, have no binding effect on any US citizen.

---

43. Wal-Mart imported some Seiko watches as gray market goods and found there were no warranties, an expensive mistake. "Florida Accuses Wal-Mart in Grey-Market Goods Case," *Wall Street Journal*, December 12, 1993, page A12.

Choosing The Supplier

Again we stress that the entity you eventually decide to rely upon for samples or product may be either an agent or a factory, but is most likely just an agent. Once you have the supplier the world loves most, then whether that supplier is a factory or an agent is of little concern to us. We have the best. Naturally, you will meet representatives of this company either overseas or in the United States. Either way, stress that everything you are doing serves the goal of building market in the United States. This is the basic value you provide to the supplier overseas, and the basis of the relationship.

Do not concern yourself whether or not you appear polite or are sensitive to the foreign culture. Many people maintain Americans must be trained in cultural sensitivity before they can do business overseas. This is nonsense for two reasons. First, the basis of the relationship is your ability to build markets. You are esteemed in direct relationship to your ability. And building markets in the United States for foreign suppliers covers a multitude of sins.

Second, few if any Americans misbehave themselves overseas. Americans are generally considered the most polite and generous of visitors in foreign countries. Those uniquely American traits we do exhibit overseas are considered admirable and charming. (We have had our problems: the Vietnamese referred to the hated Soviets as "Americans with no money.") Also, many of the agents you meet overseas were actually educated in the United States, so you may find your efforts wasted. I have met agents overseas who knew more about what was going on in the US than I did; I also met Chinese nationals who had no idea when the Tang dynasty was, or what the Tai Ping rebellion was all about. Cultural sensitivity may be sufficient for gaining trust but not necessary. What is necessary is a deal that makes sense.

Finally, before you place orders for any merchandise, check references on your supplier. Remember that the supplier is selling you something. Explain to the supplier that his reliability is critical to your success, and you need to be confident of his ability. Do not ask for references of other US customers of this supplier, they will likely not be helpful. But if this supplier is of any repute, the supplier has dealt with customers all over the world. He can give you German, British or Australian references.

Maui Sailboards, a Portland, Oregon company, once had all the elements lined up: excellent designer, acclaim from the retailers, an overseas supplier, samples and firm orders, and financing from the factory.[44] The only problem was production: although the samples were first rate, the factory had never been in full production of sailboards. Logistical problems led to a delay, causing a critical amount of orders to be canceled. Maui Sailboards held off delivery for one year, a painful decision for the principals. Beyond all of the benefits, there must be confirmation the supplier can deliver the product to specification, on time and at the fair price.

In summary, by identifying through NTDB CD-ROM research which country in the world is the most prolific supplier of the item to the US, we can contact the commercial attaché of that country for the names of likely suppliers. By letter, fax, e-mail, visits and samples we winnow down to the best supplier, which we confirm by checking references. And now that you have found your supplier and gained a sample of the item, you must cost and price the item.

---

[44] The experience of Maui Sailboards touches obliquely the untold story of O'Brien water ski company, the Colman company, HO Watersports and small business in the '70s. I would recommend any student looking for a fascinating term topic to research the experience these companies shared.

CHAPTER FIVE:

▼

COSTING & PRICING

Costing an importation is more complex than working up a price quote for an export sale, so we'll cover the harder task now and the simpler task—an export price quote—will be easy when we cover that in a later chapter.

Now that you know what you will import and where you will get it, you need to know how much it will cost to get it in your warehouse (or garage as the case may be) ready to sell to your customers. To get skis from a factory in Austria, to the Italian border, in-bond to Trieste, out of Italy across the Atlantic to New Jersey, past US Customs, and trucked inland may include thirty different steps total. Every one of those steps has a cost associated with it, and every one of those costs can be known in advance. In this chapter we will introduce the business associates who provide the information specific to your product, the cost of each step in the process, and sources of the logistical information required to import your product. In effect, these resources will constitute your continuing education structure after this book.

The most important partner in this effort is the Customs broker.[45] A Customs broker is a private company licensed by the federal government to "conduct Customs business," or in other words, fill out the paperwork the government requires to import goods into the United States. These people are not to be confused with business people who broker insurance or fish or some such other commodity. This is paperwork you may fill out yourself (if you have a social security number), but it is likely you can not fill it out yourself. Essentially, the forms are too arcane for any mere importer to figure out. But more to the point, the paperwork is so important, and your time too valuable, for you to worry about it yourself.

Customs brokers once only filled out the paperwork, but with the light deregulation we have had since the Carter administration, Customs brokers are now also very often what is called NVOCC, or Non-Vessel Operating Common Carriers. This means they can do everything a steamship line or air line can do, they just don't have any boats or planes. NVOCC's (sometimes called "NVOs") buy space in bulk at a discount and resell it to their customers, with profits and savings all around.

Your first contact with a Customs broker is when you know what you want to import and where you will get it. Of course this means you contact a broker after the NTDB research is complete. You can find them on the internet, or in the phone books of port cities. Echoing what I said about imports, the days of Customs brokers in a port city may be ending. Changes have caused some brokers to relocate all of their operations inland, such as Houston, Phoenix or Lincoln, Nebraska. You will still find small brokers in the port cities, and they offer personalized service.

Customs brokers have clerks paid from ten to fifteen dollars an hour to do the work, and the time spent is billed out at, say, $150 an hour. You are billed on the amount of time a broker spends on your paperwork, not on

---

45. A Customs broker works with importers to get merchandise into a country; a freight forwarder works with exporters to get goods out of a country. Often one company will offer both services.

the value of the goods being imported. The paperwork a Customs broker fills out is called an "entry." A simple entry of one million dollars of bananas from Ecuador may cost you some $150, but a complex entry of some $5,000 worth of pottery, textiles, and jewelry may cost $1,000 because of its complexity.

A broker's license, issued by the federal government, requires the broker "protect the revenue of the United States" and otherwise make the importer compliant with Customs rules and regulations. And here is why we work with them: trying to keep compliant is very difficult in this fast-changing world, and Customs brokers keep us out of trouble with US Customs Service.

With the enactment of the Customs Modernization Act in December 1993 (commonly known among importers as the Mod Act), importers have been increasingly burdened with additional responsibilities and con-fusing regulations. Potential penalties for non-compliance can be crip-pling in terms of time and money; new recordkeeping penalties have been added. U.S. Customs also expects importers to follow the new Reasonable Care Guidelines to show they are making a good faith effort to comply with the law.

There are certainly benefits to the changes: faster clearance for our ship-ments, all of which are inevitably "rush." There was a time when Customs was charged with looking in one of every ten boxes entering the USA, but with the explosion of world trade volume, they'd be lucky to look into one in every 10,000.

These changes can be viewed as a competitive opportunity. Starting is easier than changing. It is cheaper to start as a company that is Customs-compliant than to change an established company into a Customs-compliant company. The very act of being the first in your commodity to be Customs compliant at once eliminates exposure of noncompliance, and sets a standard others are judged against. Peter Drucker says business leadership rarely comes from the large businesses. By being compliant, your business leads the way in defining what is the "standard." And how is this?

With the new approach we can reasonably expect US Customs to draw on the experience of the Internal Revenue Service, a sister Treasury Department division, to manage the work. Recall that each entry submitted by importers gives US Customs specific information; collectively, all entries give US Customs a breathtaking database to work from in law enforcement.

In statistics there is something called the "bell curve," a graph that shows the normal distribution of a given event. It would be natural for Customs to use statistical analysis to isolate entries that fall outside the bell curve— that is, entries that show the price of the items in relation to the freight costs, or the weight of the cargo in relation to the FOB value, or the size of the cargo in relation to value, or the route of the cargo in relation to the HTS number, or simply the season a cargo is shipped, and any number of combinations to spot "problems."

Say, normally 10,000 pounds of glass Christmas ornaments cost $23,500 and have freight charges of $6,500, according to the database of previous entries of such items. A shipment of 10,000 pounds of such items that had a declared value of $20,000 and $10,000 in freight would be "outside the bell curve" and well worth examining by Customs intensively.

A possible problem here may be an importer attempting to avoid some duty charges. Say the duty is 20%, a cost of $23,500 would require $4700 in duty paid. A false declaration of $20,000 (and $10,000 freight) for the same shipment would require only $4000, saving the importer $700 in duty (feloniously), a savings that goes straight to the bottom line. Some find this irresistible.

Customs views such efforts about as well as motorcycle cops view drunk drivers. Don't expect much slack when caught. And as you can see, getting caught just got easier. Importers who have been cutting corners, and enjoying a competitive advantage because of it, have much to fear from the Mod Act.

This is not to say everyone will have to be on the bell curve to import. As long as your "paperwork is in order" you will be fine, and again, it is the Customs broker who assures this for you.

If a certain percent net profit is standard in your industry, a company illegitimately saving on duties paid can undercut in the marketplace a legitimate competitor, who pays the lawful duty rate. A company who makes products in Korea and misdeclares them "made in Mauritius" can not only deliver orders faster than importers legitimately buying from Mauritius, but with less paperwork as well. There are many more far more subtle ways an importer can cheat in the sourcing side to gain an advantage on the marketing side. Some are as yet undiscovered. The new systems cause anomalies to stand out, which can then be investigated.

By being compliant first, and being the first to be compliant, your experience "feeds the beast" with data that defines what a company in your industry looks like when compliant. You help define the bell curve for your commodity. Companies in similar commodities but whose data falls outside of the bell curve are likely uncompliant, and enjoying an unfair advantage over you. With the new capabilities, expect those taking unfair advantages to be smoked out by US Customs.

The result of being compliant is you are not bested by competitors who connive and scheme, nor do you have to connive and scheme to get the best results. You lead with your strengths—that is, best serving your customers. You compete where it matters, where it is above board and clear, at trade shows and in show rooms, where what matters is your ability to solve customers' problems with better products and services. As it becomes clearer how things are done, people begin to homogenize the process, and the bell curve becomes tighter, making fraud ever more unlikely, and making honest market competition more important.

You will sign a power of attorney with a Customs broker who serves you, but this is not to be confused with "attorney/client" privilege. That is to say, nothing you tell your broker can be kept secret.

Now, a lawyer may prudently claim that this means you need a lawyer to be safe when importing, if only to be compliant with Customs regulations. This is more true than ever, given changes since 1993. Here are some excerpts from US Customs documents on this topic:

> On December 8, 1993, the U.S. Congress enacted Customs modernization provisions under Title VI of the North American Free Trade Agreement Implementation Act (Public Law 103-182). These provisions are commonly called the Customs Modernization Act (Mod Act). The passage of the Mod Act in 1993 provided the framework for a partnership between the importing public and Customs. Under the Mod Act, Customs and the importer share the responsibility for compliance with trade laws and regulations. The importer is responsible for declaring the value, classification and rate of duty applicable to entered merchandise and Customs is responsible for informing the importer of his rights and responsibilities under the law. The Mod Act is based on two basic tenets, shared responsibility and informed compliance. Shared responsibility means that importers and Customs have a mutual responsibility to ensure compliance with trade and Customs laws. The purpose of informed compliance is to maximize voluntary compliance. The informed compliance concept imposed many publication, consultation, and notice obligations on Customs. The Mod Act fundamentally altered the relationship between importers and the Customs Service. The Mod Act shifted the legal responsibility for declaring the value, classification, and rate of duty applicable to entered merchandise to the importer and requires importers to use reasonable care to assure Customs is provided accurate and timely data. Customs retains the ultimate responsibility to "fix" the value, classification, and rate of duty. Informed compliance is based on the premise that, in order to meet their responsibilities, importers need to be clearly and completely informed of their legal obligations. Under the Mod Act, Customs will spend more time and use more effective methods to inform the public with the goal to maximize voluntary compliance and reduce the number of instances where enforced compliance is necessary. Under 19 U.S.C. 1509, Customs may examine records to ascertain the correctness and determine the liability for duty, fees and taxes due the U.S.

Clearly US Customs takes enforcement seriously. My experience has been Customs employees, inspectors, and agents are fair and helpful when they can be, and when there are problems the recourse is generally simple. Indeed, the kinds of products we import tend to be interesting, in an intellectual rather than law-enforcement sense, to Customs employees more than anything else. Nonetheless, there is no end to the regulations of which one might run afoul, but I believe a good Customs broker is enough precaution.

Simply fully inform the Customs broker you select of all you plan to do and how, and they will ask the right questions to probe for any problems. Keep in mind very often what you want to accomplish is quite legal; the problem comes when the means you want to use are illegal. By working closely with a Customs broker right from the beginning, before you import, you will begin your international transactions on the right foot.

Given a Customs broker's technical knowledge of rules and regulations, and access to costs of logistical services, they can be invaluable in inform-ing you of how things are moved, what it costs and how to comply with Customs. Nearly everything you need to know to complete your costings in advance they can offer, and for free.

And probably the most important work the custom broker will do is in the area of "transaction value" and "country of origin"—two areas of the law that would seem the most straightforward, but in fact are the most arcane.

They give you this information in advance gratis simply because they would like to see you proceed, for unless you proceed, they make no money when it comes time to charge you their fees at the time of importation.

For every product, you will do two costings: first, when you have samples to estimate a cost; and second, when a shipment actually arrives, so you may ascertain exact costs. In this chapter we will review three costings: a simple costing, an actual costing and one you can try. Within this we will also review pricing strategies.

A Few Terms Defined

Cost accounting is a massive, complicated and difficult area of study, but fortunately for us we need only figure out the costs for our small and relatively simple transactions. Let's clarify a few terms before we proceed too far:

Ex-factory price	this is the price of the goods at the factory door
+ Cartage to exporting carrier	this is the cost to get the goods to the boat or plane
+ Cost of lading on carrier	this is the cost to load the goods on the common carrier
+ Export documentation fees	usually paid to a freight forwarder
+ Bank fees	for bankers services
+ Profit	naturally
= Free On Board price quote (FOB, or the "C" in C&F) "free" of any problems	
+ Cargo insurance	more on marine insurance later in this chapter
+ International freight	one way or another, the importer pays the freight
= Cost, insurance, freight	the ultimate cost.

You may be quoted a price, or request a quote, of the price waiting at the factory door, or on the docks next to the vessel, or on the vessel, or even sitting on the docks in the USA. Any way you like is up to your preferences, and we'll discuss some of the strategies later in the chapter.

Each and every cost noted above can be provided by your Customs broker, except for the banking fees, which naturally come from your banker. There may be costs not noted above peculiar to your item, but your broker will inform you.

A Simple Overview

Let's pretend that we are bringing in dolls from Hong Kong and the price quoted for these dolls is F.O.B. Hong Kong, Hong Kong Dollars $7.49 each (HK$7.49). If the exchange rate is .1335, each doll will be F.O.B. Hong Kong, converted into U.S. dollars, exactly one dollar each. (FOB HK$7.49 x .1335 = US$1.00). Note that we make this conversion to start our costing:

First cost, FOB Hong Kong, in Hong Kong dollars:	HK$7.49
Exchange rate of .1335 converts HK$ to US$ –	
First cost, FOB Hong Kong, in United States dollars:	US$1.00
From here, all currency will be in US$:	
Duty	.08
Freight	.156
Misc.	.099
Total Cost	$1.335

The exchange rate is determined by Customs. Although there are exceptions to most of their rules, they usually use an official exchange rate figured on the date of the invoice your supplier prepares.

The next cost is the duty, the tax you are going to pay on these dolls. Consult with your Customs broker and say they advise you there will be 8% duty. That means you will pay the US government 8¢ on every dollar worth of dolls you import. Since each doll costs a dollar, the duty on each doll is 8¢. The next cost is freight, from Hong Kong to the docks in Seattle.

Freight costs can be a little bit tricky because freight charges are based on volume, not on weight. Interstate trucking freight charges are based on weight, not on volume (actually the freight rate books are set up to quote rates for both weight and volume, and whichever rate generates the greatest revenue for the steamship line is the rate used. For ocean freight, the volume rate usually yields the greater revenue; for interstate trucking, the weight rate usually generates the greater revenue).

It is not unusual to import through a port, say Oakland, for delivery to an inland point, say Denver. Your Customs broker or steamship line can assist you in arranging one freight charge for the entire transportation, both sea and land.

In this simple example, let us say the steamship line (or NVOCC Customs broker) quotes a rate of $60 per cubic meter ($60/M^3) for freight charges. For our dolls, which take 3 cubic meters of volume, the total freight charges would then be $180.00 ($60 x 3M^3 = $180).

If there are eight gross of dolls (one gross =144; 8 x 144 = 1152) in this shipment then we must divide the total freight charges by the quantity of dolls in the shipment to arrive at the freight cost on each doll ($180 ÷ 1,152 dolls = $.156 each).

Finally, we must consider any miscellaneous charges we might incur in bringing this shipment into the country all the way to our warehouse (or garage, as the case may be). If you had bank fees of some $30, plus cartage of $25 (if ocean freight is from the docks in Hong Kong to the docks in Seattle, then cartage is freight from the docks in Seattle to your warehouse), plus Customs brokers fees of $60, then your total miscellaneous charges would total $115. The miscellaneous charge per item would be ($115 ÷ 1,152 dolls = $0.099 each).

To review:

First cost	$1.00
Duty	.08
Freight	.156
Miscellaneous	.099
Total Cost	$1.335

Total cost is commonly referred to as "landed warehouse value." In other words, all costs associated with getting your item into your warehouse ready to ship to your customers is considered landed warehouse value. This would include any costs incurred stateside preparing the item for sale. If you put American glass in imported picture frames, then the cost of the glass and the labor to insert the glass and repackage the frames would be part of landed warehouse value.

It is from the landed warehouse value that prices are calculated. Every industry has a standard "markup" from cost to price, and you ought to have discovered what it is for your industry as you performed the research outlined in the previous chapter. For instance, in the gift and housewares industry the standard markup is 100%. Another way of saying this is (gross) profit margins are 50%. For example, in the case of the our doll from Hong Kong:

Cost	$1.335
x 2 (100% markup) =Price	$2.67

Of the $2.67 price (at wholesale, that is, the price charged to the retailers), $1.335 is cost, and $1.335 is gross profit. Therefore, we have a 50% profit margin (1.335 is 50% of 2.67), and a 100% markup (from $1.335 to 2.67 is a 100% markup).

Another industry may have as standard a 50% markup. Therefore, if cost is $1.00:

Cost	$1.00
x 1.5 (50% markup) =Price	$1.50

Of the $1.50 price, $1.00 is cost, and $.50 is gross profit. Therefore, we have a 33.3% profit margin($.50 is 33.3% of $1.50), and a 50% markup (from $1.00 to $1.50 is a 50% markup).

The markup varies from industry to industry,[46] but it is a rational reflection of the costs of distribution and the level of risk inherent in the task of distribution. Whatever the standard channel is for your product (as defined as the way your customers order and physically obtain your product), it is naturally the most efficient distribution channel possible. How do we know this? Because if there as a better distribution channel, all of the players in the market will have already migrated there.

Income Statement Example

Let us look at what happens to the money in an importation. If we sell one thousand of our dolls at $2.67, then we have gross sales of $2,670.00. Cost of goods sold is (1000 x $1.335= $1335.00). If we take cost of goods sold away from gross sales, we arrive at gross profit:

Gross Sales	$2,670.00
Cost of Goods Sold	– 1,335.00
Gross Profit	$1,335.00

---

46. Another resource that might help is *Robert Morris & Associates Guide to Key Business Ratios*, available in most libraries.

From the gross profit, you will subtract all of your overhead expenses, or any expense not directly associated with cost of goods sold. Expenses might include commissions, salaries, royalties, travel, rent, taxes, utilities, insurance, license, dues and subscriptions, health and welfare, and office supplies (your accountant or previous research ought to provide you with a breakdown by percentage for each of these items for use in the business plan). In gift and housewares, the expenses, or cost of sales, tends to run about 40% of gross sales. After you subtract out the forty percent, you can arrive at the net profit before taxes.

Gross Sales	$2,670.00
Cost of Goods Sold	– 1,335.00
Gross Profit	1,335.00
Less Expenses (40% of Gross Sales)	– 1,068.00
Net Profit (Before taxes)	267.00

Remember, out of the expenses come your salary, travel, meals and other business expenses,and the net profit is what is left. An example of specific expenses in more detail is given in Chapter Nine. If your company is a proprietorship, then that money is yours; if your company is a corporation, then the money is considered retained earnings, and it belongs to the corporation (which presumably you own anyway).

In the gift and housewares industry, the net profit tends to run about 10% of gross sales. Naturally, if you make mistakes, your profits will suffer, and if you are very good, you will enjoy even better than 10% net profits.

Different industries have different profit margins, again reflecting the costs of the distribution channel and the risk inherent in the business. We will discuss in later chapters how to find the best distribution channel for your product.

The mark-ups and profit margins in any business reflect the cost of distribution, plus a profit. The profit merely reflects the risk of doing the business. As a rule of thumb, the more essential the product, the lower the profit margin; the less essential the product, the higher the profit margin. The profit on wheat or rice is pennies a bushel; the profit on carnations or roses is dollars a bunch. Wheat and rice are essential. Distribution is well defined for such products, and the risk is negligible. There will always be a buyer for such essentials. Flowers are not essential, the distribution can be chaotic due to peaks and valleys of demand, and the perishability and capricious weather can make the investment very risky.

Often people ask how much money can they make in this business. From the figures presented we can give you a rough idea. Say you want to earn $36,000, net, your first year. This means after paying yourself, your suppliers, and all of your expenses, you want $36,000 extra.

If you were operating a gift and housewares import company, you know that net profits are generally 10% of gross sales. In that case, $36,000 is 10% of $360,000, so you would have to have $360,000 in sales your first year. To some this is a frighteningly large number, but to others it sounds too small. It all depends on your own disposition.

But let us examine this number closely. $360,000 divided by twelve months means we would have to have $30,000 per month in sales to equal $360,000 for the year. Still too large? If you were selling your products in all fifty states (for gift and housewares it would require about twelve different sales organizations to cover the entire US), then you could divide $30,000 by 50 states to arrive at a sales goal of $600 per state per month. And if we divide the $600 per state per month by an average of four weeks per month, we arrive at a sales goal of $150 per week per state in sales. Does this seem more manageable? Naturally you will average more orders per week out of California than you will out of Wyoming. But a $150 order is a minimum order at wholesale. If you cannot gain an average of one minimum order per week out of each state, then you ought to reconsider your product line. It may be too weak.

On the other hand, if you generate a minimum order per week per state, notice how quickly the orders build up, fast, like dot.com stocks once did on the day of an IPO. The difference is you actually have something for sale.

On the other hand, it is prudent when starting out to be careful. Certainly it is wise, if you are not comfortable with the idea of marketing nationwide, to go slow until you have gained confidence and learned the ropes. Perhaps you will market your products only in your region. But like many that have gone on before you, you will quickly see how easy it is to market nationwide.

As you start out, if you are working out of your home, you will find your net profit may be more than this model suggests because your expenses are less. You are writing off part of your home, part of your telephone, part of your car and other expenses that might have been personal otherwise. You will not have the overhead the more established companies have when you start your business, but you will still be able to charge a premium price for your products. You will need those larger profits because you will have some inefficiencies. If you fly to Chicago for a trade show and get $2,000 worth of orders, that's not terribly efficient. When you have an on-going business, you fly off to Chicago and get $20,000, $50,000 or $100,000 worth of orders. In both instances, your airfare, hotel and meals cost the same; they are fixed expenses.

Pricing Strategies

Once the costs are known, you can price the product. This may be trickier than it seems at first. Every industry is different, but each industry has pricing strategies that you need to be aware of, and use yourself.

For instance, in the gift and housewares industry, we commonly use a 100% markup from cost to wholesale. As noted above, on a cost of $1.335, we arrive at a price of $2.67 wholesale (the price we offer the item to our customers, the retailers). The retailers will take the $2.67 price and "keystone it" (double it) to: what? Herein lies a problem and a lesson.

Can you quickly, in your head, double $2.67 to arrive at an answer? Extremely few people can do it within two or three seconds, let alone instantly. The problem is most orders for product in the gift and housewares industry are placed at trade shows. The buyers are looking at thousands of products, all quoted in price at wholesale, and they must be able to quickly double their cost to arrive at the price at which they would sell it to their customers. A price of $2.67 is difficult to double mentally, so the vast majority of buyers simply pass on to other products, and not order the item priced at $2.67.

We know we must get at least $2.67 to cover our costs, but we must also homogenize the pricing to meet the needs and practices of the industry. In this case, we would price the item at $2.75, to assure an ease of acceptability once the item was offered for sale at the trade shows. $2.75 doubled is $5.50, and the retailers would actually mark the item $5.49 in compliance with normal retail pricing strategy.

Now the plot thickens! Many studies on retail pricing have shown that on most consumer items, there is no difference in the sale rate for an item priced $5.49 and the same item priced at $5.99 (or just about any other dollar point). That is to say, the rate at which an item priced at $5.49 is sold and the same item priced at $5.99 is sold is exactly the same. Therefore, if you, the importer, price your product at $2.75, the retailer is very likely to price the item for retail sale at $5.99, not $5.49. So, ought you price the item at $3.00, instead of $2.75, since the retailer is going to offer the item for sale at $5.99 anyway? This is a concern in the field of wholesale pricing.

Landed Cost:	$1.335
100% Markup–	
Necessary wholesale (2 x 1.335):	$2.67
Adjusted wholesale:	$2.75

(double 2.67 is too difficult for buyers to figure)

Necessary retail: $5.49

(since wholesale is now $2.75)

Possible retail: $5.95

(since the sale rate is the same as $5.49)

Either way is acceptable, but we strongly recommend you leave the price at $2.75, and announce to your customers the suggested retail of the item is $5.99. In this way, your customers will form an impression of your company, an impression that your products offer a wider than normal profit margin. This impression will incline the retailer to visit your company again at trade shows, and make it easier for the independent sales representatives to offer your products to the retailers.

Aside from the actual price, you must take advantage of popular price points. For instance, in gift and housewares, items ought to retail between $5 – $20 for optimum acceptability. What if we have a coffee mug that costs $1.00? It would wholesale for $2.00 and retail for $4.00.

In this instance, it would be better to package and sell the item in sets of four. Then the item would cost $4.00, wholesale at $8.00, and retail at $16.00, a much more popular price point—indeed, one that perhaps allows some retailers to mark the item $19.95 to meet the popular price point for birthday gifts.

Strange as it sounds, sometimes you must *raise* the price substantially in order to get the item to sell. We marketed a cat clock in the early eighties. It was a simple clock face with a cat image on the front. An American designer worked up the design, the design was silkscreened on the clock faces in Taiwan and the movements were imported from Japan. The clock faces and movements were taken to a sheltered workshop for the handicapped in San Francisco where the clocks were assembled, boxed, sealed and labeled with our name and item number.

The total landed warehouse value was nearly $3.00, so we wholesaled the clocks for $6.00, and the retail would normally be about $12.00 – $13.00. Once out in the marketplace, we began to receive widely divergent responses to the item. Some customers could not get enough of the item, some customers called us and begged us to take the item back.

It is normal enough to have some customers like a product, and some customers not like a product. But these reactions were extreme. We asked our independent sales representatives to look into the situation and report back. They found a very interesting phenomenon was occurring.

Those retailers who were selling the $6.00 clock for $12.00 were having a very bad time with it. Those who were selling the $6.00 clock for $24.95 were doing very well with it. It is called "perceived value." At certain times for certain products, the ultimate consumers perceive an item should cost a certain amount, and if you do not meet their expectations, they will then reject the item. Therefore, you must price the item to meet the expectations of the customers.

Quartz movement wall clocks, in the early eighties, were perceived to be priced correctly at about $24.95. If quartz movement wall clocks were priced any lower, the assumption in the mind of the customer was that the clock was junk. And contrary to what some people say, Americans do not buy junk (if they think it is junk). In 1990, the "perceived value" for wall clocks was closer to $15.00 retail. Over time, people have learned that quartz movements are cheap and reliable, so now customers' clocks are priced in the five to ten dollar range.

This perceived value phenomena seems to come into play most often when there is a change in technology, as with quartz movements. Wall clocks required more expensive electric motors up until the late 1970's. Consider whether a change in technology might apply to your product.

What if Your Price is Just Too High

I cannot remember an item or an example where the price was too high. There is always someone willing to pay outrageous prices for something— anything. A problem occurs when the price you are charging does not attract enough customers to make the importation and distribution of the item worthwhile. What should an importer do in this case?

Let's expand on the scenario.

Perhaps you price an item at $3.00 and there are many similar products in the market priced at $2.00. Customers are reluctant to buy at your substantially higher price. You have met price resistance. Let us further complicate matters by reminding you of the research, time and money put into this product. Perhaps you even have bought some of the product, sure as you are of your success. Your friends and relatives are wondering when will your company get off the ground? Peer pressure is strong. What are you going to do? How do you handle price resistance?

Cut the price? This is the worst possible decision. Once you have cut the price, you will never be able to get the price back up to a profitable level.

Enhance the perceived value? Add a little storybook to go with the doll and perhaps create the illusion the doll is worth more? This is a possibility, if you can raise the price to include the cost of the storybook as well.

The phone companies have lowered prices recently, and at the same time lowered costs faster than they have lowered prices, meaning more profit. This is right for a conservator. The cost of delivery drops faster than the perceived value. Profits widen dramatically.

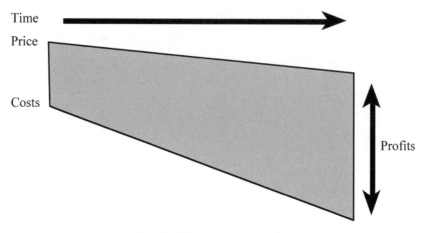

Fig. 12. Price vs. costs over time

One may as well raise prices faster than costs go up, and this is in essence the strategy of the innovator. Sadly, too many people wishing to be innovators actually end up adopting strategies that are essentially cutting the price.

Offer incentives popular with retailers, such as freight allowances or special payment terms? Any incentives are simply another way of competing on price. Every incentive you offer adds cost and cuts into profits.

The only viable response to price resistance is to either drop the idea or to completely redesign so that you develop a product with the requisite innovation for commanding a premium price.

On the other hand, what if your prices are not high enough? Occasionally, you might hear a buyer say, "Why, these are very well priced." You may freely translate this as, "Why aren't you charging more, fool?!" Although you might "reach" in price, as they say—try pushing it up to see the reaction in the market at a higher price—you must be careful for this reason: your competitors know well what your products cost. If you are getting too much, they will see that, and be encouraged to come in and get some, too. So it is possible to price your product so high that your competitors are invited into the market. The result is you may enjoy a short time of exceptional profits, but you forfeit a long time of good profits.

A Real Life Lesson in Costings

Let me start with a description of an importation of a relatively small value, from way back in my early days, and describe some aspects and flavor to demonstrate what you may find in this business. Following, I will describe document by document a typical transaction.

In April of 1979 I entered a trading room at the Chinese Commodities Export Fair in Canton (Guangzhou), People's Republic of China and came face to face with mountainous stacks of hand knotted, wool, silk and animal carpets from all over China and occupied Tibet. Many different Chinese carpet makers were present, and all were represented by the official Chinese governmental trading companies, either the China National Light Industrial Import and Export Corporation, or the China National Native Produce Import and Export Corporation.

I inquired about purchasing carpets from China, and I was informed that the Chinese Government had exclusive arrangements with the larger United States importers of carpets. Therefore, they could not entertain any orders from my company.

I begged the Chinese representatives to sell me just one little 3' x 4' carpet as a souvenir, and they agreed, if I hand carried it out of China. I did, and have that very carpet gracing my entrance, looking almost as attractive as it did over twenty years ago.

Once back in Seattle, I took that carpet around to various retailers to study the possibility of importing and distributing carpets. One retailer agreed to take a small shipment with the view to testing the market reaction. Of course, if this little test proved promising, I would test further with rugs of my own design.

Six months later, in October of 1979, I returned to the Canton Trade Fair, intent on buying perhaps a half-dozen carpets to test in the Seattle market.

The Chinese trade representatives rebuffed me again, reminding me they would not sell to any companies in the United States, except those party to the exclusive agreement. I was not concerned about the exclusive arrangement; I have gotten around exclusives before, and I did this time as well. I simply had the sales contract (Fig. 13) name Kong Shing Hong, my Hong Kong agents, as buyers and John Wiley Company (the name of my company then), as end users. It is this easy to get around exclusives in international trade.

字号
No. **79AOAS 8304**

成交确认书
SALES CONFIRMATION

日期
Date: **Oct. 16.** 19 **79**

签约地点：
Signed At: **Kwangchow**

中国土产畜产进出口公司上海市畜产分公司
卖方
Sellers: **CHINA NATIONAL NATIVE PRODUCE & ANIMAL BY-PRODUCTS IMP. & EXP. CORP., SHANGHAI ANIMAL BY-PRODUCTS BRANCH.**

电报
Cable Address: **BYPRODUCTS**

地址
Address: 23 Chung Shan Road (E. 1) Shanghai

电传
Telex 33065 ANIBY CN

买方
Buyers: **JOHN WILEY COMPANY c/o KONG SHING HONG TRADING CO. LTD.**

地址
Address: **81-85, Des Voeux Road West** HONG KONG 报 Cable Address **KWON SINHON**

兹经双方同意下列货物按照下开卖买条款成交：
We confirm having sold to you the following goods on terms and conditions set forth below:

商品名称：
Name of Commodity: **SHANGHAI WOOLLEN CARPETS** (HAND MADE)

规格：
Specifications: **SM90 4/8" Pile :**

2031/201	6×9	1	PC. RMB¥ 969.-
1772/428	6×9	1	PC. RMB¥ 969.-
1058/203	6×9	1	PC. RMB¥ 969.-
1647/387	6×9	1	PC. RMB¥ 969.-
1675/257	6×9	1	PC. RMB¥ 969.-

数量：
Quantity: **6 pcs. /324 sq.ft.** 5/8" Pile 6006/395 6×9 1PC RMB¥1221.-

单价：
Unit Price:

总值：
Total Value: **RMB¥ 6066.-** CIF **HONG KONG**

数量及总值均得有 %的增减，由卖方决定。
~~With % more or less both in amount and quantity allowed at the Sellers' option.~~

包装：
Packing: 木箱/纸板箱及麻包
~~In Wooden/Carton Cases or~~ Bales

装运期：
Time of Shipment: 在一九 年 月由上海运至 Per steamer during **NOV. / DEC.** 19**79** from ~~Shanghai~~ to **HONG KONG** with **KWANGCHOW**
允许转船和分装
transhipment and partial shipments allowed.

保险：
Insurance: 由卖方按发票金额110%投保综合险及战争险按一九七六年一月一日中国人民保险公司海运货物保险及战争险条款负责。
☐ Insurance to be effected by the sellers for 110 % of Invoice value against All Risks and War Risk as per Ocean Marine Cargo and War Clauses of the People's Insurance Company of China dated 1/1/1976.

由买方投保
☐ ~~To be effected by the buyers.~~

装船标记：
Shipping Mark: 卖方的装船标记 Sellers' shipping marks.

付款条件：
Terms of Payment: 买方须于19 年 月 日前将保兑的、不可撤销的、可转让可分割的即期信用证开到卖方，信用证议付有效期延至上列装运期后15天在上海到期。万一不能按上述装运日期出运；则有关信用证的装运期和结汇有效期允许自动延长15天。
By Confirmed, Irrevocable, Transferable and Divisible Letter of Credit to be available by sight draft, to reach the Sellers before **10TH NOV.** 19**79** and to remain valid for negotiation in Shanghai until the 15 days after the aforesaid Time of Shipment. In case shipment is not effected within the time stipulated above, an automatic extension of 15 days is allowed both for the time of shipment and that of expiration in the relevant L/C. **OR BY REMITTANCE 2748**

品质和重量：
Quality & Weight: 品质和重量以上海商品检验局检验证为准。~~Based on Inspection Certificate issued by Shanghai Commodity Inspection Bureau.~~

Fig. 13. China rugs contract

The date of the sales contract is October 16, 1979. That is the date that I personally selected the carpets, watched them be pulled from the stacks, bailed, marked for shipment, and saw the paperwork and manifests for shipment drawn up. I did not receive the carpets until February 29,1980, a full four and a half months later. Canton (Guangzhou), where the carpets were purchased, is 90 miles upriver from Hong Kong. It took the Chinese four months to move the carpets the 90 miles from Canton to Hong Kong, and the agents in Hong Kong less than two weeks to move the carpets the 6,000 plus miles from Hong Kong to Seattle. Even though some countries can produce the finest goods, their system of government may make it difficult to get delivery of the goods. China is now developing a modern transportation infrastructure, and trade with China has improved with this effort.

Nonetheless, the quality and ingenuity shown by Chinese artisans make it often worth the trouble and delay inherent in trading with China, or such countries.

Since the agent in Hong Kong takes title to the goods, they work up an invoice (Fig. 14). The merchandise is shipped to Seattle, FOB Hong Kong, after Kong Shing Hong accepted the goods shipped from China, CIF Hong Kong. Kong Shing Hong in effect took title to the carpets, and in turn, technically speaking, they sell the carpets to me. Therefore, Kong Shing Hong creates an invoice recapitulating the details from the Chinese sales confirmation. The invoice is dated and placed in Hong Kong, and appears to refer to products exported from Hong Kong, which is true. Because of this Customs might assume that the products were made in Hong Kong. If so, the duties and restrictions would be negligible. But since these carpets were made in China, the invoice clearly states in the country of origin column: People's Republic of China.

K   'G SHING HONG TRADING CO., LTD.
    HONG KONG.

81-85 DES VOEUX ROAD WEST 6TH FLOOR
HONG KONG
CABLE AND "KWONSHINHON" HONG KONG
TELEPHONE 5-491763 5-464106

INVOICE

INVOICE NO. 800128

HONG KONG   21st February, 1980.

INVOICE of............Two (2) Bales of Woollen Rugs............

Sold to Messrs....John Wiley Co., P.O.Box 12542, Seattle U.S.A.........

Order Number....79ABAS8304............shipped from....Hong Kong........to.....Seattle........

per.Oriental Importer........Despatched on....Feb. 11, 80........

Country of Origin	Marks and Number	Description	Quantity	Unit price	Amount
				CIF Hong Kong	
				RMB¥	RMB¥
People's Republic of China	S. H. 79ABAS8304 HONG KONG TO USA NO.9000—9001	Shanghai Woollen Carpets SM90 4/8" pile: 6x9 SM90 5/8" pile: 6x9	5pcs 1pc	969.00/pc 1,221.00/pc	4,845.00 1,221.00
				Amount :	RMB¥6,066.00

Exchange Rate base on date of negotiation
                    30.41 : 100

CIF Hong Kong equivalent to.....HK$19,947.39

Add: Wharfage: 2 bales @HK$4.50............................9.00
Carriage Inward: 2 bales @HK$5.00....................10.00
Carriage Outward: 2 bales @HK$5.00..................10.00
CFS Charges @HK$20.00/CBM for 0.56CBM...............20.00
Bank charges for the opening of L/C #W79/1158
            Commission 100.00
            Stamp Duty   5.00..........105.00
Insurance Premium.....................................109.71
Charges for Export Licence............................15.00
Charges for Import & Re-Export Declaration............20.50

FOB Hong Kong   : HK$20,246.60

Say Hong Kong Dollars Twenty Thousand Two Hundred Forty Six And Cents Sixty Only.

Total : Two (2) Bales Only.

Fig. 14. China rugs invoice

This invoice too states the total amount is RMB¥ 6,066.00. This is the amount the agent in Hong Kong paid on our behalf for the carpets. The agent in Hong Kong, though, does not want to be repaid in RMB¥, because that currency is useless outside China. The agent would prefer to be paid in Hong Kong dollars (HK$). Therefore, the agent converts the

RMB¥ amount into a HK$ amount of equal value (RMB¥6,066 ÷ the exchange rate of .3041=HK$19,947.39)

The agent then adds on all the expenses incurred in Hong Kong importing and re-exporting the carpets, as listed on the invoice. These are all quoted in Hong Kong dollars, so once converted they amount to no more than about US$60, for all the services rendered and fees paid. The invoice now reflects a grand total of HK$20,246.60, or about US$4,000.

On the packing list (Fig. 15), the measurements were the same on two bales which made up the shipment, but one had five pieces and another bale had one piece.

PACKING LIST

.HIPPER KONG SHING HONG TRADING CO. LTD.

STREET: 81-85, DES VOEUX ROAD, WEST 8th FLOOR.

CITY: HONG KONG.

COUNTRY ....

MARKS & NOS.   S.   H.
79 A BAS 8 304
HONG KONG TO
USA
NO.9000–9001

REF ....

Date FEB 21, 1980.

INVOICE NO......800128.

VESSEL........Oriental Importer.

SAILING DATE.............Feb.11, 1980.

DESTINATION.........Seattle.

TOTAL NO. OF CARTONS.....2 bales.

CASE NO.	DESCRIPTION	STYLE	UNITS PER PKG	MEASUREMENT	ORDER NO.	GROSS WEIGHT	NET WEIGHT
9000	SH90 4/8" pile: 6x9		5pcs	CM 260x32x32		KG 45	KG 43
9001	SH90 5/8" pile: 6x9		1pc	260x32x32		45	43

Fig. 15. China rugs packing list

Why is that? This is the kind of thing Customs agents notice that causes them to want to take a closer look. They may suspect you are smuggling Cleopatra in one of those rugs. One rug was particularly plush, twenty-five percent higher pile and much denser. Although the one plush rug bale did not truly equal the bale of five regular rugs, it is close enough. To fail to cost for volume would distribute too much cost of freight to the more plush carpet.

The carpets were subject to a curious historical event. About ten days before this shipment arrived United States Congress normalized trade relations with the People's Republic of China and granted them most favored nation status. This status gives China the same trading status as our friends, say France, Japan or Germany. The duty rate dropped from the anti-communist fifty percent duty rate down to eight percent. Instead of paying over $2,000 in duty, I paid $334.16—just one of those lucky moments.

Since textiles are quota items, this shipment required an export license. There are plenty of quota categories that never get filled and carpets out of China is an example of one such category, yet a license to export (and a visa to import) the carpets is still a necessary formality.

From this simple introductory view, let's move on to a more recent and complete costing.

An Actual Costing

Here we will outline a complete costing with all the relevant documents associated. Feel free to share these with your Customs broker, with a view to having him show you, in advance, what a set of documents relating to your shipment will look like, with all costs associated detailed. From there, you will be able to build a costing, as you will see with this set of documents. To review, we find a product, find the best source, obtain samples, cost the product the samples represent, present the samples at trade shows, and then order stock based on the demand from the trade shows. My item here is glass candles, made in Taiwan of Pyrex rod and tube, lamp-worked to resemble a wax candle in a silver candlestick, except for the fact the entire item is transparent glass. As you will see, there was a range of some dozen candles purchased, to assure a selection to please the retail buyers. The candles themselves were formed to hold paraffin oil, a safe mineral oil that burns at low temperature if wicked off fiberglass, and extinguishes if turned over or smashed. This makes these candles safer than the wax version. Further, the glass material used creates a magical ambience as the flame reflects and dances throughout the candle. The effect is heightened when the candles are grouped. The designs were occidental in inspiration, oriental in execution.

The first document is a mail entry (Fig. 16) for the samples relating to this ultimate shipment of product. Although your Customs broker would be delighted to handle the paperwork on the importation of samples, the fees he must charge would be rather expensive, and as long as the value of the goods is less than $2,000 (per conveyance, and check with your Customs broker for exceptions), you are better off having your supplier send the samples directly to you. If you direct the supplier to send the samples to your home, they may in fact show up there, although it is also possible they will only make it as far as the airport or Customs mail facility in the nearest city, and you will be notified where and when to pick up the goods. In any event, if the items normally have a duty associated with the item, it is payable (although Customs has been known to waive duties on these small sample shipments sometimes.)

Fig. 16. Mail entry form for glass candles

The mail entry form shows the form Customs uses on small shipments coming through the postal system. Later, I noted a difference between how Customs had classified my product in the mail entry and how my Customs broker had classified the item. I wrote a note to the broker inquiring about the difference, and the broker replied with proof to me the broker had it right and Customs was in error. Subsequently even Customs agreed the broker was correct.

Once the product trial at the trade shows indicates what quantities to purchase, the importer sends a purchase order to the supplier. I have always used BestWare MYOB software for my business, and I am glad to recommend it to anyone starting a small business. As a matter of full disclosure, MYOB has provided me with free software (but so have many others).

MYOB is simply the best in my judgment, and the best priced at about $90 per copy. The following is a purchase order generated from MYOB (Fig. 17).

Jo⁀ ₁ Wiley Spiers Cor⁀ ₂any
Purchase Order

John Wiley Spiers Company
5441 NE Windermere Road
Seattle, Washington 98105
U.S.A.
DUNS # 18-340-8855
PHONE 206/526-1836   FAX 206/527-4446

Purchase Order

Purchase #: 00000034

Ship To:

Forgeahead Enterprise Ltd.
PO Box 112-819
Taipei, Taiwan

John Wiley Spiers Company
5441 NE Windermere Road
Seattle, Washington 98105
U.S.A.
DUNS # 18-340-8855

SALESPERSON	YOUR NO.	SHIP VIA	COL	PPD	SHIP DATE	TERMS	DATE	PG.
		Cheapest/best				1% 15 Net 30	7/24/92	1

QTY.	ITEM NO.	DESCRIPTION	PRICE	UNIT	DISC %	EXTENDED PRICE	TX.
144	100715	7" Chamber Stick w/ Handle	$3.43	ea		$493.92	
72	100716	Oil Candle 10" stem	$4.51	ea		$324.72	
72	100717	Oil Candle 12" Stem	$4.83	ea		$347.76	
72	100718	Oil Candle 14" Stem	$5.16	ea		$371.52	
144	100696	10 " Oil Candle only	$1.19	ea		$171.36	
720	100410	Pear Oil Lamp	$1.51	ea		$1,087.20	
720	100595	Apple Oil Lamp	$1.51	ea		$1,087.20	
720	100638	Genie Oil Lamp	$2.38	ea		$1,713.60	
480	100589	Cobalt Swirl Oil Lamp	$1.88	ea		$902.40	

CALL FOR ROUTING INSTRUCTIONS WHEN READY

SALE AMOUNT	$6,499.68
FREIGHT	$0.00
SALES TAX	$0.00
TOTAL	$6,499.68
PAID TODAY	$0.00
BALANCE DUE	$6,499.68

Wholesaling Imported Glass • Exporting American Glass

Fig. 17. Purchase order for glass candles

The purchase order itself may be gratifying to the supplier, but no supplier is going to take any action until the order is backed up with some sort of payment mechanism, some sort of assurance that the importer will pay for the goods shipped. The options here are limitless, although the wisest choices can be limited to two or three options. In Chapter 7, "Financing When The Banks Will Not," I will detail those options, plus reveal why financing is not the problem in building this business. I will also fully explain the "letter of credit." In this specific shipment, a letter of credit was used to assure the supplier was paid, and to further assure I was shipped the goods as ordered, to specification and on time. For now you may examine the application form for a letter of credit (Fig. 18) and the notice to the beneficiary from the bank that the letter of credit has been opened (Fig. 19).

First Interstate Bank

First Interstate Bank of Washington, N.A. International Operations	P.O. Box 160 Seattle, Washington 98111 (206) 292-3121

Application and Agreement
For Commercial Letter of Credit

Date: 8/13/92   Bank Reference:

Please issue your Irrevocable Letter of Credit in favor of: FORGEAHEAD ENTERPRISES LTD
PO BOX 112-819 TAIPEI TAIWAN
1/F 14 ALLEY, LANE 75, SEC 3 MIN CHUN EAST ROAD
TAIPEI, TAIWAN

By:
☐ Full Cable   ☒ Brief Cable
☐ Airmail   ☐ Courier

Expiry Date: 15 SEP 92

For: (Amount and Currency) US$ 6499.68

Available by drafts at SIGHT (tenor, at sight unless otherwise stated) covering 100 percent of the invoice value of the merchandise accompanied by:

☒ Signed Commercial invoice in TRIPLICATE
☒ Packing List in TRIPLICATE
☐ Signed Generalized Systems of Preferences Certificate of Original Form A in
☐ Certificate of Origin in
☐ Certificate of Inspection issued or signed by

Insurance to be effected by ☐ Buyer   ☒ Seller.
☒ Insurance Policy or Certificate in duplicate for 110% of invoice value, covering:
  ☒ Marine Risks   ☐ Air Risks   ☐ War Risks   ☐ All Risks   ☐ Warehouse to Warehouse Clause
☒ Full Set Clean on Board Ocean Bills of Lading to order of Shipper, blank endorsed
  marked "Freight ☒ Collect ☐ Prepaid" and notify: JOHN WILEY SPIERS Co.
☐ Clean Air Waybill consigned to 5441 NE WINDERMERE RD
  marked "Freight ☐ Collect ☐ Prepaid" and notify: SEATTLE, WA 98105
☐ Truck Bill of Lading consigned to 206/526-1836
  marked "Freight ☐ Collect ☐ Prepaid" and notify:
☐ Other Documents:

Covering the shipment of: (Brief description of commodity, omit unnecessary details)

GLASS OIL LAMPS

Shipment Terms: ☒ F.O.B.   ☐ C.I.F.   ☐ C & F   ☐ Other:
Shipped from: TAIWAN   Shipped to: PORT OF OAKLAND CA USA
Partial Shipments are ☒ Permitted ☐ Prohibited   Transshipments are ☒ Permitted ☐ Prohibited
Shipment must be completed on or before: 15 SEP 92
☐ Special Conditions:

Documents to be presented within 15 days after the onboard date as indicated on the transport documents but within the validity of the credit.
All bank charges, except yours are for the account of the beneficiary.

WE, each of us agree that the terms and conditions set forth on this and the reverse page hereof are hereby made a part of this application and are hereby accepted and agreed to by us.

BANK USE ONLY	Customer's Account Number
	Signature of Officer Authorizing Credit
	Customer Current Liabilities

Applicant's Name: JOHN WILEY SPIERS Co.   Date: 8/17/92
Applicant's Address: 5441 NE WINDERMERE RD
SEATTLE, WA 98105
Authorized Signature: Title: OWNER

FX 020 (Rev 9-89)

Fig. 18. Credit application for glass candles

First Interstate Bank
of Washington, N.A.
International Banking Operations
P.O. Box 160
Seattle, WA 98111
U.S.A.
Telex: 32-9686 FIWSHA-SEA
SWIFT Address: FIWAUS 66

Irrevocable
Letter of Credit

DATE: August 14, 1992   No. CALC-33944
Pre-advised by our SWIFT dated: 920813

BENEFICIARY: ADVISING BANK:
FORGEAHEAD ENTERPRISES LTD.   FIRST INTERSTATE BANK OF
PO BOX 112-819   CALIFORNIA, TAIPEI
1/F 14 Alley, Lane 75, Sec. 3   PO BOX 59584
Min Chuan East Road   6 FLR, 675, Ming Sheng E. Rd.
Taipei, Taiwan   Taipei, Taiwan

Gentlemen:
We hereby issue our irrevocable Letter of Credit available with
     any bank by negotiation of your draft(s) drawn on us at
     sight for 100% of invoice value for the account of:
JOHN WILEY SPIERS CO.
5441 NE Windermere Rd.
Seattle, Washington 98105 USA
Up to an aggregate amount of **USD*6,499.68 **
Six Thousand Four Hundred Ninety-Nine and 68/100 U.S. DOLLARS
Draft(s) must be accompanied by the following documents:

Signed Commercial Invoice in quadruplicate
Packing List in triplicate
Full set of clean, onboard ocean bills of lading made out to
     order of shipper and endorsed in blank and marked 'Freight
     collect' and notify: John Wiley Spiers Co., 5441 NE
     Windermere Rd., Seattle, WA 98105 [phone: (206) 526-1836]
Evidencing shipment from Taiwan
                         to Port of Oakland, California USA of:

Glass Oil Lamps
Shipment term: FOB Taiwan
Partial Shipments are permitted.   Transhipments are permitted.
Shipment must be completed on or before September 15, 1992
Draft(s) must be presented for negotiation within 15 days of the
     bill of lading date, but not later than September 30, 1992

All documents must be dispatched to us via courier in one lot.
ALL BANK CHARGES, EXCEPT OURS, ARE FOR THE ACCOUNT OF THE
     BENEFICIARY.   (NON-NEGOTIABLE)
Draft(s) drawn hereunder must specifically mention the number and
     date of this letter of credit.   The amount of each draft
     negotiated, together with the date of negotiation, must be
     endorsed on the reverse hereof by the negotiating bank.

A discrepancy fee of USD25.00 will be deducted from payment
     proceeds in the event that documents are presented for
     payment or negotiation under this letter of credit, in which
     discrepancies are noted after examination and which require
     our action for approval of payment.

This credit is subject to the Uniform Customs and Practice for
     Documentary Credits (1983 Revision), International Chamber
     of Commerce Publication No. 400.
We hereby engage with drawers, endorsers, and bona fide holders
     that the draft(s) drawn under and in accordance with the
     terms of this credit shall be duly honored upon
     presentation, and that draft(s) accepted within the terms of
     this credit shall be duly honored at maturity.

Yours respectfully,

FIRST INTERSTATE BANK OF   COUNTERSIGNED:
     WASHINGTON, N.A.

_____ AVP   _____
   Authorized Signature   Authorized Signature

FK.077 (Rev 2/85)
                    CUSTOMER COPY

Fig. 19. Letter of credit for glass candles

After gaining the assurance of payment, the supplier then goes to work having the merchandise produced. From previous conversations, you will know how long this should take. After the goods are produced, the supplier will make up the documents required to assure the merchandise will pass smoothly through US Customs and into your warehouse. Precisely what documentation is required can be known in advance by having your Customs broker inform you.

In this instance we have the following documents, plus my comments: the commercial invoice (Fig. 20) is a basic document required in every shipment, it simply details the buyer, seller, date and a list of the goods, quantities and prices.

同彥企業有限公司
Forgeahead Enterprise Ltd.
P.O.BOX 112-819 TAIPEI TAIWAN

1/F, 14 ALLEY 2, LANE 75
SEC. 3, MIN CHUAN EADT ROAD.,
TAIPEI, TAIWAN, R. O. C.

TEL: (02) 5165315 (REP.)
FAX: 886-2-5015940

COMMERCIAL INVOICE

DATE:_____

TO: Messrs. JOHN WILEY SPIERS CO.
5441 NE WINDERMERE RD. SEATTLE, WASHINGTON 98105
USA

REF. NO. 6083

Destination: KEELUNG, TAIWAN TO PORT OF OAKLAND, CALIFORNIA USA

Payment: BY L/C

TERM: FOB

Delivery: SL TRADER 052E

Validity:

DATE: SEP.14,1992

Item No.	Description	Quantity	Unit Price	Amount
	GLASS OIL LAMPS		FOB TAIWAN	
	ITEM NO. 601 (100715)	144 PCS	USD3.43	USD493.92
	7" CHAMBER STICK W/HANDLE.			
	PACKING: 1/6/48			
	ITEM NO. 602 (100716)	72 PCS	USD4.51	USD324.72
	OIL CANDLE 10" STEM. 1/6/36			
	ITEM NO. 603 (100717)	72 PCS	USD4.83	USD347.76
	OIL CANDLE 12" STEM. 1/6/36			
	ITEM NO. 604 (100718)	72 PCS	USD5.16	USD371.52
	OIL CANDLE 14" STEM. 1/6/36			
	ITEM NO. 605 (100696)	144 PCS	USD1.19	USD171.36
	10" OIL CANDLE ONLY. 12/144			
	ITEM NO. 606 (100410)	720 PCS	USD1.51	USD1,087.20
	PEAR OIL LAMP. 1/6/48			
	ITEM NO. 607 (100595)	720 PCS	USD1.51	USD1,087.20
	APPLE OIL LAMP. 1/6/48			
	ITEM NO. 608 (100368)	720 PCS	USD2.38	USD1,713.60
	GENIE OIL LAMP. 1/6/36			
	ITEM NO. 609 (100589)	480 PCS	USD1.88	USD902.40
	COBALT SWIRL OIL LAMP. 1/6/48			
		3,144 PCS		USD6,499.68

SAY TOTAL U.S. DOLLARS SIX THOUSAND FOUR HUNDRED NINETY NINE AND CENTS
SIXTY EIGHT ONLY.

DRAWN UNDER: FIRST INTERSTATE BANK OF WASHINGTON, N.A.
L/C NO. LC-33944   DATED: AUGUST 14, 1992

Fig. 20. Commercial invoice for glass candles

The packing list (Fig. 21) notes the number of cartons for each item, the quantity of each item, and the weights and measures of each carton. I would criticize this packing list for failing to include the measurements of each carton. The measurements are key to a proper costing if the various items included in the shipment have different prices and sizes. If so, and if the freight charges are based on volume (as opposed to weight), then the costing could easily become erroneous. Fortunately, it did not matter on this shipment.

Forgeahead Enterprise Ltd.

P.O.BOX 112-819 TAIPEI TAIWAN

1/F, 14 ALLEY 2, LANE 75
SEC. 3, MIN CHUAN EADT ROAD.,
TAIPEI, TAIWAN, R. O. C.

PACKING LIST

TEL: (02) 5165315 (REP.)
FAX: 886-2-5015940

TO: Messrs. JOHN WILEY SPIERS CO.
5441 NE WINDERMERE RD. SEATTLE, WASHINGTON 98105 USA

REF. NO. 6083

Destination: KEELUNG, TAIWAN TO PORT OF OAKLAND, CALIFORNIA USA

Payment: BY L/C

TERM: FOB

Delivery: SL TRADER 052E

Validity:

DATE: SEP.14,1992

Item No.	Description	Quantity	Unit Price	Amount
	GLASS OIL LAMPS			

1-3	ITEM NO. 601 (100715) @	48 PCS @	4.00 KGS @	6.00 KGS
	7" CHAMBER STICK W/HANDLE.	144 PCS	12.00 KGS	18.00 KGS
	PACKING: 1/6/48			
1-2	ITEM NO. 602 (100716) @	36 PCS @	4.00 KGS @	6.00 KGS
	OIL CANDLE 10" STEM. 1/6/36	72 PCS	8.00 KGS	12.00 KGS
1-3	ITEM NO. 603 (100717) @	24 PCS @	4.00 KGS @	6.00 KGS
	OIL CANDLE 12" STEM. 1/6/36	72 PCS	12.00 KGS	18.00 KGS
·1-3	ITEM NO. 604 (100718) @	24 PCS @	4.00 KGS @	6.00 KGS
	OIL CANDLE 14" STEM. 1/6/36	72 PCS	12.00 KGS	18.00 KGS
1	ITEM NO. 605 (100696)	144 PCS	10.00 KGS	12.00 KGS
	10" OIL CANDLE ONLY. 12/144			
1-10	ITEM NO. 606 (100410) @	72 PCS @	4.00 KGS @	6.00 KGS
	PEAR OIL LAMP. 1/6/48	720 PCS	40.00 KGS	60.00 KGS
1-10	ITEM NO. 607 (100595) @	72 PCS @	4.00 KGS @	6.00 KGS
	APPLE OIL LAMP. 1/6/48	720 PCS	40.00 KGS	60.00 KGS
1-20	ITEM NO. 608 (100368) @	36 PCS @	4.00 KGS @	6.00 KGS
	GENIE OIL LAMP. 1/6/36	720 PCS	80.00 KGS	120.00 KGS
1-10	ITEM NO. 609 (100589) @	48 PCS @	4.00 KGS @	6.00 KGS
	COBALT SWIRL OIL LAMP. 1/6/48	480 PCS	40.00 KGS	60.00 KGS
TOTAL:	62 CTNS	3,144 PCS	254.00 KGS	378.00 KGS
	vvvvvvv	vvvvvvvvv	vvvvvvvvvv	vvvvvvvvvv

SAY TOTAL SIXTY TWO (62) CTNS ONLY.

Fig. 21. Packing list for glass candles

The original bill of lading (Fig. 22) is the title document in an ocean shipment, or, as the lawyers might say, it is prima facie evidence of ownership. He who owns the bill of lading, owns the shipment. The bill of lading is issued by the carrier when the overseas supplier arranges to have the carrier receive the goods for shipment onward to the importer. It is a contract that specifies when and where the merchandise will be shipped and delivered, via what routing.

When you pay for a shipment, you are actually buying the bill of lading, which in turn gives you all rights to the shipment. The bill of lading plays a key role in any payment arrangement, and in the next chapter we will address that aspect of the bill of lading. For now, we are concerned about the costs associated with the bill of lading. Since I advocate using FOB vessel in the port of origin as a price basis, one of your concerns is the cost of the freight for this shipment.

Of all the areas of costing, the bill of lading is probably the most difficult. This is one area where I would dwell at length with your Customs broker.

SEA-LAND SERVICE, INC.

INTERNATIONAL BILL OF LADING
NOT NEGOTIABLE UNLESS CONSIGNED TO ORDER
(SPACES IMMEDIATELY BELOW FOR SHIPPERS' MEMORANDA)

(2) SHIPPER-EXPORTER (COMPLETE NAME AND ADDRESS)	(5) BOOKING NO	(5A) BILL OF LADING NO
FORGEAHEAD ENTERPRISE LTD.	TGH118063	
	(6) EXPORT REFERENCES	

(3) CONSIGNEE (COMPLETE NAME AND ADDRESS)

TO ORDER OF SHIPPER

(7) FORWARDING AGENT F.M.C. NO

(8) POINT AND COUNTRY OF ORIGIN

(4) NOTIFY PARTY (COMPLETE NAME AND ADDRESS)

JOHN WILEY SPIERS CO.
5441 NE WINDERMERE RD., SEATTLE
WA 98105 PHONE: (206)
526-1836 CORRECTION TPE-3

(9) ALSO NOTIFY-ROUTING & INSTRUCTIONS

(12)	(13) PLACE OF INITIAL RECEIPT *	(9A) FINAL DESTINATION (of the goods - not the ship)
(14) VESSEL VOY FLAG 052E US	KEELUNG TAIWAN (15) PORT OF LOADING	(10) LOADING PIER/TERMINAL	(10A) ORIGINAL(S) TO BE RELEASED AT
SL TRADER	KEELUNG TAIWAN		
(16) PORT OF DISCHARGE	(17) PLACE OF DELIVERY BY ON-CARRIER *	(11) TYPE OF MOVE (IF MIXED USE BLOCK 20 AS APPROPRIATE)	
PORT OF OAKLAND, CALIFORNIA U.S.A.		CFS/CFS

PARTICULARS FURNISHED BY SHIPPER — SEA-LAND-U.S. CUSTOMS CONTAINER BOND (IT 145

MKS. & NOS. CONTAINER NOS (18)	NO OF PKGS (19)	HM **	DESCRIPTION OF PACKAGES AND GOODS (20)	GROSS WEIGHT (21)	MEASUREMENT (22)
	ITLU721846				6.580M
J W S (IN DIAM.) OAKLAND ITEM NO.601(100715) C/NO. 1-3 MADE IN TAIWAN ROC - DO - ITEM NO.602(100716) C/NO. 1-2 - DO - ITEM NO.603(100717) C/NO.1-3 -DO- ITEM NO.604(100718) C/NO.1-3 -DO-	62		CARTON(S) GLASS OIL LAMPS L/C NO LC-33944 ITEM NO.605(100696) C/NO.1 -DO- ITEM NO.606(100410) C/NO. 1-10 ITEM NO.607(100595) C/NO. 1-10 ITEM NO.608(100368) C/NO. 1-20 -DO- ITEM NO.609(100589) C/NO. 1-10		
			TOTAL: SIXTY TWO CARTON(S) ONLY		
				FREIGHT COLLECT	

23) Declared Value $ _____ If shipper enters a value, carriers package limitation of liability does not apply and the ad valorem rate will be charged

				RATE OF EXCHANGE	(24) FREIGHT PAYABLE AT BY

ITEM NO	RATED AS	PER	RATE	PREPAID .0396354	COLLECT	LOCAL CURRENCY DESTINATION
21310-60	OF	6.580CM US	38.90	USD	USD 255.96	NTD
	HD	6.580CM NT	210.00	54.77		1381.80
	DC	1.000EA NT	150.00	5.95		150.00
	FC	6.580CM US	1.50	9.87		
	CS	6.580CM US	23.10	152.00		
TOTAL CHARGES				60.72	417.83	1532.00

THE RECEIPT CUSTODY CARRIAGE AND DELIVERY OF THE GOODS ARE SUBJECT TO THE TERMS APPEARING ON THE FACE AND BACK HEREOF AND TO CARRIER'S APPLICABLE TARIFF

BILL OF LADING NO	DATE	CERTIFIED LADEN ON BOARD ON		
SEAU970483337	SEP. 14,92.	SEP. 14,92.	AT TAIPEI, TAIWAN	
		INITIAL	BY FOR SEA-LAND SERVICE, INC.	

* APPLICABLE ONLY WHEN USED FOR MULTIMODAL OR THROUGH TRANSPORTATION
** INDICATE WHETHER ANY OF THE CARGO IS HAZARDOUS MATERIAL UNDER DOT IMCO OR OTHER REGULATIONS AND INDICATE CORRECT COMMODITY NUMBER IN BOX 20

Fig. 22. Bill of lading for glass candles

You will notice the bill of lading is full of code numbers and such that in essence refer to what the item is, the markings on the boxes, and what vessel and voyage carried the merchandise. There are two areas of interest here: the box in the upper left, "shipper/exporter," filled in FORGEA-HEAD ENTERPRISES LTD; and "consignee," filled in TO ORDER OF SHIPPER. These two boxes legally form title to the shipment in an ocean bill of lading (but not on an air bill of lading, for reasons too obscure to cover here). The box in the upper left is significant because the name in the box has title to the goods until it is paid for. Generally, this will be the name of your supplier, but depending on the payment transaction chosen, it could be a bank or other third party. In essence, although you may gain responsibility for the goods once they are loaded on the vessel overseas, the supplier is unlikely to give up title to the goods until you technically pay for them, upon receipt in the US. More on this in the next chapter—for now we proceed with costs.

Notice the bottom grid totaling up various charges (Fig. 23). This is the area where you must pay the most attention. "Freight charges" is a term loosely used, and it is not uncommon for importers to be charged by the steamship lines twice what they were quoted in freight charges. The reason is there are few areas in life where more add-ons are possible than ocean freight. Fortunately, I will forewarn you here and outline what to ask and demand.

In the left column of the bill of lading freight charges you will see the item number 21310-60 which is the steamship line's numbering system. In the next column, you will see a series of codes: OF, HD, DC, FC, and CS. These will differ with each steamship line, but in SeaLand's case, they have the following meanings: OF is ocean freight charges, what is quoted in the tariff books or what you agreed to pay. The next columns say "RATED AS" 6.58, and "Per" CM—meaning 6.58 cubic meters rated at $38.90 per cubic meter—for a total charge of $255.96.

ITEM NO		RATED AS	PER	RATE	PREPAID .0396354	COLLECT	LOCAL CURRENCY	DESTINATION
					USD	USD	NTD	
1310-60	OF	6.580CM US		38.90		255.96		
	HD	6.580CM NT		210.00	54.77		1381.80	
	DC	1.000EA NT		150.00	5.95		150.00	
	FC	6.580CM US		1.50		9.87		
	CS	6.580CM US		23.10		152.00		
		TOTAL CHARGES			60.72	417.83	1532.00	

Fig. 23. Bill of lading freight charges detail

HD and DC are charges the suppliers pay to get your products across the docks overseas and loaded on the vessel. These are prepaid and noted on the bill of lading. The supplier has buried these costs in the price of the goods you are buying.

FC is a fuel charge, also known as the bunker fuel surcharge. The bunker surcharge (BSC on some bills of lading) is a fee charged in the event oil prices affect the steamship lines' profits.

For instance, the steamship line quotes a freight rate assuming you are checking around for rates, and wants to make sure you are comparing just freight rates to freight rates. You must be careful to belabor your Customs broker or steamship line to give you a "full rate" or an "all-in" rate. The charges are determined in advance and published, so you can know in advance all of your charges. The trick is to get your provider to include all the charges applicable. Another possible fee is the "currency adjustment factor," or C&F, shown here as CS. In the event the steamship line has to take the US$ you pay for freight and convert it to a foreign currency to pay its bills, and the foreign currency exchange rates will be unfavorable to the steamship line, the steamship line will levy a surcharge to come out even. Again, you may know all of these in advance, but you must be sure to ask.

There are often such items as a "CFS receiving charge," quoted in foreign currency and prepaid. Another is DDC/CFS, which refers to destination delivery charges, or container freight station charges. These charges depend on how the merchandise is packed. Almost all merchandise is shipped in containers—those twenty, thirty-five and forty foot long metal vans that are stacked on the ships in the harbors. If your merchandise takes up over 85% of the space in the container, the container will be dedicated to your merchandise, and it will be designated a container yard (CY), or full container load (FCL) shipment. Any freight rate you are quoted assumes the shipment will be on FCL basis. When the ship arrives, your container is off-loaded onto a chassis, and your Customs broker will arrange to have a trucker move the container from the docks to your warehouse.

In the event your merchandise does not take up over 85% of the space of the container (say only 50%), then the steamship line will load other consignees' merchandise into that container along with your merchandise. The shipment will be designated container freight station (CFS), or less than truckload (LTL). When the ship arrives, this container is put on a chassis and taken to a warehouse where the merchandise is unloaded and sorted by consignee. The consignee in turn is then able to pick up the merchandise. In this event, there is extra handling and paperwork so there are extra charges. These charges are normally referred to as CFS charges.

Up to this point, all of the documents were either generated or collected by the agent overseas. These documents are prepared at your direction. How do you know which documents to request? Your Customs broker, with whom by this time you have already met, will advise you and, if a bank is involved because of a letter of credit (covered in Chapter 7), they too will advise what documents they need. I would strongly advise securing marine insurance for your shipments, and would be delighted to show you the document associated with marine insurance, but alas, on this shipment, I forgot. Nonetheless, let me explain marine insurance.

The marine insurance form is usually eighteen inches long with much tiny print. Insurance is a curious part of international trade, but certainly must not be overlooked. Your Customs broker, the supplier overseas or your regular business insurance agent will be glad to arrange insurance. I recommend it strongly. And, as with just about everybody else you will work with, you do not pay any premiums until a shipment actually is imported. Indeed, if you gain a policy from an underwriter such as Chubb, insurance premiums are not paid until the end of the month in which the shipment arrived. Insurance does not cover lost or stolen goods, goods damaged in transit due to improper handling (if a longshoreman drops the container), or other such failures to perform. Such events are covered by the carrier or the party responsible for getting the work done. Marine insurance covers situations that are listed on the insurance form in the first part of the paragraph that starts, "Touching the Adventures and Perils…" These events sound quite exotic, but may indeed occur. Even more curious is how the insurance functions. For instance, one of the insured events is called "jettisons." This occurs when a ship gets into a difficult situation, perhaps taking on water, and the captain, the master of the vessel, orders several containers tossed overboard (jettisoned). The containers to which I refer here are not boxes, but the twenty, thirty and forty foot long vans you see stacked up on the ocean freighters in every harbor in the world. The weights and measures of all containers being loaded on the ship are carefully logged into an onboard computer and the captain can instantly determine which containers to jettison in the event of an emergency.

This happens often enough to warrant buying insurance. In 1991, thousands of Nike shoes began washing up along the Oregon coast, compliments of a jettison and a helpful ocean current. Newspapers reported the spontaneous "Nike swap-meets" all over the area—on weekends, people would trade the size thirteen Air Jordan left for a size nine cross trainer right.

National Geographic featured an article describing how scientists are recording the places such jetsam washes ashore. Since finding where and when the cargo was dumped in the sea is an easy matter, plotting the path becomes of interest to oceanographers in the study of ocean currents.[47]

Generally, the jettisoned containers sink or break up, as in the case of the Nikes, but occasionally a container will wash up intact, as in the case of a full container of Bang & Olufsen stereo equipment that showed up on the Florida coast in 1984, or a full container of mandarin oranges in light syrup a beachcomber found on a lonely stretch of beach in the 1970s, again in Oregon.

Of the two or three thousand containers loaded on a vessel, the captain may order twenty thrown overboard. Are you buying insurance to cover this event, to cover the possibility that your container will be thrown overboard? No, you are buying insurance to cover the possibility that you will not be thrown overboard. In a jettison situation, those whose merchandise is left on board must pay for the loss of those who were thrown overboard. The value of the merchandise thrown overboard is pro-rated among all the other consignees' merchandise on board. In the event somebody's merchandise was jettisoned, you would get a bill for a portion of the value of the goods thrown overboard.

This may sound bizarre, but it really makes sense in the historical perspective. Marine insurance had its start in a coffee shop in London in the 17th century. The coffee shop was called Lloyd's of London, and was the unofficial headquarters of the international traders at the time. Ships would arrive from the South Seas, sent by these traders to bring back teas, spices, hemp, and other products. Sometimes, a ship might have to jettison cargo, perhaps the hemp into the Straits of Malacca, to save the ship from some peril. The hemp merchant would be devastated to learn his merchandise did not make it through. At that time (and to this day), if you cannot pay your bills in England you go to debtor's prison.

---

47. "New Eyes on the Ocean," *National Geographic* (October 2000): 86.

Eventually, the traders worked out a system of assuring each other that in the event one trader's cargo was jettisoned to save other traders' cargo, those whose cargo was saved would reimburse those who lost out. From this simple concept the idea of marine insurance was born, and Lloyd's of London has grown to be the premier insurance company in the world.

In the more prosaic event that your shipment is short two cartons, appears wet or damaged, or sounds as if it might be damaged, it is very important to make a note of this fact on the bill of lading or delivery receipt. This will be the sole basis for a claim against the steamship line for damaging or losing your merchandise.

The Consumption Entry (Fig. 24) is the form the United States government requires to have submitted for every entry of merchandise into the US. The Customs broker generates this document and submits it to the United States Customs Service. This is the form you pay a Customs broker to fill out on your behalf. The information on this form is reported to the Census Department which in turn creates summaries of the data and publishes the information in the NTDB.

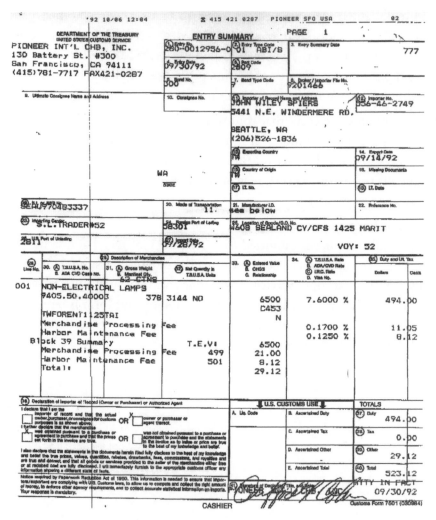

Fig. 24. Consumption entry for glass candles

Details required in the body of the form include: the country of origin, the official description, weights, quantity, price and duty rate.

Gradually the paperwork between Customs and Customs brokers is being converted to all-electronic filing. These forms will become a thing of the past, but the information will still have to be supplied.

Of course, there is always the bill from the Customs broker to you for his services rendered (Fig. 25).

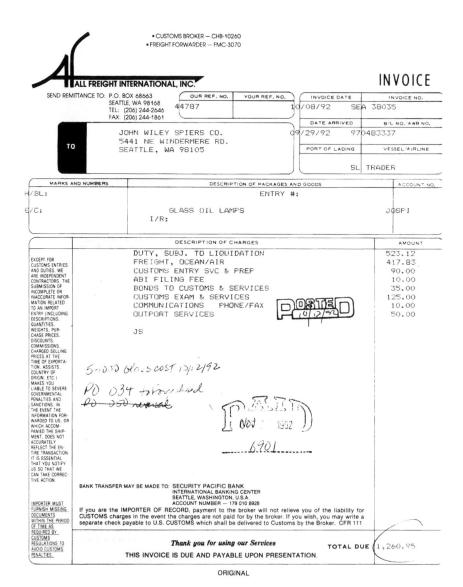

Fig. 25. Customs broker invoice for glass candles

You will note the invoice states "duty, subj to liquidation–523.12." Normally a Customs broker will collect the duty payable to Customs from you and deliver it to Customs on your behalf to assure a timely payment. This saves you the trouble of paying Customs directly and possibly missing the payment deadline. The ocean freight is handled the same way. Although this is a convenience to you, you should be careful to write out checks for freight and duty specifically to the steamship line and US Customs Service respectively, not to the Customs broker for these charges. It has happened a few times that money given to a Customs broker for Customs is lost forever when the Customs broker declares bankruptcy. Your money earmarked for freight or Customs would disappear unless the checks were made out specifically to those organizations.

The importer is required to have a surety bond, so your Customs broker will arrange this for you. A surety bond is needed in the event something goes wrong and laws are violated in regards to an importation. Customs will want to fine someone. If you, the importer, disappear then Customs will get the money for the fine from the bonding company. The bonding company in turn sends out a bounty hunter looking for you in hopes of getting its money back.

Surety bonds come in two varieties—single entry bond and general term bond. Single entry bonds will cost about $40, and a general term bond about $400. A general term bond is good for a year, while a single entry bond is good for only one shipment. The rule of thumb is, if you have less than ten shipments a year, get single entry bonds. Finally, we have the "Services to Entry," the custom broker's charges for filling out and processing the paperwork, and other various charges. Here again, question closely your Customs broker to determine what your invoice and costs will look like.

Although you will never see it in a costing, I have reproduced a copy of the relevant page of the *Tariff Schedules of the United States* for the Customs classification of this item for that year (Fig. 26). This shows how the Customs broker arrived at the number for my candles. *Harmonized Tariff Schedule of the United States* is available in most libraries, and the introduction chapters explain all the codes you see here. It is updated at least yearly.

HARMONIZED TARIFF SCHEDULE of the United States (1992) -- Supplement 1

XX
94-8

Annotated for Statistical Reporting Purposes

Heading/ Subheading	Stat. Suf. & cd	Article Description	Units of Quantity	Rates of Duty General	Rates of Duty Special	2
9405 (con.)		Lamps and lighting fittings including searchlights and spotlights and parts thereof, not elsewhere specified or included; illuminated signs, illuminated nameplates and the like, having a permanently fixed light source, and parts thereof not elsewhere specified or included (con.):				
9405.20		Electric table, desk, bedside or floor-standing lamps:				
9405.20.40		Of base metal: Of brass............................	....	3.7%	Free (A,E,IL,J) 2.2% (CA)	40%
	10 8	Household......................	No.			
	20 6	Other..........................	No.			
9405.20.60		Other..........................	....	7.8%	Free (A,E,IL,J) 4.5% (CA)	45%
	10 3	Household......................	No.			
	20 1	Other..........................	No.			
9405.20.80		Other...........................	....	3.9%	Free (A,E,IL,J) 2.3% (CA)	35%
	10 9	Household......................	No.			
	20 7	Other..........................	No.			
9405.30.00		Lighting sets of a kind used for Christmas trees...	....	8%	Free (A*,E,IL,J) 4.8% (CA)	50%
	10 4	Miniture series wired sets...............	No.			
	40 8	Other...........................	No.			
9405.40		Other electric lamps and lighting fittings:				
9405.40.40	00 6	Of base metal: Of brass..........................	No......	5.7%	Free (A,E,IL,J) 2.8% (CA) 1/	45%
9405.40.60	00 1	Other..........................	No......	7.6%	Free (A,E,IL,J) 4.5% (CA) 1/	45%
9405.40.80	00 7	Other..........................	No......	3.9%	Free (A,E,IL,J) 2.3% (CA) 1/	35%
9405.50		Non-electrical lamps and lighting fittings:				
9405.50.20	00 7	Incandescent lamps designed to be operated by propane or other gas, or by compressed air and kerosene or gasoline..........................	No......	3.7%	Free (A,E,IL,J) 2.2% (CA)	45%
9405.50.30	00 5	Other: Of brass..........................	No......	5.7%	Free (A,E,IL,J) 2.8% (CA)	45%
9405.50.40	00 3	Other..........................	No......	7.8%	Free (A,E,IL,J) 4.5% (CA)	45%
9405.60		Illuminated signs, illuminated nameplates and the like:				
9405.60.20	00 5	Of base metal: Of brass..........................	No......	5.7%	Free (A,C,E,IL,J) 2.8% (CA)	45%
9405.60.40	00 1	Other..........................	No......	7.6%	Free (A,C,E,IL,J) 4.5% (CA)	45%
9405.60.60	00 8	Other..........................	No......	5.3%	Free (A,C,E,IL,J) 3.1% (CA)	40%

Attn: John

Fig. 26. Tariff schedule for glass candles

Of course, after you have paid for the goods and cleared Customs, you must see to it the goods are delivered to your warehouse (garage?). In this instance, since I distribute out of Sparks, Nevada, I had to truck the goods there from Oakland. Your Customs broker can arrange this. Please note the total freight charges (Fig. 27) were $318.00 to go the nearly 250 miles from Oakland to Sparks. Recall now the ocean freight charge to get the same merchandise the 6,000-plus miles from Keelung to Oakland. That totaled some $417.00, all in, or $99 more for some 5,000 miles more. This is a graphic example of just how dirt cheap ocean freight is. Those vessels you see in the harbor with some 3,000 containers on board require a crew of perhaps a dozen, for a rate of 250 vans per person. Then the vessel is unloaded with each van onto a chassis pulled by a single trucker, a rate of one van per person. Once you find the best place in the world to have something made, it is dirt cheap to ship it from there to here. (Why I warehouse in Sparks although my offices are in Seattle will be dealt with in the final chapter).

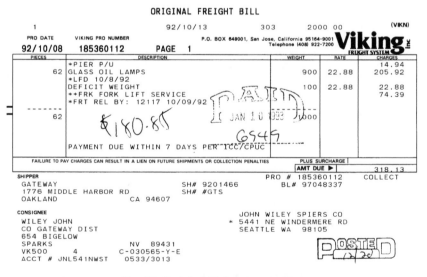

Fig. 27. Freight bill for glass candles

Now that we have all of the relevant documents for this shipment, let's cost it (Fig. 28). We convert the costs through the various currencies involved to arrive at a cost quoted in US$. In this case it is easier since the supplier wanted to be paid in US$.

	A	B	C	D	E	F	G	H	I	J	K
1											
2											
3											
4		Cumulative	601	602	603	604	605	606	607	608	609
5	FOB	$6500	$494	$325	$348	$372	$171	$1087	$1087	$1714	$902
6	DUTY	$513	$39	$26	$27	$29	$14	$86	$86	$135	$71
7	FREIGHT	$418	$20	$13	$20	$20	$13	$67	$67	$133	$67
8	BROKER FEES	$320	$24	$16	$17	$18	$8	$53	$53	$84	$44
9	BANK FEES	$110	$8	$5	$6	$6	$3	$18	$18	$29	$15
10	CARTAGE	$318	$24	$16	$17	$18	$8	$53	$53	$84	$44
11	MISC										
12	TOTAL	$8178	$610	$401	$435	$464	$218	$1365	$1365	$2179	$1144
13											
14	TOTAL QTY EA		144	72	72	72	144	720	720	720	480
15	EACH LWV		$4.23	$5.57	$6.04	$6.44	$1.51	$1.90	$1.90	$3.03	$2.38
16	WHOLESALE		$9.00	$12.00	$13.00	$14.00	$4.00	$4.50	$4.50	$7.05	$5.50
17	GROSS PROFIT		$4.77	$6.43	$6.96	$7.56	$2.49	$2.60	$2.60	$4.02	$3.12
18	MARKUP		112.5616%	115.4474%	115.0760%	117.4458%	164.3188%	137.4176%	137.4176%	132.9309%	130.7615%
19	PROFIT MARGIN		52.9548%	53.5850%	53.5048%	54.0115%	62.1669%	57.8801%	57.8801%	57.0688%	56.6652%
20											
21			Forgeahead, 62 Cartons, SL Trader 052E, ETA 10/5/92,								
22			oil lamps								
23											

Fig. 28. Costs for glass candles

In column A, I have listed the cost areas, and in line 4 I have made room for the costs and the breakdown of costs by item. The item numbers 601, 602,…609 are arbitrarily assigned by me to the items and replace the suppliers unwieldy numbers for the items. Then I simply prorate the costs per item, and arrive at a total cost, line 12. From there, in line 14, I note the quantity of each item imported, and figure the cost each. From there I take my wholesale price and arrive at a gross profit, line 17. These can then be calculated to arrive at markup and profit margin.

The part you must pay special attention to in costing is charging off freight correctly. As is often the case, this costing was simple because the freight costs did not diverge greatly among the items imported here. But in the instance of the rugs mentioned earlier, such a wide divergence occurred.

The six rugs were packed in two bales. The price FOB Hong Kong was US$4,302 total, $687 for each of the rugs except the plush rug at $866. The freight was $89, so let's assume $90 in freight. I had two bales the exact same size. I charge $45 to one bale and $45 to the other bale. If we open up one bale and find one rug, $45 freight is applied to the rug. If we open up the other bale and there are five rugs, five goes into $45 nine times. The freight is $9 each on the regular rugs.

This is an example of charging off the freight costs by volume. If you do not do that correctly, some of your products will come out overpriced, and some underpriced. When you sell them in the marketplace, the reaction will be unsound, and your business will suffer as you make plans based on erroneous information.

Keep a special eye out for miscellaneous costs incurred getting the product into your warehouse and ready to ship to customers. For example, a friend of mine imports picture frames from the Philippines. These picture frames need to have glass inserted, and some need to have their brass inlays buffed up here in the United States. These costs would be added to the cost of the goods.

When we imported baskets from China, we fumigated the baskets to control pests. Fumigation charges fell under miscellaneous costs. Although the pests, generally bugs, were harmless, they sometimes were quite large and frightened customers. One customer called us and claimed he had been chased out of his store by a bug that crawled out of one of our baskets. The man swore the bug was "bigger than a '54 Buick."

Apparently bugs were still getting through even though we were fumigating in Hong Kong. So we started fumigating in Seattle. This did not work either. Finally we complained to the fumigators about the ineffectiveness of the treatment. The fumigators investigated and in turn explained that they were indeed exterminating the bugs, but not the larvae, the bug eggs. To eliminate those eggs they would place our shipments in special tanks and suck the air out of the tanks. This would destroy (implode) the eggs and the live bugs, too.

We considered fumigation charges part of the cost of goods. This also became a sale point item with us, because with our baskets we knew how to eliminate all bugs, and we were able to charge more for the benefit than the cost would suggest.

The quantities you see here associated with the items reflect what I received in orders from the trade shows. This is of course after we have received samples of the items, and have shown them at a trade show, a step that still lies ahead in this book. For now, we need only concentrate on the technical matter of costing.

This is meant to be a guide for you to use as discussion points with your Customs broker, and there may be more or fewer documents in your set depending on the product you trade. Let your Customs broker be your guide.

Usually within a few months, but by law within a year, you will receive a scary-looking letter from the "United States Treasury–Enforcement Division" noting a penalty for private use, and looking like some sort of summon or warrant (Fig. 29). Actually it is simply a "liquidation cour-tesy notice" for your files, assuring you US Customs has closed the file on this importation and has no further interest in this shipment.

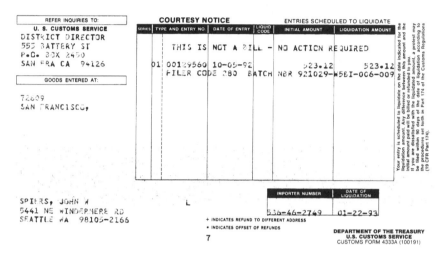

Fig. 29. Liquidation notice for glass candles

Now that I have given you my suppliers, my means, my items, my quanti-ties, my costing and everything else you need to steal my ideas and knock me off, ought I not be worried about you doing so? No, because, as I have said before, you need to have a passion for the product to compete.

If you steal my idea and come up against me in the market, I will crush you, through my formidable passion and momentum. You just won't have the passion to solve the problems that I do. I've been using this set of doc-uments as an example to thousands of students since 1993, and never has my idea been ripped off. In time it will, but not by a student, but by a conservator, which is fine by me, as explained in earlier chapters. On the other hand, what excites you most is no doubt an area I could care less about, so you are safe from me. Indeed, let me help you by sharing the design drawing from the designer, Chris Bolton, for one of the candles in question (Fig. 30).

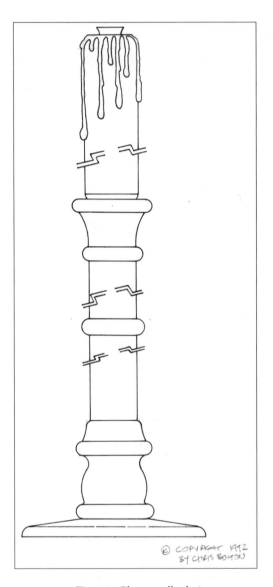

Fig. 30. Glass candle design

Summary

Of course, all costs and fees change. And there are fees you might be unaware of such as demurrage (charges for leaving your merchandise on the docks too long). It is important to do costings for every shipment to keep up on what your products cost you.

Recall those original retailers you spoke to who told you your idea was good and did not exist? Now you must go back to them with your sample, costed out, and see if they approve of both the sample and the price. If not, listen closely and adjust accordingly. When they do approve, you move forward.

Now that you have a handle on costing and pricing your products, and samples, we can begin to find the best independent sales representative to sell your imported products.

▼

CHAPTER SIX:

Selling Your Imported Products

The number one rule in importing is never buy merchandise without the orders-in-hand to warrant the purchase. An order is a legally binding contract on the buyer and the seller specifying what goods are to be shipped where on what date. It may include details such as naming by what means the shipment is to be made. The shipment is the fulfillment of that contract, or otherwise known as "the sale." An order is a contract that agrees on an event, that event being the sale.

Independent sales representatives gain orders on behalf of the importers and manufacturers by showing the importer's samples. Importers ship directly to the customer, and the customer then pays the importer. The importer pays the independent sales representative a commission on the sales generated against an order, almost always after the sale has taken place, and sometimes after your customer pays you, the importer.

It is prudent to start small and learn the ropes, risking no more than you can afford to lose. Often, though, people find this business rewarding enough to want to expand, or discover that working out of Pocatello, Idaho (or wherever), it is just as easy to get an order out of New York and ship it as it is to get an order out of Boise and ship it. Finally, the headaches associated with running a $4000 a year company are exactly the same as running a $4 million per annum company—but the income is better with the latter.

Some may argue a large import company buys merchandise before it has orders. Not really. As a buyer for a larger, established company, I would ask for the minimum order quantity when considering a product. A seller may say, "1,500 pieces," and often I would reply, "well, I can sell that many anyway." For larger companies, with, say, 5,000 customers around the United States, importers just "know" that at least 120 customers will buy a dozen each (1,440 pieces) if the item were simply displayed. So, with a more established company, I could safely buy that many.

The real question is: will this item generate 5,000 units in sales or 5 million units in its life-cycle. We importers have no idea, but the reaction from the market will tell. Based on initial orders against the samples, we can pretty well manage the distribution until we get enough experience with the item to project out what demand will be. Even then we are cautious. So it is with the small importer, and even more strictly true with the start-up year.

The fact of the matter is whether a start-up or an established company, you can easily know if you have enough demand to cover the supplier's minimum order requirements of the item. To do so, you necessarily need a sales force. Let's cover selling your product—that is, getting orders, and how to gain a sales force.

The Retail Market

The multi-trillion dollar retail economy in the United States can be broken down into three major sections: the fashion forward, the mainline retail, and the discounters. The following graphically presents this with the percentages each area has of the total. Which level is the most advantageous for the start-up importer to offer his products? Perhaps all?

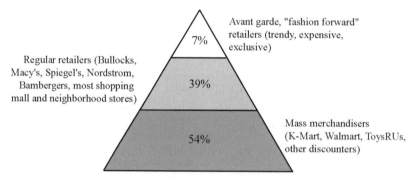

Fig. 31. Major sections of the retail market

Once we have decided this question, how do we find the sales representative best suited to help us penetrate the market? Let us begin by deciding what kind of stores we want to have carry our products.

Earlier we discussed the 54% as represented by Wal-Mart. Such stores are not a reasonable hope for us.

Fig. 31 shows that 7% of the United States' retail market is the fashion forward kinds of stores. These are the exclusive, very expensive kinds of stores catering to the avant garde. The store I compared to Wal-Mart earlier, Gump's, is an example of such a store, one of tens of thousands in the USA.

The middle level is the mainline retail stores, comprising 39% of the United States market. These stores are the common department stores, sole proprietor retail stores in neighborhood shopping districts, and most of the stores in most of the shopping malls. This group is undergoing interesting changes as the discounters begin to serve their customers better, and as the wealthier prefer the Neiman Marcus experience to the Macy's experience.

You may introduce your product at any level you wish. When deciding what store to work with as you develop your product, keep in mind retailers have a specific market to which they cater.

The Mass Markets

The 54% group is quite attractive to many start-up importers because these volume retailers place large orders. This assures that the importer will be able to meet the minimum quantities required for purchase by the supplier overseas.

On the other hand, one learns quickly that the kinds of stores in the 7% group tend to place very small orders and rarely reorder. Why put all that time and effort for such a small result?

Is the 39% group then the best compromise? Yes, but there is more to it. The 54% group, the discounters, are the "conservator" retailers that are offering popular and proven items for sale at the lowest possible price. As we have explained, your new item is neither popular nor proven. In time, perhaps, but not yet.

Also, the 54% group has buyers that are extremely difficult to contact. They are very busy, and if you do get ahold of one by phone, he will want to know what you have to sell. Remember, such buyers are primarily interested in getting the cheapest price on very popular items. Immediately there are two strikes against you. One is the fact that the buyer has never heard of you. If you call and claim you can provide the cheapest socks in the world, they will hang up on you because the buyer knows who can provide the cheapest socks in the world, and it is not you.

With all the huge socks manufacturers competing aggressively in many ways you cannot begin to imagine for that buyer's sock business, you do not stand a chance of selling your socks at this level.

You may have a relative in Argentina that is the director of a sock factory. This relative has promised you full support if you gain orders for the factory. This factory may even be the same factory manufacturing for the major sock companies you are competing against for orders from the retailer. It does not matter—you will still lose. Why? Because being a discounter is a capital intensive exercise. Your competition is willing and able to invest 99¢ to earn a penny. You will have neither the capital nor the economies of scale to compete in that market.

A friend of mine, before attending my seminar, designed an infant carrier based on the classic Oriental design usually executed in cloth. She made some minor design changes, specified a more modern fabric, replaced the need to hand tie the carrier with plastic D-rings, and brought the product to Toys-R-Us. She gained a $75,000 order for the baby carrier.

Orders from such major companies usually have two or three pages of conditions you must accept with the order (conditions you may reject, but you will lose the order). In addition to the conditions, there is usually a routing guide that stipulates how and when to ship. Many situations are covered: where from and where to; how much weight will determine what trucker is to carry the freight; and what to do in case of delays.

The order had some conditions I found objectionable, but my friend could not object since she had already accepted the order. Remember, in the United States, an order is legally binding on both the buyer and the seller. The condition that most concerned me was the "chargeback for failure to make the delivery window."

A chargeback is a common way for retailers to punish their suppliers for failing to meet all of the retailer's demands. For instance, a retailer may require you, the seller, to put the retailer's purchase order number on the bill of lading covering a shipment. If you fail to comply, the retailer deducts a fee (or "chargeback") from the payment of your invoice. These fees normally run anywhere from $25 to $50, but for more egregious failures to comply with the order, up to $250. The chargebacks are supposed to reflect the cost the retailer bears because of your error. In this instance, the retailer may need the purchase order number on the bill of lading so the receiving clerk can quickly find the store's paperwork relating to the incoming shipment. When the purchase order number is not evident on the bill of lading, the receiving clerk must drop everything and research the order in the main office. This waste of time costs the store money, so they "charge you back."

Some stores abuse this practice, and try to lower their costs by charging back on a variety of pretexts. That was not the case in this instance of the baby carrier.

A delivery window is a specific time the retailer wants the merchandise to arrive. For instance, a retailer may define a delivery window on an order as Tuesday, March 1st, between the hours of 7am and 8am.

The baby carrier order in question featured tight delivery windows of this nature and a $250 chargeback for failure to meet the delivery window. That may seem excessive, but it accurately reflects the capital at risk for a huge operation like Toys R Us. Such a store cannot afford to have management, labor and paperwork waiting around for product to show up. They pre-plan when the shelf space will be free so customers see only shelves bulging with merchandise, and usually in concert with some form of advertising. Failure to deliver on time is costly for the stores.

To further heighten the suspense, the $75,000 order was to be divided between 50 stores! Some quick calculations proved, at the very tight margins this deal was generating, it did not take many late deliveries to wipe out all of the profit.

A company like Mattel can demand trucking companies deliver their products to meet the delivery windows. Mattel moves so much cargo that the trucking companies gladly organize their schedules around the needs of Mattel. Can someone working off their kitchen table with a measly $75,000 order (actually 50 orders of $1,500 each) command such cooperation?

Had she run into some kind of delay in manufacturing or importing, she may have faced order cancellation and even a lawsuit for the failure to perform as contracted in the purchase order. The expense these major retailers incur in administration and advertising is vast, and can be recovered only if they sell your product. If you fail to deliver the product, you will have to "make whole" the retailer, that is, pay them what they lost. Often you will see the ads placed in newspapers by Target or Sears that say something to the effect of "due to a manufacturer's delivery problem, the pharmacy style lamp advertised in our March 10 circular is not available." These ads are placed at the expense of the offending supplier.

To make a saga short, by the grace of God our friend with the baby carrier was able to ship on time and without many problems. But that was the end of the business, because she could get no reorders.

The failure to get reorders reflects another reality. The shelf space at these stores is watched closely by suppliers and, in a way, fought over. The sales representatives of many companies visit the stores to observe what products are gaining shelf space. This shelf space represents income to the sales representatives.

If a product like the baby carriers shows up, a sales representatives may buy one and send it back to their company headquarters to find out how low in cost the item can be made. Naturally, a huge corporation can make the item very inexpensively, compared to people working off their kitchen table. If the item is popular, there will be reorders, but they will go to someone who can provide the item at a lower cost. A patent will not protect you in this instance, since the designers will simply improve the item to the point it is superior to yours and make a patent moot.

Finally, these large retailers tend to pay very slowly. As your creditors demand payment from you, you in turn are trying to demand payment from people who know they can make you wait. It is cheaper for the store to have you to wait for your money than it is to borrow money from a bank. As you and tens of thousands of other vendors await payment, the retailers in effect enjoy interest free loans at your expense. Yes, you can add interest onto the statements, but when they pay up sans interest charges, you'll be so glad to get paid that you will ignore the fact the interest was never paid.

The Regular Retail Markets

The mainline retailers and the fashion forward are actually one in the same market. Certain retailers, like Neiman Marcus,[48] actually cover both segments in one store. If a sales representative covers the 39% segment, he will also cover the 7% segment, or vice versa. On the other hand, the sales representatives covering the 54% segment work only that area.

Although some readers may still hesitate to walk away from a segment that is 54% of the entire United States retail market, keep in mind the regular and avant garde retail markets equal 46%, and that is of a multi-trillion dollar total.

And to contrast these stores, note that it is a very easy process to gain orders from the retailers serving the upper segments. It is an easy process to fulfill the orders, which are normally straightforward, just a matter of packing the items in a box and shipping it via UPS to the store. Often you are free to deliver the items yourself, if the store is local.

You will get only small orders from these stores. Over time, as your products prove to be more and more popular, the stores will place larger and larger orders with you. You will not expose yourself to the danger of a large order, or having "all of your eggs in one basket."

---

48. Also affectionately known in the trade as "Needless Markups."

There will be very little competition. Nobody will be stealing your ideas, because, for the small orders you are getting, it is not worth anybody's effort. Your competition will be limited to who has the best designs, not who has the lowest prices.

And finally, these stores pay on time.

People are amazed to hear of small business people getting appointments with Nordstrom buyers and such upper-end stores. Your ticket into the Nordstrom buyer's office is the fact that you are a new company. This is where such buyers find the new and different items that their customers expect from Nordstrom.

As a matter of fact, department stores pass out purchase orders quite freely. But what would you imagine an opening order from Nordstrom, to cover three stores would be in dollar volume? I have received plenty of those (Fig. 32).

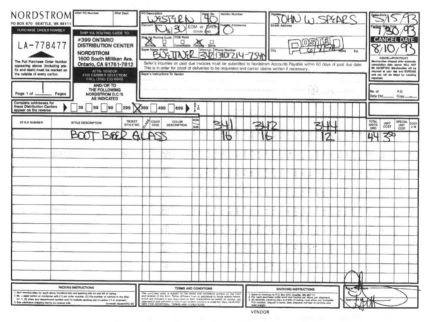

Fig. 32. Sample Nordstrom purchase order

Will the Retailer Go Around Me?

We know without a customer we have nothing. We explored the problem of defining a good customer, and agreed that at the small business level it is the better stores, upper end retailers, that make our best customers.

Then we explored which comes first, the customer or the product, and we outlined how those companies we see thriving came up with their product. And then we learned that those companies we see thriving in international trade are the ones very often started on the basis of a problem solved, a problem experienced by the founder, and the founder having the "why don't they just..." experience.

We visualized which stores in our area would sell such an item, and then we tested our bright idea by asking, as a customer of the store, if they have the item which we have conceived.

If they do have it, we buy it, and move on to another idea.

If they do not have it, we push up through the clerks to the buyers to make sure. We keep pushing until we are told our idea is good, but does not exist.

This process also yields, naturally, more ideas for us to fold into our original concept, improving yet more.

Eventually we leverage the retailers' confirmation of our idea as good and non-existent into samples of our item from the best source in the world. These are leading suppliers, and as such feel pressure from competition on their main lines, and are always searching out new product lines to produce. We return with our samples of the item which was deigned good and nonexistent, and we surprise the retailers by switching from their "customer" to their potential supplier of a needed item.

The first question every buyer asks every sales rep is "what is new?" Store buyers spend 80% of their time looking for 20% of what they sell. They spend 20% of the time looking for 80% of what they sell. 80% of what retailers sell is the same old-same old; that is easy to find, just phone in a reorder. The other 20%—the new and different items that retailers must have to keep the store fresh, interesting and attractive to their customer base—this 20% of the stock takes 80% of their time to find. This is only natural; the 20% is new and different, thus hard to find.

So when we return with the samples of items we've already determined are a good idea but nonexistent, we are a boon to the retailer. We have a new item to offer, one they already believe to be a good idea…but it now exists!

But now we have a problem: won't the retailers to whom we show our idea steal it from us, or cause it to be stolen from us by going around us to the factory direct?

The short answer is no. It cannot happen in any meaningful sense, for a structural reason.

Let me first confirm a few important points that you may intuit, causing your concern. First, if in fact we are working with first rate retailers and first rate suppliers, the two probably already know about each other. Expect this.

Second, the improvements in communication and transportation world-wide would make this "going around you" even easier today. And since they badly want new ideas, shouldn't they hurry things along and go around you?

So why won't they go around you? Why can't they go around you?

Let's back up and fill in a few blanks. Earlier we eliminated the prospect, if ever there was one, of selling to such stores as Target, K-Mart, Walgreen's or Walmart: too big for us. The other end of the spectrum is orders too small for us. Every basic accounting book can show you how to run a break-even analysis, a formula for determining how small of an order you will accept. This is necessary because some customers only want a mini-mum order amount, and you need to be prepared to quote a minimum figure. For gift and housewares the figure is $150.00. Any order less than $150.00 will actually be a money loser for a small gift and housewares company, because it will cost more to process and ship the order than the profits allow. We'll learn more about minimum order requirement, and how to find what it is in your industry later.

But now let's go back to the stores we will commonly serve, better stores such as those one-of-a-kind stores in every community, the boutiques, and the specialty chains such as Smith and Hawkins. We also mentioned in the class such major, upscale chains as Macy's, Neiman-Marcus, Nordstrom and Saks as potential customers. Know, though, that these big names will likely never be more than 20% of your sales, and the one-of-a-kind upper-end stores will be about 80% of your customers.

I have sold to all of the stores, and more, and mail order catalogs, over the net, you name it, they are my customers. When my company was new, stores would place orders for my product. Teaching face to face classes I often poll the group to ask what they think the dollar value of an order a store—say Nordstrom—offers with their initial orders.

People commonly say $50,000, $100,000 and $5,000 and other such reasonable amounts, especially if the order is for multi-stores.

What if these numbers were wrong? What would it mean if even major stores, when buying a product, placed orders more towards the minimum price dollar range?

What if an order to a small company like yours from a big company like Nordstrom was normally in the minimum range, say $200.00?

If small orders to small companies were the rule, even from large buyers, then what would this mean about the reality of building a new business, and as a side issue, what would this mean in regard to retailers "going around us?"

As you can see in figure 32, the total amount is $154 even though the goods are being distributed to a variety of Nordstrom stores.

If small orders are the rule, then one of the values we provide in business is to buy the supplier's minimum order requirement, and break it up among various stores from which we've received orders. Indeed the German word for wholesaler is "grosshandler," one who buys 144 to sell out a few at a time, taking a profit for the trouble. Indeed, this is partially a value we provide, acting to some extent as a grosshandler.

We can expect that the supplier's minimum order is far greater than a buyer's minimum order, meaning we must aggregate perhaps hundreds of orders from customers in the United States to cover the supplier's minimum production requirement.

So say the supplier requires a 2000 piece minimum for an items that costs your $4.00 each, and you sell these for $10.00 each. And your customers normally wish only 24 each minimum order for their stores, so merely $240.00 worth. 2000 divided by 24 is about 85, so you'd need to aggregate minimum orders from about 85 stores to cover the supplier minimum production run.

This is, as I mentioned in previously, our main strategy. Of course, we are only speaking with maybe a half dozen retailers locally to get started, and that is not enough business to cover the suppliers minimum production requirement. Next we'll see how we get to enough customers around the USA to cover the supplier's minimum production requirement.

But back to the problem of the buyer going around you directly to the supplier.

Buyers have absolutely no idea what will sell and what will not. Nor do sales representatives, nor anyone else. Don't take my word for it, ask them, they will tell you themselves. What buyers do, if they see something that looks like a good idea and doesn't exist yet, is give it a try.

They will try an absolute minimum order, and see how it goes. In fact, everything new they try is always a small test. The orders you see on the order sample above from Nordstrom is not unusual—it is typical. Not only typical, but common. Just about anyone can get an order from Neiman Marcus or Saks or Nordstrom; your ticket into the store is the fact you are a new and small business. This is traditionally where they find their "new" items—the items for which they spend so much time looking.

These test orders, initial orders, the store throw out like confetti. At trade shows the buyers walk up and down the aisles casting them about, hither and yon. They even have a pretty good idea how many of these orders will never be shipped to them, since some small companies never really get around to "starting."

Getting these orders is so common and so easy, it presents a problem to some entrepreneurs. Initial orders from retailers such as Saks and Nordstrom cause the new business owner to rejoice, borrow massively, stock a warehouse as high as they can afford, and wait for success, based on a few initial, confetti-ish orders.

Orders are meaningless. They are necessary for a business, but not sufficient. Beyond orders, even from Saks and Nordstrom, we need reorders, or we do not have a business. To believe you've succeeded because major stores have bought from you is an error. Unless you get reorders, you've got nothing.

The reality is, retail stores never take risks. They minimize risk by testing our small orders, and in fact throw them out, as I said, like confetti. So, on the one hand, we must get orders from many stores, but on the other hand, orders from many stores is rather easy to do. Also, we have the added benefit of many stores to work with, of feedback coming from a wider market than you may have originally conceived.

Earlier I hinted that a larger order necessarily would be a tip-off that something was wrong. Say you were at a trade show, and among the orders, you were to receive from a company a $5,000 order. You being a start-up company, I would only need to hear you received a sizable order to know you were about to be robbed. I would not need to know what your product was, nor who the customer was.

The reason is that since retailers never take risks, to find one buying a large amount means they have no intention of ever paying for what you will ship. You would protest, the company is twenty years old, with excellent credit references. And then I would be sure you were being robbed.

Since it is so egregious to place large orders with new companies, I would know that the company you received the order from is going out of business. Yes, they have three excellent credit references they gave you, but they have another fifty dissatisfied suppliers they did not mention.

They also have a bank who holds a perfected security agreement on the retailer's home, and the retailer is some $300,000 short in the balance sheets, owing the bank and others. Unless the retailer comes up with the money before shutting down, the retailer will lose his home and all personal assets. Bankruptcy is not an option, because the bank gets to take the home, whether or not the retailer is incorporated.

So here is what the retailer does. The retailer places as many $5,000 orders with as many importers and manufacturers as possible, and offers the three excellent credit references. The vendors check the references, and ship based on the sterling feedback. The retailer receives the goods, puts them on 50%, 75%, maybe 100% off sale, who cares? The retailer has no intention of ever paying for the goods anyway!

The goods pour in, blow out, the retailer pays off the bank, keeping his personal assets secure, and no doubt enjoys a tidy sum left over, and closes up. We importers and manufacturers who shipped are holding unsecured notes, but we can sue. Since it is too large for small claims court, we go to civil court, where it will cost no doubt at least $5,000 to get a judgment for $5,000. And of course we will win, but now that we are at zero, we can now go through the process of collecting our judgment, an expensive process when we are an unsecured creditor. The harder we try, the more we lose.

Now please understand, the vast majority of retailers are as honest as you or I. But it only takes one early on to ruin your company. How to keep from being robbed by the unscrupulous few we will learn in the chapter on finance.

Small orders are normal, and make our business rather likely and easy. No retailer in his right mind wants the risk and capital encumbrance of the minimum order requirement of a supplier overseas—especially on a new and untried item such as ours. Large initial orders are an anomaly, something of which to be wary.

Reflect on the value you provide in the market place, the role you play: you introduce new items to stores desirous of such items, you help overseas makers expand sales to the United States.

Since the idea of "finding something cool overseas" or "having a source of cheap whatever" is so commonly thought to be the way of international trade, I could easily affirm that was the case, spend these pages rattling off import and export rules and regulations, get you all ready for international trade, and turn you loose—and when you fail you'd blame yourself, and all the effort wasted. But that would be no fun for me, so I prefer to teach what works, in spite of the fact that trying to wean people away from the false approach is rather tedious.

For those insistent they have a wonderful product from overseas: prove it with orders. At zero cost to you, you can find out immediately, before you invest a dime, if there is any interest in what you believe will sell. Simply walk into the stores you expect to sell the item, show the buyer or owner, and see what they say. Try this soon and tell me what they say. If it does not work out, you can try what does work—what I lay out in this book.

And once you have the supplier and customer established, as I lay out, the rules, regulations, logistics, finance, organization, license—all become exceptionally easy.

Having said all of this, let me also make the point that over time, as your product becomes more and more successful, in fact people do steal your idea. But this is years later, after you are "done" with the idea, have made your money on the item and leave it to others to chew on what are now your scraps.

Now on to the task at hand: we need to find the very best possible independent sales representative for the market segment we wish to serve.

How To Find the Best Independent Sales Representative for Your Products

We have found a product in your field of interest that solves a problem and provides a value; retailers have confirmed it is a good idea and does not exist; we have found the best place in the world to have it made; we got samples and costed the item. We had the original retailers confirm we got the samples right; and now we must find the best very best independent sales representatives possible, to see if we can get enough orders to cover a minimum production run of the supplier. Although you have spoken to some retailers, you need to contact many more, if nothing else to aggregate enough test orders from retailers to match the minimum order amount of the supplier overseas.

The way most importers market products is through independent sales representatives, as explained earlier. So, to sell your product, you must find independent sales representatives, and preferably the very best. Independent sales representatives can lend you credibility, informally check credit on your customers, know who to sell to, and know when to sell. They provide you endless tips about packaging, pricing, improvements, distribution, and, in general, teach you about the business. They are likely to assist you in building your representative network nationwide. Finding the best independent sales representative for your product is easy when you simply ask yourself, "Who is the best judge of an independent sales representative's effectiveness?" The answer, of course, is the retailer, your customers. No other source or opinion matters!

Simply ask the retailers you've already spoken to, the ones who originally told you, "Your item is a good idea, and does not exist," for the name of an independent sales representative the retailer thinks would be best for your product. You may get a few different names from a few different retailers, but ultimately at least one name will come up most often.

Every independent sales representative will be glad to meet with anyone who has a new line. But when you call an independent sales representative and mention that, "The handbag buyer at Nordstrom says you are the best rep in the territory," you at once communicate your own seriousness and professionalism. From an independent sales representative's point of view, many people would like to see their products sell, but few have the savvy and discipline to do the support and paperwork required to sustain the business. So it is important you present yourself well.

You may also be surprised at what the buyers tell you. Buyers may tell you they buy the kinds of products you are selling in Los Angeles or New York . If this is true, then you must contact the appropriate independent sales representative in that territory. Either way, you will gain this name from the local buyers with whom you are making friends. The local retailer most likely will name a local rep, and that retailer no doubt occasionally places orders with reps in other cities for like products. Because of this, it is likely a local retailer can name reps around the country for you, as well as locally. Also, the local rep likely mentions connections he has found to reps in other territories, and vice versa. Your job is to mine these veins of gold.

When you meet the independent sales representative, be prepared to give a review of your products, what you have accomplished to date, and the direction you are planning to go. Then sit back, answer questions and let the independent sales representative begin to teach you all about the business. All of the questions you have that weren't answered in research the reps can handle. Also, the MBAs talk about something called the "concept of the offer." These are the details in pricing, packaging and so on that the reps will advise you on, and help shape the presentation so your line will gain the most advantage in the marketplace.

When I say "the line," let me clarify that usually a product is actually a range of items. In an earlier example, I spoke of a mountain-climbing pick-ax. In reality we would come up with five or six models to introduce, each with different features. The glass candles you saw in the costing earlier started out as a single item, but of course I needed at least twelve models to interest retailers in buying a selection for their customers, and actually developed 24 initially. As reorders came in, I could tell which three were hot designs, and which three were dead. I could dump the three dead items, and introduce a few new ones based on new ideas and expanding the theme that sold well.

If the independent sales representative declines to take on the line, find out why, and learn what you have to do to be represented by the best. When you have learned that, go improve your company as suggested by the independent sales representative.

Generally, independent sales representatives are willing to take on lines to test. But if the line performs poorly, then they will drop the line. This casual approach may disconcert you. Again, this business is in your blood, yet these other people may view it as just one of many possible lines to carry. If they do take your line, then you must discuss a contract.

The Contract With An Independent Sales Representative

When the independent sales representative agrees to take on your line, should the two of you negotiate a contract? My experience of independent sales representatives is that they generally dismiss the idea of a contract. "Why have a contract? You give us samples, we get you orders, you pay us a commission, what could be simpler?" Also, an independent sales representative may be unsure whether your line will warrant continuing after a few weeks, so why get tied up in contract negotiations?

So forget about a contract, but do draw up a "memorandum of understanding." This is a quick, professional document laying down your expectations for this independent sales representative. Remember your independent sales representative (rep) is also representing as many as a dozen other companies. The independent sales representative's "deal" with you may get confused with his "deal" with another company. Sometimes this results in disputes that can harm an otherwise good working relationship.

To avoid this problem, you can briefly discuss the following points:

1. The territory this representative will cover. Name the state or area, and keep this in mind as you contract other independent sales representatives.

2. The dates this agreement is effective. Try to keep this no longer than a year at a time. You will have many issues to discuss each year relating to your agreement and performance.

3. Whether commissions are paid against sales, and the definition of sales. Try to maintain the principle that you, in essence, pay commission on revenue. If an independent sales representative writes a $1,000 order, and you are able to fill only $800 worth of the order, naturally you pay commission only on the $800 you ship. Now what if the customer only pays $500 on the account (or nothing) before going out of business? My position would be the rep must refund the commission, and some independent sales representatives would dispute that. Work this out in advance!

4. Whether all orders from a territory, regardless of source, will be considered commission sales. Perhaps you receive in the mail to your office an order from Pocatello, Idaho. Idaho is your Seattle independent sales representative's territory, but you know the Seattle sales representative has never set foot in that town. Will you give the rep commission on that order, an order he knows nothing about? If not, you ought to inform the independent sales representatives of that plan.

5. Whether the independent sales representative will get commission for orders he writes in unassigned territories. We think certainly.

6. What happens when a customer crosses territories to write orders? This is a particularly touchy issue because it affects both ego and income. Some people feel these are the two most important aspects in a rep's life.

For instance, your Chicago rep has been making a presentation of your line to the Spiegel catalog company. The Spiegel buyer, interested in placing an order, notices the product on display in New York at another rep's showroom. The Spiegel buyer places an order with the New York independent sales representative. Naturally the Chicago rep claims credit, and the New York rep says "prove it, we have the order to prove we did our work!" The Chicago rep has had both ego and income bruised. This can make for a very nasty situation.

Some buyers even exacerbate the problem by purposely crossing boundaries to place orders. A Chicago buyer needs as many orders as possible written in New York to warrant the cost of spending a week in New York at company expense.

Two possible solutions exist. One solution is to state flatly the principle "he who writes the order gets the commission." The other is to split commissions when a buyer crosses the territorial lines. Since splitting commissions is management intensive, and might still lead to some ill will, I recommend the "he who writes..." formula. The most important point to keep in mind is the way you handle this with one independent sales representative is the way you must handle it with every other.

7. Determine when the commissions will be paid, and the rate of commission. Generally, commissions are paid by the middle of the month following the month the sale occurs. For instance, an independent sales representative may write an order in January stipulating an April delivery (or sale). You ship in April, and pay the independent sales representative a commission by May 15. It is important to be prompt with this arrangement, because many states have laws automatically doubling the commission due salespeople 46 days after the commission was earned. This formula assures you do not violate the prompt-payment-of-commissions

laws. Remember this is only one example; many industries use different formulae and timeframes for reckoning commissions. As we mentioned earlier, this is another point to discover in your research on the industry you enter.

Independent sales reps are paid a commission on each sale. How much and when a sale occurs is different in each industry. In the gift and housewares industry, we pay independent sales representatives a commission of 15% on sales, garments 8%, and I have seen anywhere from 2-24% depending on the industry. This means on a $2 sale, a commission of 15% generates a 30¢ commission for the independent sales representative. If you recall from the chapter on costings, a $2 sale represents $1 cost of goods, and $1 gross profit. So the 30¢ commission comes out of a $1 gross profit. This is the time to ask yourself, is it fair to give the independent sales representative 30¢ for merely gaining an order, leaving you only 70¢ to pay for all of your expenses and to cover your risks? If you make no profit, the independent sales representative still gets the commission. Should we not look at ways of cutting the independent sales representative out of the picture?

Many companies attempt this and ultimately fail. One way is to hire in-house sales representatives. In-house sales people often mislead their employers when reviewing prospects and performance. Being on the company expense account, they have no interest in economy. They all too often pad the expenses. And, they may well pad orders, knowing if they lose this customer, their job is more secure since the company is just that much more reliant on keeping representatives in the field trying to gain new business. Is the in-house representative really spending a "working weekend" in Vail, Colorado prospecting new accounts, or is something else going on at company expense?

Even if you are expert at managing a sales force, you will never motivate and manage the in-house sales staff as well as the independent sales representatives do themselves. I've seen studies that show the independent sales representatives are far more efficient than the in-house sales staff. Padding expenses cheats only themselves; reps do not travel extravagantly, and write more orders on each call because they represent more lines.

Finally, independent sales representatives speak frankly with you. If your line looks bad, or if your new products are in poor taste, he will challenge you. If customers complain, you will be informed quickly. The bottom line is you simply cannot run a sales staff as efficiently as the independent sales representatives run themselves.

Another way is to eliminate a sales staff altogether. Simply show your products at the trade shows around the country, and hire local people at minimum wage to take orders with you during the trade shows. This might work for a while, in an extremely strong market, but customer service will suffer and soon you lose touch with your customers; then your sales will dwindle.

Since there is no alternative to the independent sales representative and there is money in your budget to pay them; since they provide tremendous value; and, since your competitors use them, you must use them, too.

8. Decide whether any sales targets or quotas will be established. At least informally these are always in place. An independent sales representative will have a vague idea in mind, an expectation, of what he can do with the products he is representing. Ask your independent sales representative to annually project his sales of your product. This serves two purposes. First, the independent sales representative commits to a number in which he has an ego investment, a powerful motivator. Second, you can see how this matches your expectations, and help in the planning of your company's growth.

Earlier you determined the production capacity of the overseas supplier, and from the independent sales representatives you determine the sales potential. It is essential to the soundness of your business that these figures are within each other's range. This exercise affirms you can reasonably expect to sell what you can make, and you can make what you can sell.

9. Whether any incentives will be established for salespeople. The answer is no, generally. The point in contracting independent sales representatives is to avoid managing and motivating a sales force. On the other hand, you might want to turn unreasonable independent sales representatives' demands for concessions into market-builders for yourself. For instance, a New York rep might claim, "Although 15% commission is standard, you must pay us 20% because New York is a much more expensive place to operate." True in some respects, but other efficiencies like market concentration exist, making the advantages and disadvantages of operating in New York a wash for the independent sales representative. Nonetheless, in this instance you are being squeezed by your independent sales representative, and you must respond. Ask the independent sales representative what dollar value will be generated in New York. If he quotes proportionately low, compare it to other markets and ask the independent sales representative why you should pay more for less performance. If he quotes proportionately higher than other markets, agree to pay 15% (or whatever the standard is in your industry) on sales proportional to other territories, and 20% on sales above the norm, calculated each calendar year.

In this way the independent sales representative is focused on building sales for your product, yet is only rewarded for exceptional sales. As subtly as possible, each year push up the base target to make the 20% commission level. Also, knowing New York is performing proportionally higher than everyone else, mention this to your other independent sales representative and wonder aloud why they are not quite up to snuff. Play one rep off against another.

Working this aggressive angle requires you know the relative sales potential of each territory in the United States. This we will learn in the chapter on financing.

10. Who will pay for samples, and in what quantities they will be available? This is tricky, because on one hand you do not want to give samples away to the independent sales representative. The reps break, lose, sell,

give away and loan out samples forever, especially when they can always get more from you. On the other hand, you want the independent sales representatives to have enough samples to promote the product.

The independent sales representative does not want to pay for samples if he can avoid it, and on an untested line may flat out refuse. If this is the best independent sales representative for the territory, are you going to keep looking for an independent sales representative over this issue? Certainly not, and the reps know that.

How can you reconcile the independent sales representatives' refusal to pay for samples with your need to control the expenses associated with samples? The standard practice is to "memo bill" all samples. A memo bill is an invoice that states the wholesale value of the products delivered as samples, and requires that the invoice be paid before any replacement samples are shipped. There is no time limit on a memo bill. If the item is discontinued from the line, the sample must be returned, or paid for. Naturally the independent sales representatives will not pay any invoices, but with this stipulation you are free to deduct the cost of disappearing samples from the commissions you owe the independent sales representatives.

Some importers let the samples be billed at cost, which does promote the practice of independent sales representatives and their employees buying your products as samples for personal use. This can be beneficial within bounds. Testimonials are powerful sales tools. If an independent sales representative says to a client about your product, "I have one in my home," it will often promote the sale. On the other hand, you want to limit this activity somewhat. Remember, an independent sales representative earning 15% on a $2 wholesale price might be tempted to order 1,000 of your items at $1 cost on his own account and resell himself at the $2 price, netting an easy extra $700. (1,000 items at $2 = a $2,000 sale, and a 15% commission = a $300 commission; to take that same order and buy 1,000 "samples" from you at $1 each and reship to his customer at $2 each generates a gross profit of $1,000, $700 more than the $300 a mere commission would generate).

Therefore, include wording to the effect that "samples are available in quantities adequate to the task of promoting the product."

11. How will samples be shipped, and on whose account? Be low key on this, simply saying the representative pays the freight as part of the memo bill on the samples, to be deducted from commissions. If they object strenuously, then compromise by agreeing to pay all surface freight for samples. This is reasonable, but by all means avoid paying the cost on air freighted samples. From an independent sales representatives' point of view, all samples need to be shipped Federal Express overnight service. This is extremely expensive, and rarely necessary. If they absolutely need it overnight, they can pay for it. You will be amazed at how rarely samples are truly needed overnight.

12. Will export shipments be allowed? Try not to get in the business of exporting imported goods. The paperwork involved quickly wipes out any profit or fun. As we explained earlier, it is far better to have your products shipped directly from the overseas factory to customers in third countries. But in the event a Harrods buyer wants to place a small order with your company, insist that the payment be in advance and the goods be delivered to a United States address. Most foreign buyers have consolidators in the United States that gather these small orders for export. It is an expense the buyer would rather avoid and make you pay, but with a firm policy you can avoid the expense and leave it for them to pay.

This could be said of Canada and Mexico as well, except with NAFTA, trade with these countries is becoming far more difficult and the paperwork has been increased, so some traders have found it prohibitive to sell to Canada and Mexico, or import from there.

Working With an Independent Sales Representative

While discussing these points with the independent sales representatives, they will be concerned about your ability to perform as well. It is one thing to develop a wonderful product, but do you have what it takes to do the paperwork, keep records and service the customers?

Many polls have been conducted to determine retailers' major complaints, which naturally are concerns of every independent sales representative.[49] You must communicate to the independent sales representative the fact that you are aware of these concerns and will not allow the problems to be a part of your business. Keep in mind that you pay the independent sales representatives, but they work for the retailers. Vendors such as you come and go, but a relationship with a retailer is the lifeblood to the reps. To cover these complaints, make sure the independent sales representative knows you, the importer, intend to:

1. Endeavor to be an industry leader by introducing new lines at least semiannually (industry leaders are rarely the biggest or oldest companies, if ever). Here again, the importance of competing on design is paramount. By bringing out a new line every six months, you answer an important question the reps face every day: what's new? Keep in mind the new lines do not have to be great, just new. Often the new lines will flop. So what? You only had samples anyway. New lines are added to existing lines to expand your offerings. As a rule of thumb you want to drop about 20% of your line each year, and replace it with more products, likely better products. Establish a criterion for whether an item is kept or dumped. A rational test is to decide if the product sells four times a minimum order required by the supplier. For instance, if the supplier requires you buy $5,000 dollars worth a year, four times $5,000 is $20,000, at cost. Convert this to the wholesale amount, that is, $40,000. Therefore any product experiencing sales of less than $40,000 at wholesale per year is targeted for dumping from the line. The reason for the "four times the minimum" criterion is that, to be most profitable in gift and housewares, I expect to have four inventory turnovers per

---

49. *Giftware Business* publication began polling retailers in the early 1980s and has found the complaints to be fairly consistent over the years.

year. In other words, in general I expect my products to be in my warehouse for no more than three months before they are sold.

These policies keep your line fresh and active. I understand that at the 3M Corporation, a division is excluded from the bonus plan if more than 20% of their product line is more than five years old. Such stipulations encourage conservators to get out in the field and appropriate new products.

2. Ship orders as accurately and completely as possible. There is no excuse for not shipping accurately. Ship only what is ordered. Far more difficult is to ship completely. As your company grows, your product offerings will grow. A company with four million dollars in sales may have 400 items in its product line. Since these products may come from various suppliers, and even different countries, it is difficult to have all products in stock at the same time.

Fulfillment rate in the gift and housewares industry is about 80%. This means of every $1,000 in orders, about $800 will actually be shipped; about $600 of it will be shipped on time and the balance will be back ordered. Know what the averages are for your industry and make sure your experience falls within the averages. Certainly do better if possible and if doing better costs you nothing extra, but do not do worse. Garment companies, like Generra in Seattle, aggressively pursue as high a fulfillment rate as possible. Generra's corporate goal is to have 85% fulfillment rate.[50]

3. Maintain sound records. I am always surprised how the independent sales representatives are so concerned whether the importer can handle the paperwork. It seems simple to me, yet it must be a problem, because it is always a major question. The chapter on organizing your operations should be sufficient to meet their concerns. At the heart of the concern is whether you keep records accurately enough to assure the independent sales representatives gain just compensation for the orders they write. Maintain sound records. If any of your associates,

---

50. Information taken from Generra internal documents received unsolicited and anonymously.

customers, reps or suppliers gets a sense that your records are disorderly, expect to be treated harshly. They will expect to be given the benefit of the doubt in all disputes, and they will treat you contemptuously because they expect you to fail soon. With such excellent and inexpensive computer hardware and software available there is no excuse for poor records. I operate strictly with Macintosh hardware and use MYOB by BestWare (PC Version available, too—both about $90) as my software. I paid about $2,500 for computing capability superior to capability we paid over $140,000 for in 1982. Today you can have it for less than one thousand dollars. There is no excuse for unsound records.

4. Answer inquiries and complaints promptly. Inquiries are potential orders, and complaints are both the opportunity and means to improve your company. Ignoring or failing to act on inquiries and complaints is an early warning of business failure. Customers order from you with a view to turning a profit. If they have to ask questions or voice complaints they are wasting time. Swiftly answer complaints and inquiries and go one step further: consider the cause of the question or complaint and attempt to take action that will prevent such a question or complaint from happening again.

5. Adjust billing problems promptly. Nothing disinterests a customer more than wasting time with billing problems. A quick way to slow the income is to leave billing problems unresolved. Some department stores purposely confuse billing issues to delay and reduce payment. Your billings, or receivables, are one of the two areas where problems can occur that are fatal to your business. The other is inventory, which we will study in the chapter on managing the company.

A Foot In The Door

Once an independent sales representative has agreed to take on your line, usually the first question is, "What can you do for my customers?" The question is in reference to advantages you will give his customers, incentives your independent sales representative may offer to the retailers so they are more inclined to buy your products.

These incentives come in many varieties. One is quantity discounts. Although this is common practice, it is appropriate only to the conservator. A small business, the innovator, cannot generate the economies of scale that warrant quantity discounts. At a seminar I taught I found on the floor a piece of paper with an anonymous example of this point. I reproduce it in its entirety:

●   ●   ●

The Folly of Price Cutting

On the basis of 25% profit, a cut of:
5% requires 18% more dollar volume and handling 25% more merchandise.
8% requires 35% more dollar volume and handling 47% more merchandise.
10% requires 50% more dollar volume and handling 66 2/3% more merchandise.
12% requires 69% more dollar volume and handling 92% more merchandise.
15% requires 112% more dollar volume and handling 150% more merchandise.
20% requires 300% more dollar volume and handling 400% more merchandise.

In other words, if you cut price 15% on a $100 sale, it is necessary to sell $212.00 in volume and you must handle two and one-half times as much merchandise before you can make a profit of $25.00 to which the original $100.00 sale entitles you.

●   ●   ●

Or in the way a Certified Public Accountant put it: "increase sales and go out of business." His pithy comment is in reference to the fact that some 80% of all new businesses are defunct within five years, and most of those that do go out of business experience a sales increase just before closing. This sales increase is either part of an orderly liquidation process, or more commonly the result of a price cut that increases sales but does not generate enough revenue to keep up with expanding costs.[51]

Another concession the independent sales representatives may request is "full freight allowance." The freight charges due the trucking company or UPS for carrying merchandise from your warehouse to the retail store is the responsibility of the retailer. They expect to pay any such charges, but naturally are delighted if they do not have to. Some companies entice orders from buyers by offering to pay any freight charges. In essence, this is another way of competing on price.

Yet another concession might have to do with "advertising dollars," referred to as "advertising co-op plan." Generally very complicated, such plans often require a year-end accounting, just when everyone is eager to close the books and long after any bookkeeping errors have occurred. It is just these sorts of minor errors, long ago committed, that keep customers from paying you. For example, a common plan might allow a retailer to deduct up to 3% from your invoices to pay for up to 50% of the cost of advertising your products. On a $1,000 invoice, your customer may deduct $30 toward the cost of an advertisement featuring your product. If the ad cost $60 or more, the customer can take the whole $30. If the ad cost less, say $40, then the retailer may only deduct 50%, or $20. Few legitimate ads cost this little, but when a retailer features many products on one page, the page must be prorated among everyone else's products featured on the page. From an administrative point of view, this is like trying to manage a train wreck in progress.

To encourage your retailer to advertise your product is a powerful way to build sales, but you certainly do not want to get caught up in the co-op craziness.

---

51 Daniel Jack Chasen, "Anchor Systems: how a sudden success crashed and burned," *The Weekly* (Seattle, June 27, 1984): 22. The leading computer retailer in Microsoft's home town grows rapidly and blows it, for reasons common to many failed enterprises.

Small-business importers can promote their products by a method of advertising allowances. Offer a simple ad allowance, 3% is normal, 5% is generous, but we offer 10%, to entice the retailers to advertise the product (the 10% if you recall is our net profit). The program calls for a straight ad allowance on any order for which the merchandise is advertised, and the ad must mention the name of your company. This offer is made to every retailer, regardless of size, but of course only the bigger stores and mail order houses accept it.

The 10%, or say $100 on a $1,000 order, seems substantial, but is negligible when taking into consideration the obvious cost plus the hidden costs of administration of co-op plans. All retailers have an advertising budget, and they will advertise products, allowances or no. But $100 would not pay for the color separations to produce the ad, so in effect you get a lot of benefit for the $100. Since almost all retailers already have advertising budgets (I have heard from 3% to 15% of sales), this ad allowance simply tips the scales toward your product. The 10% looks substantial and is impressive to any buyer whose aggressiveness in getting concessions from vendors is subject to review—that is, pleasing to superiors. Also, it provides a discipline to divert requests for quantity discounts and freight allowances, for which you gain nothing for the inevitable reduction in revenue. ("Do you have a freight allowance?" "No, but we have an aggressive ad allowance.")

The important question is: does it promote sales? My experience has been, yes, it does, in three ways:

1. The store orders a bit more in anticipation of the increase demand from the ad.

2. The store reorders (at times even assigns an SKU number or logs you in for automatic computer-programmed buying), because inevitably somebody tore out the ad and put it on the refrigerator for two months and then came in looking for the items. Since none of the reorders are against an ad, no discounts are given for reorders. Some studies show that 50% of

sales generated by an ad will occur within 30 days after the ad appears. The next 50% will occur over the following four months.[52] Those people who keep trickling in asking for your product encourage the buyer to reorder your product. Unless the buyer advertises again, no discounts are given on these reorders.

3. Since the ad allowance is used only by stores with some power in the local market, it puts all your would-be promotion dollars concentrated into tight local markets. Other retailers in the area see your product advertised, in effect "approved" by the heavy hitters, and inevitably the smaller stores in the area get on the bandwagon and fuel what will seem to you a feeding-frenzy around your product.

The discount is taken only against "proof-of-tear sheet." A tear-sheet is a copy of the ad literally torn out of the magazine, newspaper or catalog in which the ad appeared. In this manner, it is simple to administer. The retailer mails you a check for $900 along with the tear-sheet, and you can zero balance your accounts receivable. No tear-sheet, no discount allowed. This method has been proven over time as very effective for small businesses, and how big businesses who were once small, like Nike, did it.

Radio ads can be accepted as well. In that case, the radio station has a log of everything broadcast and will provide proof the ads were broadcast.

Many independent sales representatives will encourage you to print up full color brochures of your product line to help them sell your product. Never, under any circumstances, should you produce such brochures. They are expensive, quickly out of date, and serve no purpose. You will see brochures passed out at trade shows, and many independent sales representatives will give them away as well. We have yet to see a brochure write an order. If the independent sales representative does not write the order, the customer will not be writing an order later, with or without a brochure. If an independent sales representative truly needs pictures for

52. See William Cohen, *Building a Mail Order Business* (John Wiley & Sons, 1996).

road work that prohibits him from carrying around many samples, then put picture sleeves in a three-ring binder and make one catalog of your line. The cost may be $6–8 per catalog, but you'll need no more than a dozen or so, and they can be constantly revised. Better yet, put your catalog on a website (and certainly, as you begin this business, search the web for businesses who do what you hope to do). Old-fashioned catalog sheets will cost you a minimum of $500 each run.

The Independent Sales Representatives as Research and Development

Initially we develop products based on what interests us most, and we temper our own inclinations with input from the very retailers we imagine will sell our product. Those retailers will refer us to the very best independent sales representative, who in turn will gain us more and more customers. Eventually, we have more customers than we can communicate with directly, especially as we go nationwide. Therefore, we must shift the primary contact from ourselves and the customers to ourselves and the independent sales representatives, who will provide the contact with the customers.

Customer feedback is critical to improving your product lines and spotting the new trends. Your customers will also complain about problems with your company, which you must heed. You must develop a means to keep the independent sales representatives giving you the feedback from your customers. Develop a simple one or do a web search for business feedback forms and adopt one that best suits your product and market. The forms might be sent in weekly. Focus first on getting the independent sales representatives in the habit of sending in the form; later you can start directing the quality of the content of the form. Reps hate paperwork, so you may have to tie the payment of commissions into the receipt of the feedback form. Make a habit of reviewing these forms and responding to every point brought up on the forms by way of a review memo, mentioning what action is being taken in response to the feedback forms. This will encourage the reps to keep sending the forms.

Also survey your customers directly, offering them a small discount on their next order if they respond.

How To Build a Nationwide Sales Representative Network

There are two ways to accomplish this goal. One is fast and expensive, the other is slow and cheap.

The fast and expensive way is to simply repeat the process we recommend for finding an independent sales representative for your local market. That is, fly to every major market in the United States and spend a few days meeting with leading stores to show them your line and ask who is the best local independent sales representative. In the gift and housewares industry, this would require visiting about a dozen major cities. It may take more or less time in other industries.

The slow and cheap method is to ask your local independent sales representative to recommend another independent sales representative in the other markets. All of the independent sales representatives in a given industry tend to know one another. They have worked together at one time, or carry similar lines and visit regularly at the premier trade shows. If they are doing well with your product, they can recommend you to their fellow independent sales representatives in other cities.

Then it is a matter of sending samples to the independent sales representatives recommended to you. You follow up with telephone discussions. It is not ideal, but the price is right.

In either event, when speaking to the independent sales representatives, do inquire about the organization the independent sales representative is running. The following is a list of legitimate concerns an importer should ask about:

Independent Sales Representative Agency Questionnaire

1. Agency sales power:

   A. How many field sales representatives does your agency have?

   B. Is the owner actively involved as a salesperson?

   C. What is the number of office personnel?

   D. How many offices or showrooms do you have?

   E. What hours do the showrooms and offices keep?

   F. What trade shows do you exhibit at, and what are the dates of the shows for the coming twelve months?

2. Growth patterns:

   A. How long has your agency been established?

   B. What is your present sales volume?

3. Describe the territory covered by your agency:

4. Product lines:

   A. How many lines do you represent?

   B. Are your present lines compatible with ours?

   C. Do you feel there would be any conflict or unfriendly competition?

   D. What do you consider the minimum sales you need to justify handling our line?

5. Customers:

   A. Describe the kinds of customers you currently are contacting.

   B. Are they compatible with our product line?

   C. Who are your key accounts?

With this information, and a memorandum of understanding between you and the very best independent sales representatives, you are ready to begin working with the customers whose orders you will begin to receive, and you must concern yourself with your relationship with them.

Terms and Conditions

Earlier I recommended you obtain a copy of the product catalogs and price lists of your competitors, as identified in working with the *Directory of Importers*. Along with the catalogs and price lists, your competitors will include a list of terms of sale. These terms are in essence the expectations and requirements inherent between the buyer and the seller for each order. You must survey the terms and conditions of sale among your "competitors" and adopt a similar set. Although the terms are generally a recapitulation of the uniform commercial code, each industry does tend to have particular conditions that need to be spelled out for newcomers and customers from other industries. For example, the following is a typical set of terms and conditions for the gift and housewares industry.

Terms & Conditions of Sale

Terms: *Net 30 from date of invoice; 1.5% per month will be charged on unpaid overdue balances; no anticipation discount.*

Net thirty means the customer is expected to pay the invoice amount for the goods within thirty days of invoice date. Note it may take a week or so from the day you ship the goods, that is the invoice date for the customer to actually receive the goods. Therefore, the customer pays three weeks after receiving the goods, but 30 days after invoice date. The customer will put a check in the mail thirty days after the invoice date, and it may take a week for you to get the check. Commonly retailers wait as long as possible to pay; the longer they wait, the less they have to borrow from the bank. Retailers can be trained to pay in a timely manner, and we will look at this shortly.

Some companies offer "1/10, Net 30." This is an early payment discount meaning the customers can deduct 1% of the invoice value if they pay within ten days, otherwise they pay the full amount in 30 days. Such enticements cost a company plenty because all retailers that pay late take the 1% percent anyway. On a thousand dollar invoice, when a check for $990 comes in, you will not refuse it and begin collection procedures for the shorted ten dollars. The retailer knows this; therefore I recommend you never offer early-payment discounts.

Charge the legal limit in interest for past due amounts. If someone owes you $500, charge them the $7.50 a month in interest, compounded.

Retailers may attempt to turn your interest charges around on you. Being cash rich early in the year, a retailer may order $1,000 worth of Christmas ornaments in January to be delivered in October. If the retailer pays in January will you pay 1.5% interest, since you charge that amount on past due amounts? This is called "anticipation." The ten months in advance plus thirty days normally allowed equals eleven months of interest, or a 16.5% discount, or a payment in January of $835 for merchandise the retailer would normally have to pay $1,000 dollars for in November. If you recall from the chapter on costings, you would go out of business quickly with this program.

Prices: *Prices are shown at wholesale on the price list that accompanies this catalog. Prices are subject to change without notice and will be billed at prices in effect at time of shipment.*

Normally you do not change prices more than twice a year.

FOB: *Seattle, Washington*

FOB stands for Free On Board, meaning the merchandise is loaded on to a common carrier and all freight charges from the point mentioned—Seattle in this instance—are at the expense of the retailer. Often an importer will warehouse in a major city like Los Angeles, but maintain offices in another city, even another state.

Minimum Order: *Minimum opening order is $150.00. Reorders under $100 will not be accepted.*

I have lost the formula for determining the break even amount of each order, but I know for gift and housewares it is about $92. Every industry has minimum order amounts, and note the stiffer amount required for an opening order. This reflects a desire to weed out "one-shot" customers.

New Accounts: *We require a credit application. Please supply five trade references with complete addresses and account numbers. To expedite a shipment while we check credit, you may send full prepayment. Sorry, no COD or pro-forma orders will be accepted.*

Checking credit is an important task for you, and we'll cover it in detail in the next chapter, especially in the context of getting financed.

Newly Established Business: *Businesses lacking sufficient references should arrange prepayment.*

Prepayment is the best plan, although few retailers will accept it. If you find someone who wants delivery immediately but cannot wait for a credit check, suggest prepayment. Another version is to accept partial prepayment. Tell the customer you will ship immediately the order if they prepay 50%. Often you will ship only 50–75% of the order initially anyway, so the risk is minor.

Minimum Quantities: *All orders must be written in multiples of the minimum quantities as quoted on the price list. Orders which do not conform to minimums will be automatically adjusted to the nearest correct multiple.*

Usually you are in the business of importing gross quantities of goods, and then repacking them against smaller orders from customers. As a strategy to save money, you have your supplier efficiently pack inner cartons of your gross quantity master packs to match your minimum order requirement of your customers. If your minimum order is packed in fours, and a customer orders six, you will ship the customer eight.

Buyer's Name and Phone Number: *All orders must include the buyer's full name and phone number. Without this information your order will not be processed.*

This information is critical for resolving order problems, collecting payments if the account goes past due, and for following up for reorders. Naturally, get an e-mail address as well if they are willing to give it.

Delivery: *Delivery of orders will be three to five weeks after receipt of orders, and subject to credit approval & availability.*

Back Orders: *Our overseas factories are occasionally subject to delays beyond our control. Although we make every effort to ship quickly and completely we draw your attention to our backorder procedures: backorders on new items are not canceled, regardless of age or value; backorders on established items which are either five months old or less than $50 cost are canceled. You may specify any other alternate instructions regarding cancellation of orders or backorders as you wish.*

Cancellations: *All cancellations must be received in writing.*

Priority: *Orders are shipped on a first come first served basis, so there is some advantage in ordering early and leaving open cancellation dates.*

Discontinued Items: *Due to manufacturing or other considerations beyond our control, items may be sold out and discontinued without notice. Please accept our apologies if merchandise which you have selected is unavailable because of this.*

Returns: *No merchandise may be returned without written authorization from John Wiley Spiers Customer Service. Unauthorized returns are subject to a 15% restocking charge plus all freight charges.*

Do not accept returns, even if the retailer requests authorization. Returns are a problem because some retailers make a habit of trying to return what they did not sell. This practice improves the store profits because the store never needs to hold sales to get rid of slow selling merchandise. Except in a case where you broke the contract (the order), never take merchandise back from a retailer. To do so harms your company and may put it in legal jeopardy.

The harm to your company comes in a lack of remuneration for your efforts. It is expensive to gain orders, buy merchandise, ship it and invoice it only to have it returned. The legal jeopardy comes if the retailer is failing; in a bankruptcy the courts will hold your company liable for the value of any merchandise returned. The merchandise is the asset of the retailer, and the first call on those assets legally belongs to the holder of the perfected security agreement (normally the bank).

Examples of you breaking the contract might be the buyer specified a July 1 ship date, and you shipped July 15; the customer ordered blue sweaters and you shipped red; or the merchandise is defective (nobody orders defective merchandise). As you will see below, merchandise damaged in transit does not warrant a return authorization.

Returns often come in the form of a customer refusing a UPS shipment for no acceptable reason. Such customers are a nuisance, and the 15% restocking charge policy eliminates them from your customer base. For instance, if a customer refuses a $500 shipment, upon return reverse the invoice, restock the merchandise, and create a new invoice for $75 (15% of $500) plus freight charges both ways. The customer certainly will not pay the restocking charge. The amount will go into bad debt, and you will refuse to do business with this customer in the future. Although this seems self defeating, in reality there are so many good customers who play by the rules that there is no need to accept returns and other such nonsense. Indeed, for the good of your company, you must allow them to go "bad debt" to assure they will not waste your time in the future.

As a company which competes on design, I have had customers actually come back, pay the restocking charge plus interest just to get back in my good graces.

Claims: *Claims for damages, shortages, substitutes or defectives may be made only by writing or faxing John Wiley Spiers Customer Service. Please do not telephone. Claims should be made within one week of receipt of shipment and must include the order number or invoice number, item numbers and quantities involved, and a brief description of the problem.*

Damage or Loss in Transit: *All shipments leave our warehouse properly packaged for shipment and in good order. The common carrier (UPS, trucking lines, etc.) signed a bill of lading accepting the merchandise for delivery to the buyer and attesting to the good order of the shipment. As soon as the bill of lading is signed by the common carrier, the merchandise ceases to be our asset and becomes the asset of the retailer, that is, the buyer (our asset is the accounts receivable). If there is damage or loss incidental to the carriage and delivery of your order, then you must file a claim with the common carrier. John Wiley Spiers Company has no authority or responsibility after the carrier accepts the goods. ICC rule 19 provides for your protection: in the event there is any damage or loss apparent, you have the right to make note of that or any other exceptions on the bill of lading the common carrier presents to you, before you sign it. The notations you make on the bill of lading are the sole basis for your claim with the carrier. Occasionally, there is damage not apparent until the boxes are actually opened; in this event please leave the merchandise in the box and call the carrier to send out a customer service representative to write up the claim. John Wiley Spiers Company will gladly assist any customers who feel they are not getting prompt, courteous service from the carrier in the course of filing any claim.*

Shipping Terms: *Shipments under 150 pounds are sent via UPS, and the charges are added to your bill. Over 150 pounds we ship via a freight carrier, freight collect. Please indicate "UPS only" on your order if you do not wish to receive truck shipments. Sorry, no freight allowances are available.*

Every retail store buyer worth his salt will try to have you pay the freight from your warehouse to his store. Simply refuse; this is just another form of competing on price.

Credit Policies and Open Account: *We are pleased to extend net 30 terms to our customers. Our commitments to our factories and our bankers require that any customer unable to pay within 30 days be put on prepaid only status. Any customer unable to pay within 60 days will be referred to collection.*

If you use just what is in italics above, you would have a set of terms and conditions for the gift and housewares industries. If the version you obtain from competitors in your industry varies from this list, your independent sales representative would be the best person to explain the differences.

The terms and conditions may seem harsh and unfriendly, but they are the foundation for an equitable relationship and therefore cannot be trifled with. Certainly you want to be friendly with your customers, but express your friendship in ways that promote your company. A good way to do this, now that desktop publishing is so accessible, is with a newsletter. Send your customers a monthly or quarterly rundown on your company, reprints of government data on trends for your industry, and your own views on trends and their implications.

How to Gain Orders: The Battle Plan

I must stress every industry is different and this example is only one, albeit popular, industry, gift and housewares. But, from this example you will be able to extrapolate what you can expect from other industries and the natural strategy for success.

This is a good place to state again the number one rule in importing: Never buy inventory until you have orders! (A participant in one of my seminars told me he gets paid before he buys product: he is a yacht importer, and he is fully prepaid before he lays the keel).

There are two problems that kill import companies. One is inventory-related, the other is accounts receivable, or slow-paying customers. Following the number one rule in importing assures that you will never have inventory problems. The rule is observed by old established firms as well as start-up importers.

This rule does not contradict what we have laid out thus far; certainly you will get samples of your product to take to the trade shows, but you will not buy inventory until you have orders from your customers. You may have to buy *samples* to gain orders, but certainly not inventory .

There is a difference between the start-up innovator and the established innovator in following this rule. The start-up innovator must strictly follow the rule to assure success and avoid crippling inventory problems. As for accounts receivable, I will cover that in the chapter on operations.

How do importers gain orders against samples before they buy any inventory? How do they follow the number one rule: never buy inventory until you have orders?

The Time Line and Strategy

Using what you have learned about sales representatives, showrooms, customers and trade shows, I will now lay out the plan of action for starting your business. So far you have been doing research, developing a product and positioning your company for success. Now is the time to put your product to the real test. Up to now, your feedback has depended on a few retailers. It is possible they gained their enthusiasm for the product from you. You still don't know if the larger market is interested in your product. Will your product be as popular in some faraway city as it is in your home town, especially if you are not there to promote it? By working with the reps, who also show their other clients' products at the trade shows, you can prove your potential with orders.

Trade shows come in cycles, and the gift and housewares trade shows come twice a year, for twelve weeks starting in January and again in mid-June. Each weekend within this twelve week cycle a new show starts and runs for four to five days. Major cities like New York and Los Angeles make sure their schedules do not conflict, but you might find smaller markets like Boston running the same time as a major market like Chicago. Like a surfer waiting for the right wave, you must wait for the right cycle to launch your product. If you introduce products between cycles, the reps may be bored with them by the time the shows come around, just when you need the most enthusiasm.

We know the lion's share of retail sales take place in the fourth quarter—that is, Christmas time. But when do the retail store buyers place orders for the products to be sold in the fourth quarter? January, Spring, Summer, Fall, November, a year before? Just about any answer is partially correct. In January in Atlanta the first gift show of the season is held and it is common to see department store buyers placing orders with the Christmas ornament importers for delivery in September. These are the same buyers that a week earlier put their entire Christmas ornament stock on 75% off sale. The buyers know they must get orders in early, especially with importers. And why September delivery? September is the end of the third quarter, not the fourth quarter. We will address that later in this section. Although retailers are fairly consistent as to when they want their merchandise delivered, they are very inconsistent as to when they place their orders for merchandise. This is true of individual retailers and retailers as a whole.

Factors such as personal plans, financial concerns, even weather can change an individual retailer's habit. And retailers as a whole can be motivated by such macroeconomic factors as interest rates, recessions, and so on to change industry-wide patterns.

But the fact that the trade shows do exist, and follow a consistent schedule, allows the start-up importer the opportunity to test his product further, and ascertain demand.

Let's begin with a few assumptions. The first is that whatever you are importing—say, cordless telephone headsets—has a 2,000 piece minimum order requirement from the supplier. You in turn are requiring any orders from potential customers to have a four piece minimum, or $100 worth. Now we know we need at least 500 orders (500 orders at 4 pieces each) to equal the 2,000 piece minimum of the supplier overseas.

We also know we have a twelve week trade show cycle starting in January. Having obtained samples of our item from the supplier overseas, the reps show the product at the trade shows one week after another.

If your samples are limited, you must overnight express samples from one city to another between shows to assure a complete exposure in the cycle. This practice is very common and reps will not have a problem in cooperating with you on this, although they will want you to pay the freight.

After the twelve week cycle is complete, you must assess the situation. The best case scenario is you gain 500 orders at 4 pieces each and you proceed with the plan. What is the worst case scenario?

In my seminars the answer is always "no orders!" I disagree. The worst case scenario is 150 orders, or 175 orders. Too few to meet the minimum of the supplier overseas, but still quite a few people have placed orders. Recall that orders are legally binding on both the buyer and the seller. This scenario may very likely occur in your case. What to do?

The suggestions I get in the seminars range from lower the price and try to sell more, to get the supplier to lower the minimum. Neither of these plans addresses the central problem: the designs are not very good. Psychologically this can be devastating, and in denial you may go ahead and order merchandise for which you have not enough orders. If after prime exposure your product cannot meet even a minimum order, simply pull the item and start again. Aren't you glad you only have samples, aren't you glad you don't have a garage full of this product?

The effort is not entirely lost. Although the twelve weeks of exposure did not yield initial success, it certainly gave you enough feedback to develop what would sell well. Pull your item and redesign your product to what people do want to buy. Reintroduce the item in the following cycle.

Redesigning is simpler than you might think. During the course of gaining even too few orders, you will get so much input into your offering that very quickly you will have an idea of how to improve and salvage the item.

In any event, it is very fortunate that you, the innovator has not invested in inventory of an item that does not sell well.

And even if you learn the item is simply not worth it after all, it is an item you care about, and you may have the only one in the world. My home is full of such items, not commercially viable, but very pleasing to me. Picasso's favorite question to ask people was "Do you like what you have?" Yes, very much, even if the world in general does not care for some of the items.

But remembering the Uniform Commercial Code law that states an order is a legally binding agreement between the buyer and the seller in the United States, what are we to do with the orders we have gained? We have decided not to ship those orders because the demand is too low to bother with; it would be foolish to buy thousands of an item when we have orders for only dozens. If we do not fill those orders are we not going to get sued by those retailers to whom we fail to ship against their orders?

The answer is no, you will not be sued. The orders you are getting are minimum orders. No retailer in his right mind will place an order much greater than your company's minimum requirement. The first order from a retailer is always a test order. The retail stores, even those with which you have been working closely, will start with a small order to test their customers' reaction to the product; therefore the orders are small and insignificant to the retailer. No retailer is going to bother suing you over some unshipped $150 order (on the other hand, JCPenney and other large stores most likely will sue you for damages if you fail to ship a $50,000 order).

Nonetheless, do not simply ignore the orders if you decide not to purchase from the supplier against the too few orders you have received. Do notify your customers, perhaps via postcard, that you will not be shipping their order. In this way, far from harming what reputation you might be gaining, you enhance your reputation. Retailers mistakenly buy enough poor selling merchandise without having you go out of your way to bring it in for them. If a lack of orders suggests an item is not sufficiently marketable, let those poor retailers that did order from you know that you will not be shipping—

and why: too few retailers ordered! In this way, the retailers getting such notices from you will admire you for your forthrightness and savvy. And furthermore, any retailer counting on your product, perhaps for a Christmas display or other circumstance unknown to you, will not be aggravated when you notify them far enough in advance to find an alternative.

One of the saddest situations I often see is the entrepreneur who is so sure of his product he buys a garage full before he has fully tested the item in the market. The product fails, and the entrepreneur learns why, in the process, but cannot correct the problem because all of his capital or credit is tied up in the wrong product in the garage. I got a call from one such case in which an importer had a load of something called slim-tea. One simply drinks this tea and loses weight. Unfortunately, nobody believed it, and the fellow was stuck with a 700 year personal supply of slim tea. He forgot the rule—never buy without orders in hand.

Let's go back to the best case scenario. If you gained 500 orders at 4 pieces each, you have met the minimum of the supplier overseas. If those orders are all of minimum amount, or $100 each, you have 500 orders x $100 = $50,000 in orders. Next chapter we will cover what it takes to get financing, and from what sources.

Assuming it takes a full month to get your financing, and you open the letter of credit in early April, the supplier manufactures and ships by late July, you receive your goods in early August, and begin shipping to your customers.

Now we come back to the question of why retailers often want merchandise shipped in September. September is back-to-school month, and a sure test of what is hot and what is not for the coming fourth quarter sales. Retailers will place small orders with very many suppliers and let the back-to-school crowd react. Maybe 10% of the suppliers they order from are hot. The retailers, based on the back-to-school response, can pick the winners and place their reorders.

Nordstrom has a sale every August on their new Fall items. The sales lasts until say September 15, and then the products go up in price to regular season pricing. Is this not backwards? On sale first, and then raise the prices? Are Nordstrom buyers unaware of good business practices? Of course they know what they are doing. Nordstrom has a wide range of items for sale, but shallow stock levels at this time. Based on the reaction to the sales, the buyers can tell which of the five women's winter coats is the hottest design. In turn, they can write a million dollar order for the coats, and the manufacturer begins production and shipping coats out every day to supply the demand.

If you are one of the lucky ones to warrant a reorder, then that is a good indication you are on the right track as far as your designs go. Unfortunately, by following this method you will not have any merchandise to fulfill reorders. You cannot fill reorders because as a start-up importer you have not bought more than is warranted by the early orders, and as an importer you certainly cannot get supplied from overseas in time to satisfy the reordering customer. When you are more established you can order some extra, but never when you are starting out.

To proceed with the time line, you ship in August, September and on until you have filled your orders. Thirty days after you have shipped each order, the payments from your customers can be expected. This money you use to pay debts and yourself. Based on your experiences for the year, you plan your strategy and lines for next year. One factor that greatly influences your further line development is reorders. Did you get any?

Reorders

An order is an indication of interest. Reorders from customers confirm you are on the right track. The first order from the retailer will test interest on the part of the ultimate consumer for your product. This reorder is the only indication of potential and opportunity for your company to grow. It is the reorder that makes the initial investment in time, expense, creativity and infrastructure worthwhile. Your first orders only allow you to break even; it is reorders that earn you profit. And when those reorders come in, it is time to offer the customer more products, allied to what you initially offered, and therefore likely to be of interest to the retailer. In the gift and housewares industry we must have new items to show at least twice a year.

If you gained no reorders, you know your lines were good enough to attract attention, but the ultimate consumers were not terribly impressed. They did not buy your products from your customer, the retail store. Then you must, as they say, go back to the drawing board and redesign the line entirely, as though you had gained too few orders. You will have ample indication of what would sell at this point, based on the exposure of your item to the marketplace.

So reorders are critical to your success, but if you buy only to meet the needs of orders in hand, how can you handle a reorder? Following the number one rule, if a retailer has tested your product in September and wants to reorder your proven product in October, can you deliver more merchandise within a reasonable time frame, say by Thanksgiving? You have no merchandise in stock on speculation that you might get orders. This would be contrary to the number one rule. We established earlier that it might take 120 days to have merchandise in the warehouse ready to ship to the customer. An October order would mean the soonest we could deliver would be February. The best you could do would be to make the appointment to write a reorder (or have your independent sales representative do so), and explain that you have "sold through." The popularity of the item was far more than you expected and you have no more in stock. Since you are sitting in the buyer's office, you would be glad to take an order now and let the buyer be the first to get a reorder delivered. Certainly an order for February will be less in quantity than an order for October, but it will be an order nonetheless and well in advance.

This strategy I learned from friends of mine importing picture frames. I. Magnin & Co. wanted to reorder their stone and coral picture frames in October and my friends agreed to meet the buyer in the store. The buyer asked for late October delivery and was told the earliest my friends could deliver was February. The buyer was astonished. My friends explained Bloomingdale's and Neiman Marcus had cleaned them out. This was a very clever strategy on my friends' part. The claim was true, and the I. Magnin & Co. buyer felt at once slow and timid. The I. Magnin & Co. buyer wrote an order, albeit smaller, for February delivery, and begged our friends to save the red coral frames for next year since the buyer was going to feature the item in all catalogs and all stores.

It is not a crime to sell out of merchandise (referred to as "selling through"). Indeed, it is to be preferred above all other possible scenarios. You can easily solve the problem of too little merchandise. Too much merchandise is a very difficult problem to solve. But some business people, especially most salespeople, act as though it is a crime to sell out.

If you sell out, initially the strategy is to put off retailers' reorders for a future date. As your company grows, you can add on a little to your orders to your suppliers to cover reorders that "you know you can sell anyway."

So assuming the best case scenario, you gain sales, customers, possible reorders, and certainly enough information to develop more and newer products and grow your business. Although you have written a business plan (as I will detail in a later chapter), and proved there is a market, you have not conducted a market study, nor do you need one (your orders obviate the need for a market study). The means I lay out here are used by those you see thriving.

Two Concerns

This time frame assumes your independent sales representatives will be gaining orders in January for delivery in August at the earliest. Since the sales representative is paid after the sale, that is after you ship to the customer, the representative will be working for you in January but not be paid until perhaps September. Why would they do this? The answer is simple but hard for some entrepreneurs to take. Simply put, your company and its product lines are insignificant. The vast majority of a rep's income is derived from the conservator's product lines. Having your line will not make or break the rep; having to wait for the few dollars the innovator will owe is of little concern. You may grow into a significant part of the rep's business, but certainly not to start. But you do provide a value to the independent sales representative.

The independent sales representative is trying your products on pure speculation. The first question out of every buyer's mouth at trade shows or in-store sales calls is, "What is new?" Who knows what will or will not be successful? Certainly no self-respecting rep would hazard a guess. When a buyer comes in and asks, "What is new?" the reps says YOU are what is new.

It is innovators like yourself that provide something new for the retailers to look at. This is why the independent sales representative takes on your line. If none of the customers who ask what is new buy your product, your samples will be shipped back to you.

The large conservator companies do not show what is new. In the late 1980's Waterford Crystal laid off a thousand workers due to a drop in demand for their products. My sources indicated the drop in sales was a result of consumer boredom with the Waterford line. Designs over 100 years old get tiresome. Conservators must appropriate ideas once in a while to stay in business.

The next problem has to do with the number one rule: how many people will be willing to place orders in January for delivery in August? Of the people who ask what is new and see your product, maybe half will be willing to place test orders. Of the half that are willing to place test orders, maybe half will be willing to wait until August for delivery. The half not willing to wait until August will of course promise to come back in July and place an order for August. How many of those will come back in July? Zero, correct.

What you will net is very few orders with this system, fewer than you might have received had you not followed the number one rule and purchased stock before getting orders. Remember that an average of just one minimum order of about $150 per state per week generates yearly sales of over $360,000. Keep that in mind when pressure is put on you to break the number one rule in importing. You do not need to run the risk.

When importing as a small business, or any importing for that matter, you need never run any more than negligible financial risk. You are unlikely to succeed if you do take personal financial risk. It is unprofessional to do so, and this requirement accounts for the high level of discipline and professionalism among successful importers.

As a side note, when does this become a full-time business? As soon as the samples are on the independent sales representatives' showroom shelves, you ought to be free days to work on this business. For many start-up companies, this means the principal delivers pizza at night, or something more creative, until the income is sufficient to support yourself. My boss in San Francisco remodeled a flat into a duplex, rented out the top half and earned enough to pay the mortgage and eat. There is no stopping the trader moved by passion.

Having progressed through the program to gaining orders, we now need to attend to getting finance.

CHAPTER SEVEN:

▼

FINANCING WHEN BANKS WILL NOT; PAY AND GET PAID

We want a loan to buy merchandise to ship to our customers. So the task now is to show that any loan we get will be repaid. Will the money we borrow disappear when we send it overseas to buy the merchandise? Will the exchange rate between the two currencies involved fluctuate and wipe out any hope of a profit? After we receive the merchandise from overseas will the people to which we ship the merchandise pay us? Do we have effective means of collecting from any customer who is slow in paying, or tries not to pay? Until we can answer these questions, we can offer no assurance of our ability to repay any loan.

Recall in Chapter 6 how we arrived at the best case scenario in which you gained 500 orders at four pieces each, and you have met the minimum order requirement of the supplier overseas. If those orders are all of minimum amount, say $100 each, you have 500 orders x $100 = $50,000 in orders.

How much money does a gift ware importer need to borrow to buy the product from the supplier overseas to satisfy the $50,000 in orders? With a 100% markup, or 50% margin, we need exactly half of the $50,000, or $25,000. We need $25,000 in financing to buy the product from the supplier, and we will then use the product to fill the orders we have in hand, and gain $50,000 in receipts for the sales against the orders we are holding in hand.

What kind of position are we in when we go looking for financing, and we show the $50,000 in orders as proof that we can turn a $25,000 loan into $50,000 in about nine months? Obviously this is a very strong position. Some entrepreneurs expect to get financing because of their business plan even though such plans only guess that a customer may exist.

In any event, we have shown we can get orders, but we still need to show we can repay the loan. Orders show we can merely get sales, yet is it proof we can repay the loan? The loan is being used to buy the product necessary to fill the orders. The orders are from many retail stores. We must show we will not lose the money when we send it overseas to pay for goods, nor lose it by not being paid by our customers after we ship the goods.

Necessarily those stores who order from you will expect and demand you ship (sell) to them on open credit, as is customary in the wholesale business. Open credit means you ship and give them some time to pay, normally 30 days. You will be risking whether or not you will be paid when you ship to the customers in fulfillment of those orders. In effect, you will be taking a risk yourself, just like a banker, of not getting paid, and therefore, not repaying any loan. The problem is some customers are unworthy of any credit from you.

Therefore, three tasks remain before you get any financing:

• first, you must show you know how to make a payment to a supplier overseas without losing the money;

• second, you must demonstrate you know how to determine which customers are creditworthy to ship to; and

• third, when inevitably some customers you've shipped to prove in fact to be unworthy (that is, slow pay or going out of business), you know how to effectively collect from such customers what they owe you.

Without these skills, lenders risk you shipping the orders out but never getting paid yourself, and thus never repaying the lender. In short, you must learn the mechanics of international payments, and you must learn how to issue credit and manage receivables domestically. Only then can we look at the best source of finance.

Letters of Credit

The essential problem in international trade finance is credit and payment. If an importer wants to buy something from Indonesia, does he send a check to the Indonesian in advance? What if, after cashing the check, the Indonesian cannot or will not ship? What recourse does the importer have? Realistically speaking, the importer has no recourse.

So from the importer's point of view, the Indonesian must first ship and then the importer will pay. What if the Indonesian ships first, and the importer, after receiving the goods, cannot or will not pay? What recourse does the Indonesian have? Here again, none.

Centuries ago the problem was solved as banks became widespread. The solution is the letter of credit—a bank guarantee to the seller that the buyer will pay if the seller conforms to the requirements of the buyer as stipulated in the letter of credit. Because of the security a letter of credit offers, the seller overseas may confidently manufacture and ship the goods to the importer, assured that, having met the conditions of the letter of credit, the importer's bank will pay the exporter's bank. The importer is assured the seller ships the merchandise as agreed or the bank will not pay the seller.

A bank charges fees for opening, amending if necessary, negotiating, and closing letters of credit. The fees are negotiable, but can run a minimum of approximately $150 for a $5,000 letter of credit. If less than $5,000 it is probably better to work out some other payment arrangement such as cash against documents, which we will cover later in the chapter.

The Mechanics of the Letter of Credit

After the letter writing, meetings, product development and marketing effort, the time will come to place an order with the supplier and open a letter of credit. The steps are illustrated in Fig. 33. Assuming you have orders to warrant a purchase from a supplier overseas, you, the importer, will:

1. Place an order detailing the quantity, quality, delivery date, price, etc.

2. The exporter will send you an order confirmation.

3. You will apply for a letter of credit, and put up collateral in the form of cash (established importers will draw on their line of credit, to be described shortly).

4. Importer's bank will advise the exporter's bank of the letter of credit.

5. Exporter's bank advises the exporter the letter of credit has been issued. (Smaller exporters may use your letter of credit as collateral with the exporter's bank to get a loan to buy the material overseas to make your product!)

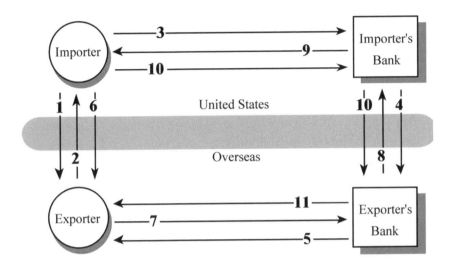

Fig. 33. Steps in a letter of credit

6. After manufacturing the goods, the exporter creates the documents your banker and Customs broker told you to require when you originally obtained the letter of credit (invoices, packing lists, certificates of origin, etc.). Furthermore, upon delivery of the goods to the steamship line, the exporter obtains the original bill of lading to include with the other documents.

7. The documents created and collected by the exporter in step six are presented to the exporter's bank.

8. Exporter's bank sends the documents to the importer's bank (no money changes hands yet).

9. The importer's bank advises you the documents have arrived and will note any exceptions (such as variances between quantity ordered and quantity shipped, misspellings of names on the documents, etc.).

10. If the exceptions are minor, you will accept the exceptions and the importer's bank will simultaneously release the funds for the merchandise to the exporter's bank.

11. The exporter's bank pays off the exporter (less the fees, principle and interest on any loan). At this point, the exporter and the banks are satisfied financially, and you have the documents allowing you to pick up your goods and effect the transfer of title.

This ought to seem simple and straightforward. It is not particularly difficult. But there is a problem with the system that might not be immediately apparent. The full appellation for the letter of credit is "irrevocable documentary letter of credit." This means the letter of credit cannot be canceled (irrevocable) and it is documentary, meaning it assures that the documents, the paperwork, are in order.

If the letter of credit assures only the documents are in order, what about the shipment? What if the 200 cartons of shoes you ordered are somehow defective? Or if you were shipped red sweaters instead of blue sweaters? What if the shipment is not what you ordered? What recourse do you have? For all practical purposes, none. The bank makes sure that if any exceptions exist, you first agree in writing to accept those exceptions, thus relieving the bank of any liability.

Banks gladly charge their fees (say a base of $150 and 1/4 of 1% of the amount of the letter of credit), with the implied assurance the letter of credit will protect the importer. If there is a problem, a loss of money for any reason, ultimately the bank will not pay. Letters of Credit are covered in rules written by bankers for bankers, specifically in a document called Uniform Customs and Practice for Documentary Credits, or UCP 500. Under the aegis of the International Chamber of Commerce (ICC), banks worldwide meet in Paris and make the international banking rules. As the ICC website notes:

Because its member companies and associations are themselves engaged in international business, ICC has unrivaled authority in making rules that govern the conduct of business across borders. Although these rules are voluntary, they are observed in countless thousands of transactions every day and have become part of the fabric of international trade.[53]

And so it is "the rule" that banks do not lose money on letters of credit. In essence, the theory is if a bystander (i.e., the bank) accepts an offer to help two parties in a transaction, it will be one of the two parties who must pay if there is a loss, not the bank. Without going into details, if it were any other way, it would be quite easy to steal from bankers.[54]

Then there is the problem of the letter of credit itself being fraudulent. What security there is, is only as good as the bank providing the letter of credit. Here your bank will advise you as to the reliability of the "corresponding" banks. From time to time there will be stories about a series of fraudulent letters of credit issued, such as an *Asian Wall Street Journal* article from April of 1993 in which Robert Steiner reports the Agricultural Bank of China warned bankers it would not honor a series of some 200 letters of credit issued by the bank, valued at over ten billion dollars, because they were fraudulent.

But, as mentioned in the introduction, relationship is a critical factor in international trade. The very process we go through developing a product that provides a value, the careful steps taken to test out and build this business, as a side benefit, fairly well eliminate any interest in us on the part of thieves. That is not to say there can be no problems, but if you have taken care to find the best suppliers, they will make good any error. And there will be errors, since every company, domestic as well as overseas, occasionally makes mistakes.

---

53. http://www.iccwbo.org/

54. A useful review of letters of credit can be found in the book, *Letters of Credit in International Trade*, by Matti Kurkola (New York: Ocean Publications, 1985). Kurkola admirably lays out the realities of letters of credit, and the problems, then advocates in essence a one-world government to solve the problems. Never mind that the system works well-as with so many people not actually in business, the tendency is government first, ask questions later.

The only protection you really have in international trade, at the small business level, is your relationship with the other party. The relationship is necessarily based only on the potential for making money, or once trade is established, the consistent profits for all concerned. Since contracts and letters of credit have no force of law, every deal must be a "momentum-deal." That is to say, if the contracts and letters of credit fail, the deal will still go through with all parties honoring their commitments, because the deal itself is good business. The work that led up to the agreement to buy and sell, and the surety that the importer has a market for the goods once imported, makes certain that if some minor aspect of the deal falls through, such as the letter of credit not being perfect, then momentum takes over and the deal is completed anyway.

For instance, years ago I placed a late order for some Christmas tree ornaments. The ornaments were little wooden sports figures playing baseball, soccer, tennis, and other sports. The ornaments sold surprisingly well—hence the late orders to the factory. The factory accepted the late order, but turned it over to a third-rate subcontractor. The subcontractor made the ornaments, but packed the ornaments in their individual poly bags with the glue and the paint still wet. You can imagine how they looked when I received them.

This was about $6,000 worth of ornaments, manufactured in Taiwan. I complained, and the supplier went to remarkable lengths to make good. Taiwan at that time did not have a convertible currency. Unlike Deutsche Marks, US$ or Swiss Francs, outside of Taiwan the NT$ was useless. Generally under these conditions the best the importer can hope for is to recover the loss through some sort of arrangement such as a discount on future orders until the loss is covered (say, the Taiwanese company will invoice the next $20,000 worth of goods at $14,000). Aside from the complexity and inconvenience, there are possibly US laws being broken.

Instead of the usual solution, the exporter explained he could not send currency out of the country, but he would be willing to give us US$6,000 worth of travelers checks when next we met. He could not easily bring that kind of currency out of Taiwan, but he could certainly give them to us to take out. And this is precisely the solution we hit upon. (Keep in mind when taking currency across US borders you must declare the amount if it is US$10,000 or more. It is not illegal to transport amounts larger than that, but it is illegal to do so without reporting it. US Customs often secretly searches the baggage of US citizens traveling over- seas to find currency violations).

Another time I imported 12,000 dinner plates all of which appeared "bowed." The center of the dinner plates rose to a mound; these plates couldn't possibly be used to serve dinner—any steak or potato placed on these plates would slide to the edge. These plates would be better for squeezing lemons.

I notified the supplier in Nagoya regarding the problem, and he found it incredible. I insisted and the supplier (actually an agent for the manufac- turer of the plates) flew to San Francisco to inspect the plates, which he did one by one. The supplier managed to salvage about 3,000 of the 12,000 plates. The agent confirmed the loss to the factory which in turn replaced the defective plates, air freighting the replacements in sufficient quantity to keep our customers satisfied. The balance came by regular sur- face transportation. In any event, all of the freight charges and replace- ment cost were at the expense of the supplier.

An importer may recover 99% of duties paid to the United States Customs if the imported goods are either destroyed or re-exported. In this instance, the supplier wanted the defective plates back (to recycle?). I obliged, and at considerable trouble and expense to the suppliers, I was made whole.

The first story comes from a small company, the second from a much larger company. In both instances, the sellers made good. Why? Because they want your future business. And more to the point, the sellers overseas make good because that is standard procedure in these countries. Korea,

Japan, Taiwan, Germany, Hong Kong and all of the other thriving trading centers of the world excel because the traders in those areas produce first rate goods, to specification, on time and at a reasonable price. These people are not getting rich ripping off customers.

Getting burned overseas is easy if you are looking for a quick buck or flashing money around with no particular value to provide. I too have heard stories of American importers being "taken" by suppliers overseas. In every instance I know of, it was the American's fault for being so foolish and unreasonable, for having standards and practices that first rate exporters would not abide, or for failing to conduct a first class operation.

Might having a quality control agent overseas ameliorate the problem of defective goods? The question you must ask yourself is, "Do my competitors use quality control agents?" If not, then you cannot. Quality control agents usually charge about 5% of FOB value, and you cannot afford to pay this if your competitors do not pay such fees. You must do what your competitors do, and in most industries that means to simply find and rely on the best suppliers.

The garment importers commonly use quality control agents, and a client of mine looking to import tuxedos for a chain of rental stores examined the need for paying a 5% quality control fee. Since the initial purchase was about US$300,000, the quality control fee would amount to about $15,000. The would-be importer quickly realized that she could travel first class to Hong Kong for a week and do the quality control check herself and save over $10,000.

But why use letters of credit at all if they are not 100% safe? Simply put, letters of credit are better than no security at all. They at least show the buyer has credit. Some countries will not allow trade to be conducted without letters of credit, so that the banks can control the foreign currency flow. And many exporters overseas simply will not deal with new customers on any other basis. Again, the only real security in international trade is your relationships.

Currencies

Aside from letters of credit, banks trade in foreign currencies. On the macroeconomic level, whole industries are affected by currency fluctuations, and commodity dealers have been known to be wiped out by even a small shift contrary to expectations. George Soros is possibly the dean of currency traders, and is quoted as saying to the effect he makes money punishing stupid government decisions. After the Asian currency debacle of the late 1990s, the prime minister of Malaysia bitterly complained—referring to Soros—that "one man could wipe out forty years of a nation's efforts." At a July 26, 2001 Senate hearing, Chairman Alan Greenspan noted it is not exchange rates that matter in international trade, it is the economic health of the partners. Soros wiped out forty years of central planning and economic malady.

Often I am asked in what currency should international trade be conducted, US dollars or the foreign equivalent? The question is good because on top of all the other factors we must deal with, currency fluctuation in effect means the price we pay for our goods fluctuates, up and down. The essence of the question is who runs the risk of currency fluctuation? And the answer is the importer always runs the risk. In some instances that means the currency will be dollars, and some instances it will mean foreign currency. Ask your supplier what currency he would like to use, and go with that.

Yet currency risk is a minor factor at the small business level. Recall how we do not compete on price like the large businesses, we are not afraid of handsome profits to begin with therefore we have more room to absorb any shocks in the fluctuation. Also, we tend to trade in several small shipments over time, as opposed to the more efficient large shipments conservators tend towards. Therefore, we are able to react more swiftly to adjust price or arrange some hedge when our exchange rates trend unfavorably.

Currencies are commodities like wheat futures or pork bellies. The price of a foreign currency changes from day to day. You can get different prices from different currency traders on any given day. Quantity discounts are available on money: the more you buy the less you pay.

If buying a foreign currency to pay a bill overseas, you would simply contact any large bank in your area and ask for a quote for the currency you desire. You must ask for a "buy" or "sell" quote, for there are two different rates. You want to buy foreign currency so you need the sell rate (the words buy and sell are used from the bankers point of view, so a sell rate is the rate at which you buy and the bank sells).

Here are the currency rates for the Hong Kong dollar (HK$) versus the US dollar (US$) as quoted by First Interstate Bank on August 14, 2000:

	The bank is buying at	The bank is selling at
HK$ into US$	.1215	.1335
US$ into HK$	8.23	7.49

According to this graph, on this date, and at the $5,000 transaction level, US$100 is equivalent to HK$823 when the bank is buying, or HK$749 when the bank is selling. Or the HK$ is bought by the bank for a little over 12¢ and sold for about a penny more.

The problems and opportunities arise as the currency fluctuates. For instance, say a Hong Kong supplier lends you HK$180,000 in 1981, when the exchange rate was .21. For simplicity's sake, we will assume there is no interest involved and ignore present value theory. The only requirement on this loan is that it be repaid in 1984.

The borrower takes the HK$180,000 in 1981 and converts it at .21 to US$37,000. The $37,000 is invested or otherwise profitably used until the time it is to be repaid, in 1984. In 1984, the borrower finds the relevant exchange rate is now .1335, which means the borrower needs to use US$24,030 to buy HK$180,000 in order to repay the loan. Therefore, the borrower has earned about US$13,000 for doing nothing on top of any profit from the use of the original loan. The lender in Hong Kong is not out anything; he can still use the HK$180,000 at the time of repayment for pretty much anything he could at the time of the loan. The price of a newspaper, a lunch or a condominium has not changed, although the currency rates have fluctuated. Yet the borrower has gained very well (and must remember the US$13,000 profit must be declared as income to the IRS). And naturally, just as easily, a borrower in a different time frame could find that Hong Kong dollars became more expensive over time and get stuck trying to find enough dollars to buy HK$180,000 to repay the lender.

Currency speculation is a tricky area and large companies sometimes have their entire profit for a year substantially helped or hurt by currency fluctuations. They use big business tools to hedge their exposure, such as forex contracts and rate swaps.

A small business must rely on much simpler tools for hedging risk in currency exposure, and here is the height of our means: almost all small business importers are dealing in consumer items, for which the lion's share of sales occur in the fourth quarter of the year—in other words, Christmas. The retailers are paying the importer in January and February, but the importer is not ready to buy new merchandise yet. So almost all importers are "cash-rich" in the first few months of the year, but not ready to buy until, say, June.

It is with this pool of money that the importer must work wisely. If dealing with Italy, the importer must decide, after being informed by reading the Wall Street Journal and other commerce journals, which way a given currency is going. Is the lira going up, meaning it is getting cheaper, or is it going down and getting more expensive? If the lira is getting cheaper, hold on to your US$ and buy the lira just when you need it. Since the lira has been getting cheaper, you will be able to buy more lira for your money.

If the lira is getting more expensive, buy the lira now and put it in the bank (yes, this is possible). Since the lira has been getting more expensive, you will be able to use "older," cheaper lira, and therefore get more for your money. This is all we can do at the small business level.

In April of 1985, I suffered the worst currency shock in twenty-five years when the yen became 25% more expensive in less than a month—a month that caught me off guard. Yes, I lost money on the one deal, but overall for the year did just fine, since each deal we do is rather small and just one of many over a year. We are insulated from too much shock by our size.

Currency fluctuation problems are often opportunities to improve your business. As the Yen became more expensive in the early 1980's Japanese products became more expensive. Many importers abandoned Japan as a source and went to Korea looking for alternate suppliers. Responsible Korean companies were happy to accommodate the new customers and performed very well. There were also instances where orders were taken but not delivered on time because certain suppliers overbooked production and came up short. Those importers that failed to make contact with reliable sources got stuck. Those who stayed with Japan got delivery—they also get quality. Remember we compete on design, not on price. Quality and delivery are two very important elements not to be overlooked.

At the same time many importers switched to Korea and overwhelmed the production capacity, Japan found its production capacity underutilized. People who contacted Japan during these times when "Japan was too expensive" found eager, creative interest in their proposed product. You can expect upper management's close attention, fast turnaround on samples, and first rate workmanship on production. Certainly Japanese products cost more, and by charging more your sales will be less. Certainly prices out of Korea are lower, but can they also deliver? As the wise have said, 50% of something is better than 100% of nothing.

A client in the home heating business found a miniature heater in a Japanese hotel room that simply plugged into the wall socket and generated tremendous heat quickly. Checking out of the hotel on his way back to the states, the tourist left his name and address with the clerk asking to have his interest in the heater expressed to the manufacturer. When the fellow arrived back home within 24 hours of checking out of the hotel, he received a telephone call from the manufacturer's agent requesting an appointment to meet him in Seattle! Not all suppliers respond with such alacrity, but it does contrast the conventional wisdom that "expensive" countries hold no opportunities.

Prepare yourself to be facile with currency exchange rates for the countries with which you plan to do business. At least once a week in major newspapers, and every day in the Wall Street Journal, the exchange rate for almost all currencies is published. You can access up to the minute rates on the internet. Pretend you have $10,000 and each week buy and sell currency based on the rates quoted. Get a sense of the trends in the currency in question. This simple exercise will allow you to quickly convert in your mind foreign to US currencies and vice versa when dealing with foreign suppliers.

With prudent means for assuring we don't lose the money we send overseas in payment for our merchandise, we now can look at assuring that our customers pay us.

Checking Customer Creditworthiness

Most retailers will provide you with a set of credit references if they are new customers. Credit references are critical in this business because you will be giving your customers time to pay and in effect acting as a banker, inasmuch you are loaning them the value of the goods for some set time, in this instance thirty days. Not only do you want to avoid nonpayment, but also slow paying customers.

To do so you must check the credit references of all of your new customers. The credit references are the customer's other suppliers (your competitors), banks and perhaps a credit information agency such as Dun and Bradstreet.

Since about 80% of your customers will be small operations, Dun and Bradstreet or other organizations will be useless for determining creditworthiness. Being small, there is no cost-effective way for Dun and Bradstreet to make an assessment. Dun and Bradstreet simply calls small companies and asks the proprietor to rate himself. The information is not reliable. On the other hand, Dun and Bradstreet is good for assessing large corporations, but large corporations are only about 20% of your business and your independent sales representative can give you a better sense of the creditworthiness of local large corporations than Dun and Bradstreet can.

Banks are worthless when checking credit because if their client is failing in business it is not in the bank's interest to let you know. It is better for the banker to have you ship that $1,000 order they know cannot be repaid. The proceeds from the sale of your merchandise, as well as the merchandise of many other hapless importers, will go to the banker to repay any loans due the banker. Even if the banker artlessly misleads you and you think you have the basis for a suit against the banker, he knows you cannot as a practical matter press your suit. Privately I have the utmost confidence in bankers, but every industry has its bad apples, and we can't be naive when protecting our businesses.

This leaves your competitors as the only reliable reference of creditworthiness. I use the term competitor in the broader sense: not only do I mean the companies selling products very much like yours, I also mean any company that a given store may buy from. Sometimes people are surprised to learn that competitors are the only reliable reference of creditworthiness. The retailer is not only reliable, but happy to share credit information with you. This informal sharing of information efficiently protects importer/wholesalers and other distributors from retailers experiencing business failure. By sharing their experience with you, competitors expect you to reciprocate when the opportunity arises. Realistically speaking, it is not the owner of the company, but a clerk, that responds to your credit inquiry. And as an unknown entity nobody cares if you get orders anyway.

There are some problems to avoid in checking credit. First, I ask for five references when the industry standard is three. I ask for five because every retailer has three suppliers they pay well, with which the retailer maintains good relationship as business falters. If a retailer has been in business a few years but cannot name five references, I know the retailer is in trouble, even though I cannot ascertain with whom. Another version of the five reference trick is to contact competitors that would be likely suppliers of the retailer even though not given as references. Any retailer selling baskets will have an account with a company called Kwan Yuen; if Kwan Yuen is not listed as a reference, check with Kwan Yuen. I have often found derogatory information on retailers and avoided problems with this method. This assumes you have a good idea of who your competitors are, and you will from having done the research outlined in earlier chapters.

Full addresses and account numbers are required for credit references because your competitors will not give credit information over the phone (too disruptive), and generally go slow in replying if an account number is not available.

Although many retailers come prepared with credit reference sheets, it is a good idea to prepare your own credit application. Usually this is a two-sided form with the owner and buyer information to be filled out on the front and a list of likely references preprinted on the back. Such a list may be compiled for your industry by getting a list of exhibitors at a major trade show. The list is helpful because your customers do not have to think of references and you do not have to look up addresses when writing credit inquiries.

With this reference form in hand you can then mail a credit inquiry to your competitors. The common format for credit inquiry form is in essence a two-sided return-reply form folded one way to be delivered to the credit reference, and folded another way to be delivered back to the inquirer. Postage both ways is provided by the inquirer. The essence of the inquiry is three part: how long has your competitor dealt with your potential customer, how much credit has your competitor extended to your potential customer, and how long does this potential customer normally take to pay.

Perhaps three of any five will reply in a timely manner (within two weeks) and you will make your decision whether to extend credit based on the replies.

In addition to any credit references, you will often find the independent sales representatives will help out. After an order is written and the customer has left the showroom, the rep may write a note on the order such as "watch out," or "seems shaky," or better yet "good customer." Although these notes are advisory, they are usually reliable.

Never accept COD (cash on delivery) or pro forma orders. Most retailers have standing instructions in their stores to refuse all COD shipments. This is a legacy of the years in the 1960s and 1970s when unscrupulous people would send unordered merchandise COD to other companies. Often these shipments consisted of office supplies or some other benign product sent COD at inflated prices—hence the standing instructions. Nowadays, companies engaging in such illicit activities don't bother with sending merchandise COD, they simply send out invoices for merchandise. Never mind that no merchandise was ever shipped—often enough these bogus invoices are paid because they look plausible enough and they are for supplies every business uses. Enough bookkeepers find it easier to pay the $79.00 invoice rather than try to research it. When you license your business, you will begin to get such invoices. Simply throw them away.

Because of the standing instructions, too often a shipment designated COD by the buyer will arrive at the store only to be refused and sent back at your expense. The only exception to the no COD rule is if credit cannot be approved and you suggest COD (still better is prepayment) to a buyer with poor credit who desperately wants your merchandise now. In this instance you can ship and make delivery within a few days and the buyer can have a check waiting for UPS at the cash register. However, for the busy buyer to remember an agreement at a trade show and follow through with informing the staff and preparing a check for an eventual shipment is very unlikely.

Pro forma shipments must never be accepted. In a pro forma situation, you pack up a shipment and send an invoice for the full amount to the retailer. In turn, the retailer will send you a check for the full amount. Once you receive the check, you release the merchandise to be shipped. Simple enough, except the plan rarely works. Your customer simply will not get around to sending the check, and valuable merchandise is literally tied up.

Dealing With Problem Accounts

If your receivables slow down you will find it difficult to keep your business afloat. On the other hand, by aggressively pursuing receivables, you can improve your profits.

I reduced a company's average collection period (the time it takes to get money in from sales) from 60.21 days to 48.25 days, a reduction of 20%. The effect on the business was dramatic.

Taking a reduction of twelve collection days in the year's year-to-date sales figures, and assuming an interest rate of 8%, a savings of $5,275 was generated in just a nine month period:

YTD SALES x (REDUCTION IN COLLECTION DAYS x INTEREST RATES) = SAVINGS

$1,978,100 x (12/360 x 8/100) = $5,275

Furthermore, a company always borrows money. By generating an extra $5,275, the need to borrow is reduced by a like amount, as well as the costs of borrowing the amount.

Many importers expect to experience about 3% bad debt. A way to make your company more profitable than your competitors is to lower that bad debt to something like 1.5%. The effect goes straight to the bottom line: assuming you have $100,000 in sales each year, reducing bad debt from 3% to 1.5% puts $1,500 more profit into your pocket.

To lower the bad debt and increase your average collection period you must be aggressive in receivables collections. Far too many businesses simply get tough on credit checking, and hope that will keep bad debt and slow pay down.

Unfortunately, the process of collections most businesses employ assures that a company will experience both slow pay and bad debt. Let's look at how most companies collect receivables, and then the effective way of collecting receivables.

How Not To Collect Money

Most import/wholesalers give their customers thirty days to pay, and if the customer does not pay in the agreed amount of time, the import/wholesaler waits at least a month before taking any action.

Most retailers pay their bills on time, but the few retailers who do not pay on time can easily break your company. Most of those who do not pay on time are merely seeing how far they can go before paying—again, using the importer as a banker (if you do let them get away with this, you are, in effect, competing on price). Some of those who do not pay on time are planning to use you to pay for a golden parachute.

Never accept an opening order that is more than triple the minimum order, per store. For gift and housewares, this means I would never accept an opening order for more than $450 per store. Of course if a Nordstrom buyer came in and wanted to place a $2000 order, I accept it because it would be split up and sent to five different stores, and therefore within my rule. No competent, honest buyer would place a large opening order for anything new. A minimum order is a good starting point to test the item.

If it does well, the buyer will place a slightly larger order, and then grow slowly from there. Let me review and nuance.

Why not accept a $5,000 opening order from a store? It is not an uncommon practice with retailers going out of business to order as much merchandise as anyone will send them, and then hold a liquidation sale. With two hundred wholesalers happily shipping about $5,000 each to the retailer, the retailer has a million dollars worth of merchandise that would normally sell for two million dollars. By offering the merchandise at 50 to 75% off, the retailer quickly brings in revenue of at least a half million dollars (another example of increasing sales and going out of business).

This half million dollars goes first to the retailer's banker to pay off any outstanding notes. The banker has a perfected security agreement on the retailer's store and private property, so that is both sensibly and legally the highest (and only) priority to the failing retailer. Once the bank is satisfied, the balance, a couple hundred thousand dollars, goes into the pocket of the retailer who simply closes down and forgets about all the other debts.

What about the million dollars owed the two hundred wholesalers? Those two hundred wholesalers are spread around the country and eventually resign themselves to the fact that it will cost them far more than $5,000 to collect their $5,000. They write it off. The retailer is off the hook, but a new import company might fail under the weight of such a bad debt.

The retailers who employ this tactic know new importers are particularly vulnerable to this scam because they are usually desperate to have a retailer compliment them with an order for their products. A policy of refusing all large orders will protect your fledgling company.

Whether a slow-paying retailer plans to make you a banker or simply rip you off, they can count on the standard collection procedures to enable execution of their plan.

Once the receivable is 60 days old (or 30 days past due), businesses will send out perhaps a statement of account, or a letter of inquiry encouraging the customer to pay.

By ignoring the letters until legal action is threatened, retailers can learn how far they can go before they really have to pay. The importer unwittingly provides this information in the form of letters and telephone calls. I will quickly outline the common progressive collection technique:

Day 1	Merchandise shipped	Invoice sent out.
Day 30	Payment due	Optional statement sent out.
Day 60	Payment 30 days past due	Importer sends polite inquiry letter.
Day 75	Payment 45 days past due	Importer sends second letter, asking for payment, and suggesting concern.
Day 90	Payment 60 days past due.	Importer calls customer, and requests commitment to pay. Customers says will pay in a week.
Day 105	Payment 75 days past due.	Send letter threatening collection.

At this point, most customers who abuse credit privileges will pay up, noting they can go at least 100 days without paying you with no ill effect. Thereafter, they will count on getting 100 days to pay from you. Those who are going under will simply ignore you, so the clock keeps ticking.

Day 120	Payment 90 days past due.	You either call or write with your final notice demanding payment.
Day 145	Payment 115 days past due.	Collection agency begins letter writing and telephone sequence all over.
Day 235	Payment 205 days past due.	Collection agency gives up, recommends a lawsuit.

Lawsuits are probably not cost effective, and in any event you have probably learned the company has gone out of business, and you have no one on whom to serve papers. You do what most people do—you write off the debt.

Collection agencies charge a percentage of the invoice value with a minimum base charge. Invoices over sixty days old (thirty days past due) generally command a 25% collection fee. The fee jumps higher as the receivable ages. By the time this was turned over for collection, the fee would be at least 50%.

Statements of account are generally a waste of time and postage. Your customer received an invoice, and if they cannot handle that properly, the customer has problems. Certainly send a statement to a customer who requests one—sometimes they lose an invoice or the paperwork gets confusing. But to automatically send out statements is poor business practice.

The collection method outlined above, although common, is not the way to collect money.

How To Collect Accounts Receivable

The most effective way to collect receivables starts when the order is written. Although the Uniform Commercial Code of the United States lays out the rules of the road for business, it is important to establish the terms and conditions of your company's relationship with customers, as it says in the Bible, in the beginning.

Every new customer ought to get a copy of your terms and conditions, as outlined in the next chapter, either from the sales representative or mailed by you to each new customer. As noted above, the customers may have thirty days to pay. With this in mind, I outline the effective way to collect receivables:

Day 1	Merchandise shipped	Invoice sent out.
Day 30	Payment due	No statement sent out.

Day 60   Payment 30 days past due   Collection letter sent out from collection agency, restating the terms and conditions, and demanding immediate payment.

A collection letter at this point introduces a dynamic situation. Retailers are astonished to be put in collections so swiftly. Also, retailers feel confident they can delay payment to importers because their slow payment is just between the importer and the retailer. The fact that a third party is introduced ruins the intimacy that permits the retailer's abuse of credit privileges.

Day 65   Payment 35 days past due   Retailer calls apoplectic about being turned over for collection.

Notice the change here. The importer never bothers with collections. The retailer is calling the importer about an invoice, not the other way around. When a retailer calls us about a past due invoice, I say there must be a mistake, because the retailer certainly pays his bills on time. When I pretend to check the records and establish the retailer has not paid his bill, I quickly blame the aggressive credit practices on my bankers who force us to behave so tough, and then assure the customer the collection will stop as soon as the check is received.

I have not wasted any time collecting money owed me, I look innocent, the problem remains with the retailer who will find relief only by paying the bill. Finally, the retailer will not be late next time, knowing that his credit is at risk if he is. For those retailers going under and simply cannot pay:

Day 75   Payment 45 days past due.   Collection agency notifies customer the account will be turned over to an attorney in two weeks.

Day 90   Payment 60 past due.   An attorney files a lawsuit against the retailer.

Although you probably will gain nothing from the lawsuit, it is worthwhile to proceed. Those "golden parachute" retailers described above will pay you off rather than risk having their plans ruined by news of a collection suit.

Clean receivables make backers happy. The import/wholesaler decides when someone has gone bad debt. It can be at 90 days or 180 days. By writing off any receivable before it is beyond 90 days old, your company appears better on paper to bankers and backers. Furthermore, the aggressive collections will actually improve your profits as described before.

This collection program also requires a special collection agency. Most collection agencies attempt to get the money for you, and then charge a hefty percentage of what is collected. There are also collection agencies that provide, in effect, letter writing services. The importer chooses the content and frequency of the collection letters by means of a transmittal form purchased from the collection agency.[55]

Once you have a past due customer, you fill out the name, address, amount owing, invoice number, etc, on the transmittal form and mail it to the collection agency. The collection agency inputs the data into a computer and generates the letters until you send in a stop order, that is, when you get your money. Although this is a fully licensed collection agency, the letters direct the slow payer to send the past due money directly to you, the importer. The collection agency does not touch your money. The collection agency makes their money sending out these very effective letters. The transmittal forms cost a few dollars each, a handsome profit on letter writing.

The collection agency also has staff attorneys to file the lawsuits as required.

Most retailers are honest and cooperative. They are certainly critical to your success. And there are so many good retailers out there, there is simply no reason to work with those customers that are any trouble at all. This cuts both ways though; there are far too many good suppliers of

---

55. I use Transworld Services in Rohnert Park, California.

products for retailers to put up with any nonsense from importers. By having clear policies and procedures to promote good relations, an aggressive collection program avoids cash problems.

We now have the methods of gaining orders that prove we can sell merchandise bought with money loaned. We know how to avoid losing that money when sent overseas to pay for the goods. We know how to check creditworthiness of our customers, and further we know how to collect aggressively if and when a customer is not cooperative in paying for the goods we shipped. With these skills in place, we now seek financing.

Realistic Finance Sources

At the small business level the resources considered for financing are usually something in this order: self, customers, banks (and Small Business Administration loans), friends and relatives, suppliers, professional investors.

The most risky scenario is if you have your own money to spend. If you are forced to borrow, your lender usually requires some sort of plan and security before any money is lent. This forces you to work at a higher level of competence then you might if you were risking your own money. Borrowing money serves as a check on your passions. When you are blinded by your own desires, it is good to have a cold-blooded money-lender reining you in.

Your customers would be a great source, and in a conceptual way they in fact do "finance" your business. But in reality none of your customers will ever take the risk of financing your purchases. Don't even ask, because it upsets their expectation that you are solid enough to serve them.

The ideal situation is to have a line of credit with the bank. As you know, a letter of credit is an instrument for making a payment. A line of credit is access to loans, like a credit card. Often letters of credit are backed by a line of credit. Unfortunately, no bank will give a line of credit to a start-up company, under any circumstances. Maybe you have been to "Small Business Development Days" where bankers proclaim their programs to assist the small businessperson. In fact banks do not assist the "undercapi-talized" small business people generally, and the start-up business never. Bankers wave their banner at small business development symposiums, saying "we're here for you!" But if you visit them one-on-one, they will say to the start-up company, we didn't mean *you*.

A banker friend of mine explained banks, as part of their charter with the government, must use their resources to aid in community development, hence the programs to promote small business. This is at odds with the federal regulations that dictate the "mix of risks" a bank can carry. So the stipulations and requirements of the terms of the bank are usually impos-sible for any small company to meet.

Realistically banks are repositories of the collective capital of the commu-nity, in the form of savings deposits, that must be lent out in safe invest-ments. Therefore, it is foolish for banks to assist small businesses. To put it bluntly, the vast majority of small business ideas are not good risks. The money lent by banks would be wasted, and probably *cause* the business to fail, because the money would be lent too early. Nonetheless, very many small businesses are started and many of those succeed, all without help from the banks. The simple reality stands: if you provide a value, invest-ment dollars will flow to you from non-banking sources.

Some small business people speak with resentment of bankers, but really ought to be glad bankers do not recklessly invest our money in businesses like ours. Loan officers have an inside joke: We are willing to lend you money precisely at the moment you don't need it. I believe bankers ought to speak freely and simply announce that they don't want to see you until you are successful.

Nonetheless, you want to work with banks as soon as you meet the quali-fications. And you can "meet the qualifications" earlier than most if you work with the reality of the system. Very early on send a seasoned loan officer your business plan and financial statements (even if they are laugh-ably impoverished) for you and your company. Make sure the bank you choose is large enough to have an international department; and don't be afraid to use the same bank as your local competitors. And keep in mind the foreign banks—a Banque de Paris or a Hong Kong & Shanghai Bank—may be more sophisticated and helpful in dealing with the foreign supplier, although such banks are often more selective in taking customers. Include a cover letter saying up front that you know the loan officer can do nothing for you now, but things will change. After doing this three or four times a year, meet for a half hour with this banker and begin to discuss under what conditions they would begin to extend you a line of credit. Eventually, when you want the bankers help (you will never *need* their help), you can build on your already budding relationship.

The banks will finance your company when you have met their criteria of a worthy credit risk. To gain a line of credit from a bank, you will have to meet at least the following conditions:

1. A three year successful track record. You must have been in business as an importer for three years and provide audited statements showing you are making a profit. The profit need not be large, just consistent and growing.

2. A deal that makes sense to the loan officer. Loan officers must take their plans for lines of credit to a loan committee at the bank. The loan committee plays advocatus diaboli, and the loan officer must defend his or her plans for your company. If the loan officer is ignorant of your business, it is unlikely the proposed line of credit can be supported. It often helps to use the same bank as your competitors, since the loan officer will then understand your business.

3. A ten year potential. The banks do not want to go through all of the trouble of meeting you and setting up an account for a one shot deal. They want to work with customers who plan to be around for years.

4. Full collateralization. Essentially, a line of credit will equal the value (never more, often less) of your company, liquidated today. Some loan officers will bristle at any definition so exact, preferring to believe there is

some art and risk in banking, but there is not (or certainly should not be). You might consider bankers pawnbrokers, with you pawning your assets for working cash. With the aforementioned elements in place, the banker will figure your line based on your assets.

The first most valuable component of your company is any cash. If your company has been around a few years and you tend to have $60,000 in the bank on any given day, then the bank will lend you that amount. This may seem silly to borrow cash against cash, but that is part of what is occurring. You need that $60,000 for your day to day operations. You cannot at the same time use it to pay for imports. But you can borrow against it to finance imports. For the bank, the key document in the banking relationship is the perfected security agreement. In essence, your bank has first call on all your company's assets. If there is a problem paying the bank back, they will seize the $60,000. The telephone companies, suppliers, employees, insurance companies, and government agencies that the importer intended to pay with the $60,000 simply will not be paid because the bank took it.

The next most valuable asset is the accounts receivable (what your customers owe you). Accounts receivable are created when the importer ships against orders from the customers. When the importer ships, that is considered the sale. The original order from the customer, a copy of the invoice for the goods shipped against the order, and a copy of the bill of lading (or UPS log) constitute the documentation of an account receivable (A/R). If you ever need to sue a customer for collection, or place a claim with a judge to recover from a bankrupt customer, you will need these documents, or you will have no claim.

Accounts receivable are considered liquid assets. They can be sold to companies called factors, but factors earn their profits by purchasing accounts receivable at lower than face value (say 10%). If a factor buys a million dollars worth of accounts receivable for $900,000, the factor can expect to earn about $70,000 over a few months time (assuming a 3% bad debt rate). The importer may want $900,000 now more than $1,000,000 over the next few months, and the factors are happy to help out. For purposes of a loan, a bank will discount the accounts receivable much more than a factor, to assure the bank will recover full value in the event of a business failure. It is not uncommon for banks to discount the value of your receivables some 30%, and this assuming the accounts receivable are creditworthy customers who are also within payment terms.

After accounts receivable, the next most valuable asset of the company is inventory. Working from the cost you paid for the merchandise (not the selling price), the bank will discount the value of your inventory by 50%. Banks do not want to inherit your inventory. They want to be assured they can unload your assets in the event they must seize them.

Your business may have acquired other assets (cars, real estate, etc.) that can also be taken into consideration when determining your line of credit. To review above we have:

Asset	Value	Value to Bank	Line of Credit Value
Cash	$60,000	100%	$60,000
A/R	$200,000	70%	$140,000
Inventory	$500,000	50%	$250,000
Other	?	?	?
Line of Credit			$450,000

So this imaginary company may have nearly three-quarters of a million dollars in assets, but can only hope to get about a half million in a line of credit.

As part of the line of credit, the banks exercise an "abundance of caution" and will require that you back up the company assets with your private assets as well (your home, your car, etc). You will be required to take out a life insurance policy upon yourself, naming whomever you wish as beneficiary, except again the bank will have first rights to the proceeds of the insurance if you should die and the business not be able to repay the loan.

The specific instrument giving the banks first call on all of your assets is something called a UCC filing or a "perfected security agreement." This condition is why incorporating to limit financial liability is not reasonable. It is the bank from which you want to protect yourself; they make sure you cannot limit your financial liability. Incorporate when your accountant tells you to, for tax reasons, not for legal reasons.

Finally, you will negotiate your salary with the bank. They will allow you to draw out some reasonable amount but want you to keep all other monies in the business where they can quickly seize them in the event of business trouble. A salary is the last area where you can bleed your business dry, leaving nothing for the banks to recover.

Once assured of repayment, the bank is ready to give you a line of credit, in this instance a $450,000 line of credit. In short, the banks are not a likely source.

With banks routinely rejecting start-up businesses, congress funded something called the Small Business Administration (SBA) to assist in loans to small businesses. Whenever the government dictates to banks how they must act, the banks become less competitive and profitable in equal measure. Naturally the banks resist compliance until the government promises to cover, at taxpayers expense, any risk from the bad business practices mandated by the government.

In the case of the Small Business Administration, the government is in the business of making the bad loans through the banks that the banks prudently refuse themselves. The program has the highest failure rate of any loan program. Companies that are involved in the program have less chance of succeeding than companies not in the program.

Two factors contribute to this high failure rate:

1. you must be turned down by three banks as a bad risk before you can apply for an SBA loan (the bank then makes the loan, but with the US

taxpayers guaranteeing the loan). Therefore, SBA loan candidates are on shaky ground to start.

2. A banker has explained to me the following more complex factor: banks must maintain certain liquidity ratios demanded by the government. Sometimes, demands for credit or opportunities for profits dictate that they dive into this ready cash. To avoid violation of government regulations, they quickly replace the cash by declaring the SBA loans in default (technically most of them always are) and liquidate them for government money, and all is well for the bankers.

The interference from the government in the form of compliance in having the loan eliminates any value. As a friend of mine who participated in the loan program relates, "You can get an SBA loan, or you can run a business. You cannot do both, so you have to pick one." It appears the paperwork required to obtain and comply with the loan program is so onerous that if your poor business plan doesn't kill your business, the paperwork and compliance of an SBA loan will.

If your business is on a sound footing, defined as a market proven with orders, there are other sources of financing available. To thrive you will need to focus all of your creativity and energy on the opportunity manifest in the orders. To dilute that focus by giving any concern to government regulations attendant to a SBA loan is to beg for failure.

Another source considered is friends and relatives, a natural source of finance. Although their interest rates may be low, the interference factor and emotional tax is usually too high. Also they grew up with or actually raised you and probably don't take you seriously—"prophet in his own land" and all that—or, more damaging, they remember you in your younger days. In any event, they likely do not have the business savvy that other lenders normally provide.

Your foreign suppliers, are under certain circumstances a reasonable source of finance. Quite the opposite of disrespecting you, they often treat every American as if he were Bill Gates. This may not be only for initial backing but for growth as well. If in your second year orders showed a five-fold expansion in sales-potential, a bank would still have to decline. Too risky. On the other hand, a supplier is most eager to help expand sales of their manufactures.

When I began teaching in 1984, people would often ask for recommendations as to the best source of financing for their proposed import company. I would draw the following on the chalkboard:

	Import	Export
Orders:	Easy	Hard
Money:	Hard	Easy

As I drew the chart, I would explain that in importing orders were very easy to get. Too easy, as a matter of fact. Because of the excellent refinements in the US markets, there are specialized trade shows for virtually every conceivable product . A friend of mine decided to import venison sausage from New Zealand with an idea of selling it to delicatessens. He discovered the deli products trade shows that take place in every major market of the US each year. At these shows the many buyers for delis come to place orders for their regular products and to search out new and interesting deli products. My friend found the buyers very receptive. He gained many orders, but cleverly only bought enough venison to cover those orders.

The reorders were paltry due to slow sales in the delis, and federal laws prohibiting the transportation of deer meat to states that restrict the sales signaled the unlikelihood of success with this particular product. Contrast this fellow's prudence with the multitudes of others who have bought excessive amounts of products based on the initial reaction of trade shows. To mind comes the fellow that called me regarding a garage full of "slim tea" he owned. Apparently he received many—although naturally small—orders from a variety of stores, perhaps a few thousand dollars worth. Based on this "success" he bought tens of thousands of dollars worth of the tea in anticipation of the great business he was going to do. No reorders came in, and the tea is slowly rotting in his garage. Again the number one rule: buy no inventory until you have orders from customers.

In exporting, the orders are hard to get. If you want to make a sale to Argentina, you probably will have to travel all the way to Argentina and make your presentation in Spanish. You will be competing against not only other American companies, but the German, Japanese and so on. And you may find that although your product is essentially identical to the Tanzanian's product, they win the order because some obscure export subsidy made theirs cheaper. Quite a contrast from the US markets.

But in exporting, financing is very easy. If you get an order, then the buyer overseas must open a letter of credit to your benefit for the value of the goods. You are the beneficiary, and are in effect guaranteed payment. Often exporters use letters of credit from customers overseas to get the financing to buy the very product they are exporting.

But if orders are easy in importing, the money, financing, is hard. When I first began teaching I would not mention the fact that I had received financing from suppliers overseas. I felt this would create an unfair expectation in people's minds, "if the teacher can get financing from overseas, why can't we?" Over the years I have found that not only have I gained financing from overseas, but just about everyone involved in international trade is in some way getting support from the suppliers.

That is not to say you can call up suppliers overseas and say, "I am in business, send me cash." There are some elements that have to be in place. How much money can we expect a foreign company to invest? Such questions cannot be answered directly, but do deserve some reply.

First, let us define "invest." In this instance we mean the supplier will send you enough product on credit to meet proven demand. This is the extent of the supplier's "investment." The suppliers will not send you money to market goods or for any other purpose (although we have seen this occur on rare occasion).

The suppliers overseas are not getting rich because they are stupid. They recognize a good investment and are able to act on it when presented. It is up to you to present a program your suppliers can back. In studying what elements must be in place before you can seek backing, we have identified at least four. There may be more, but in a review of many companies now enjoying financing from overseas, these four stand out:

1. New product. This is the funnest requirement. When I say new, I mean just a little bit new. I have discussed this more fully in the chapter on finding products, but to review, the importer wants to develop a product that is at the same time new enough to command a premium price (it is price blind), yet not so new as to require explanation or advertising. The amazing part of this is how little it takes to come up with a new product. For those who like to have concepts quantified, I say never more than 20% new.

2. New market. If you try to sell something a supplier already makes, he will not back you, because you will just be stealing business from another of his customers.

3. Orders in hand. We have seen how to accomplish this in the previous chapter.

4. Relationship. This is probably the most overlooked requirement.

Anyone raised in the United States enters the field of international trade at a great disadvantage—and it is a result of the benefits of our legal structure that puts us at such a disadvantage. The tremendous economy and opportunity available in the United States is a tribute to our legal structure. Without it, we could not possibly enjoy the opportunity and prosperity that comes from having rational and fair rules to follow. Our legal basis allows you to proceed with confidence that the agreements you are gaining towards cooperation on some stated goal will be honored. To put it another way, in America, if someone does you wrong you can sue and expect justice.

As an importer by profession who has been teaching, consulting and writing on international trade since 1984, the two critical areas I have found most fascinating are managing risk and finding customers.

Every country has its legal system, and everyone involved in international trade experiences a similar conflict of expectations that makes for uncertainty, or worse, in international trade. For example, in the USA, we have the Uniform Commercial Code, a sort of "rules of the road" in which any transaction occurring within the US economy is supported by a legal structure (the root of "legal" means "protected"). Nonetheless, we may be aware of the differences and thus afraid to risk international trade, or perhaps worse, be unaware of the differences and presume a security not there, with disastrous results.

In international trade, even with "conventions" and "trade agreements," no such legal assurances and protections are in place. There is the Paris-based ICC which maintains the UCP for letters of credit, and there is Lloyd's of London for insurance. But even with these innovations and traditions, international trade is different from domestic trade, and in that measure uncertain. And as uncertain it is for Americans due to the differences between domestic law and international trade conventions (such as when and how title transfers), the differences for us are as pronounced as for Italians who compare the international system to their Roman law, and for the French who compare it to Napoleonic law, and as it is to the Japanese…and so on.

Our strengths are our weaknesses. We enjoy the prosperity of the United States, but we do not look beyond our own efforts to see the foundation of our prosperity. Consequently, when we work with suppliers overseas, we do not take into consideration that a yes answer may really be a no answer;

we may not expect the comment "interesting" from a foreigner to mean "hell, no!" and we may not realize that a contract with an entity overseas is legally worthless.

The American Bar Association does not recognize the phrase "international law," because no such practice exists. Sovereign countries certainly join conventions (as long as it is convenient), but when they choose to repudiate any such treaties they do so. Some American lawyers claim to practice international law, which of course is silly. An American lawyer in California may have a Japanese national as a client, but the lawyer is simply practicing California law on behalf of his client, no different (one would hope) than the service given to any other client. Some lawyers even capitalize on the pretension of being international lawyers and charge their clients more for such work!

The United States Supreme Court has even ruled that if an American overseas fails to abide by a contract with another American overseas, there is no jurisdiction in the United States. So remember there is no legal basis and certainly no recourse if deals go awry in international trade.

For most this is a terrifying realization. The risks seem insurmountable. But keep in mind the US is the world's largest international trading country, in both imports and exports. It is said we consume about 25% of the world's production. International trade is growing rapidly and quite successfully for those who operate fully informed of the realities.

Recall there are 350,000 importers in the United States bringing in some $656 billion (and growing); and the top one thousand importers account for some $400 billion of it, or $400 million each on average. The remaining $256 billion in imports is spread among the remaining 349,000 importers, for a average of some $775,000 each in imports. Either way, there is vast trade at the small business level.

With no assurances available in international trade, on what basis does an importer proceed? As stated, the number four element is relationship.

Without building a solid relationship with the supplier overseas, your chances of succeeding are very close to nil. Certainly you want the best supplier possible, and I have covered the process for finding the best in the chapter on that topic. But once found, how does one develop a strong relationship? Does one take sensitivity seminars to learn to never pat an Asian business partner on the head (do Americans business people pat each other on the head)? Does one learn to keep the pointy end of a slice of pie turned away from the King of Thailand (I'll keep it in mind the next time we have pie with the King of Thailand). Does one learn to never turn up one's heels to an Arab (again, how would one come into such circumstances)? Such seminars are unrewarding except for the humor. It is not even important to speak the foreign language. I know an American who speaks Japanese fluently but insists all conversations and agreements be in English. This is the rule rather than the exception. The reason for this is clarity; foreigners almost always speak English better than Americans speak the foreign language. Certainly the ability to speak a foreign language is critical if one is to be considered educated, but not necessary if one wants to import.

The simple fact of the matter is most of the people involved in international trade overseas do so because they have been exposed to the US, most likely because they went to school here to begin with.

We cannot rely on contractual law or our sensitivity and appreciation for their culture to bind our suppliers overseas to us. The tie that does bind is our value to the suppliers overseas: we build markets for products of their manufacture in the United States. The products may be of our design, but it is still their manufacture. And this is the complete and exclusive basis for their interest in you. Therefore, remember to base every conversation and correspondence on this point: the action proposed will result in stronger markets in the United States. If the point can't be made, wait until you can.

With these four elements in place, you can begin the process of securing financing from overseas. Keep in mind that you are a small company, and the amounts you may be asking for are actually quite small. If you hope to have a multimillion dollar business, you do not need commitments for multimillion dollars. It will take time for your business to grow, and your first shipments will rarely need to exceed a few thousand dollars. When this is shipped against the orders you have received, you will take your profits, pay the supplier, and do more business next time.

Let us assume your first foray into the market netted you $20,000 in orders. Then you need about $10,000 to pay for the product (assuming an industry with a 50% gross profit margin). Of that $10,000, the supplier probably has $8,000 invested. When you have the four elements in place, what risk is there to the supplier? Very little when one considers the alternatives. What would it cost the supplier to come to the United States to build a market for new product, even if he knew how to proceed? Far more than $8,000, and there would be no assurances he might succeed. On the other hand, you have the proof of the orders to assure success. From another angle, a mere $20,000 aggregate orders for all the time and effort does not warrant putting a high pay salesperson working on the task for some large corporation.

Why would a foreign company be interested in backing you in the first place? Just as the US government aggressively promotes exports with a wide variety of subsidies at taxpayers' expense, so foreign governments do likewise. When, as a result, some companies overseas take advantage of these foreign government programs, the effect may be that you are the beneficiary of a foreign government export promotion scheme. Also, as Americans buy more foreign-made goods, foreign companies earn more and more US dollars. Overseas, huge corporations and small companies alike have excess US dollars. And the best place in the world to invest US dollars is in the United States. At the macroeconomic level, foreign entities invest heavily in American real estate, business and securities. It is reported that Manhattan real estate is owned largely by the Dutch, the British hold the largest portfolio of American businesses of all the foreign countries, the Germans are heavy players in the New York stock exchange and the Japanese own 47% of downtown Los Angeles.

At the microeconomic level, modest sized companies overseas too are flush with US dollars. For a small exporter of footwear, where is the best place in the world to invest any excess US dollars? Again, the United States, but more specifically, it is best to invest in the distribution channel of the product the exporter manufactures. This is true for the manufacturers of every product imported into the United States.

The most likely source of funding is the one you will encounter only as you go through the process of actually building your business, as laid out in this book.

Twice in my career I started an importing company: once before I was recruited away to an old, established company, and now in my current business. Both times I had an experience that others tell me is near universal. As I went through the steps, such as are outlined in this book, naturally people would ask about the business I was starting. I would tell them where I had started, what my goals were, and how far along I was in the process. Often people would make a comment along these lines: "Well, if you get to the point where the customers are ordering, give me a call." Or perhaps, " I've got some money to invest; when you need financing, let me know." Indeed, in 1985 a participant stood up in my class and said, "I am a CPA with money to lend. If anyone in this class gets orders, but cannot find financing, give me call." Needless to say, this caused quite a stir in the class.

After nearly twenty years of saying this, and getting many calls from students with questions on some problem advancing their business, never have I been asked for a source of financing. When the questions have to do with a problem in distribution or a strategy in marketing, I can tell they are well beyond any finance challenge. I think I know why I never get a question on financing: as you go through this process, you will have the same experience I have had, and everyone else has: You will tell people, especially those who ask, what you are doing. Some of those will people will suggest you call them when you are ready to borrow money.

In some industries, like the garment industry, this is so formalized the people who lend in such a manner are called "factors." In essence you pledge the value of your orders against the loan to buy the garments for your customers. The factor collects the receivables from your customer, subtracts the loan principle and any fees, and gives you the balance.

Finance is *a* problem in business, not *the* problem. *The* problem is getting customers. If you solve *the* problem, all of the other problems, such as where to locate your warehouse, what kind of computer to get, how to get financed, what you business card should look like, and all the others fall into place. Notice how I slipped finance in that list of mundane items? That is because that is where it belongs. If you cannot find financing yet you have all the elements in this book laid out, contact me, and we can discuss it.

From my own experience and what others show me, whether from friends, relatives, or suppliers overseas, financing has never been a problem. So is there no role for banks in small business international trade?

Banks play a role in almost every international trade transaction, in importance just below the Customs broker and the overseas agent. Specifically, banks issue letters of credit, facilitate the transfer of title of the goods, convert foreign currencies into US$, and vice versa. Of all these functions, only a bank can issue and accept letters of credit; the other functions alternative entities can perform.

As you go looking for backing, keep all options open. Remember this is a business need, and treat it as such; lending money is a competitive business. Literally shop around for the best deal on money, and go with that. If you are looking for $5,000 to buy product from overseas, approach each potential lender with a full disclosure of your activities so far and your current situation (in other words, a business plan). No doubt you will follow the advice to have the four elements in place mentioned earlier in this chapter. Ask the potential lender to make you an offer on what terms he will lend you the money. Under such conditions we have never had difficulty finding financing. And we often have competing offers to choose from.

Cash Against Documents

In the event you do not have a line of credit with a bank but you are getting backing from some local source (friends, relatives) and you want to minimize bank fees, you may be able to secure "cash against documents" terms. In essence the supplier agrees to send the original documents (including the bill of lading, the prima facie evidence of ownership) with the banks acting as COD courier. No letter of credit is opened; you promise to simply pay the bank cash for the documents when the merchandise arrives. This is not popular with suppliers overseas because if you cannot or will not pay when the merchandise actually arrives, the supplier overseas is stuck with their merchandise on the docks of a land far away. But it is not unheard of in some smaller transactions.

Lockbox

There are occasions a backer supports your efforts and agrees to eschew the banks at first. Since the deal is so small and your efforts are so genuine, the security of bank participation is not desired. In such a case, what are the mechanics of moving the money? Let's say the exporter is willing to ship you $10,000 worth of merchandise. There are two extremes to consider, one we will call the handshake, and the other we will call the lock box.

On the handshake basis the exporter ships you the goods and you pay the exporter after you get paid. This is least attractive to the supplier, but not uncommon. The lock box is far more attractive to the supplier, but less common.

A lock box is simply a bank account like any other except the individual holders cannot gain access to the account without agreement from all the holders.

In a lock box situation, the importer, exporter and a bank agree that all payments on invoices will be directed to a bank. The invoices will be mailed from your company to customers, as you ship against orders the reps gained on your behalf. The invoices will list what was shipped and the prices, the total due, and all other details including your name and phone number, but the address to which the customer remits will be a post office box number. And you the importer have no access to the post office box to which the payments are sent.

The post office box belongs to the bank, which as agreed, collects the checks and deposits them into a "lock box" account. At some interval and on some percentage as pre-agreed between the importer and the exporter, the money is divided up. In the case of a gift and housewares company, it would be divided 50/50.

Although this sounds very complicated, it is quite common, and requires nothing special on the part of the bank. To them it is another business account, on which they earn about a dollar on each check processed and an account fee for maintenance (with a minimum of about $100 per month). This might seem high, but the work is labor intensive.

There is a method to even further assure the foreign supplier. The supplier has you sign a perfected security agreement (also known commonly as a UCC filing) that is then filed with the secretary of state for your state. Blank perfected security agreement forms can be found in just about any stationery store. Once executed this is a legal document that gives an exporter overseas who would ordinarily have no rights in the United States the first right to the assets of your company, which probably amount in fact to only the goods the exporter ships to you. In this way you bind yourself financially responsible to the supplier overseas. Again, this is US law, not "international law."

One might get the impression that fear of getting ripped off motivates much of the activity in international trade. Although we must never lose sight of the market as paramount, money troubles can hurt a business, as do labor troubles, management troubles, utility problems and so on. Money is just a tool in business like labor, management, or equipment.

I doubt anyone would go into this business to engage in fraud. Trouble is far more likely to to be from simple mismanagement. After receiving merchandise on credit from a supplier, an inexperienced importer may find himself a bit overwhelmed. As one friend described it, each day he has to control a blizzard of paper that blows in from the door, phones, faxes and e-mail.

In the midst of this challenge, paying back the supplier may be a lower priority than getting the shipments out to the customers. I have seen a few instances where a company bought computer equipment and software to handle the rush of orders and subsequent accounting. The outgoing shipments caused the owners to overestimate success; the company bought top-of-the-line hardware and specially modified software (which never did operate properly). When it came time to repay the supplier, the money was tied up in computers and other over-estimated needs. Naturally, there was no further cooperation from the supplier.

Therefore it is prudent to consider the option of the lock box even if the supplier is willing to back you on the basis of a handshake. With the lock box, the fledgling importer is forced to get by with what he has, and cannot squander, especially unwittingly, the company's revenue.

My seminar at one point was entitled "Importing on a Shoestring." Two participants in my seminar from that era who subsequently started businesses and stayed in touch were having fun with the title. One said to the other, "Sure, some shoestring! A $25,000 shoestring so far." The listener related this to me because his company was roughly equally advanced, yet he had put no more than a few thousand dollars into it. Why can some people with very little resources grow a company and others require much more to do the same? Simply put, people achieve their goals with what they've got. If they have plenty to spend, they spend plenty. If not, they get creative.

Ted Turner is famous for his business acumen and turning a rather small business into possibly the world's foremost TV channel. At one point he was tens of millions of dollars in debt and criticized for being so reckless. Turner explained the television network he went into debt to build could be sold at any point in its growth for a profit far in excess of his debt, even at a "fire-sale" price. He fit the criterion of an entrepreneur Peter Drucker discusses in his book *Innovation and Entrepreneurship*. According to Drucker, an entrepreneur takes negligible financial risks. And so it should be with you. Certainly you will expend some money getting started, but whether it is mere hundreds or tens of thousands depends on how much emphasis you place on providing a value and how creative you are in approaching each apparent need to expend.

Hope For The Best

The ideal financing method for small business in the United States would be a copy of a program widely used in Bangla Desh. Essentially ten individual borrowers apply for a loan to an agency as a unit. The borrowers are liable for the loan jointly and severally. In other words, all are expected to repay the loan; if any one of the ten cannot, the other nine are required to make up the difference. The debt becomes theirs. Because of this requirement, the borrowers carefully select their "partners," and even more carefully monitor each other's progress. Goodwill and cooperation among the borrowers is tremendous. The failure rate is very low, and success rate surprisingly high. And the average loan amount is $67 per individual.

Peru has a similar program that is working quite well.[56] But with banking laws too onerous to allow such beneficial creativity, and the tendency for government SBA programs to bog down in political corruption, it is unlikely we will ever see such practices in the US. Then again, perhaps

56. Nancy Sherwood Truitt, "Microlending to Peru's Poor is Becoming Big Business," Wall Street *Journal* (September 20, 1996): A15.

some entrepreneurial banker will revolutionize small business banking with something proven in third world countries.

Until that day comes, and between now and the point, where you can get financing from the suppliers or other likely sources, where do we come up with the money for postage, letterhead, airfreight charges for samples and so on? These come out of your own pocket. And what if we want to buy a thousand dollars worth of product to test in a variety of settings? John Gordon, a friend of mine and author of the book *Profitable Exporting* (published by John Wiley & Sons), was quoted in a newspaper, in response to an inquiry as to where most small business people get the money to start their business. He replied, "They whip out their VISA card and get a cash advance." Sue Scott of Primal Lites, a company covered by at least a half dozen entrepreneur magazines, says the same thing. But using a bank card to finance the start-up of a company is bank fraud, so don't do it.[57]

Economists speak of the "moral hazard" of credit too cheap, and credit too cheap is the result of too much money being printed, which becomes clear if money is lent at too low of interest rates. The net effect is asset inflation—that is, goods become overpriced to soak up the excess printed dollars (a current example is internet stocks). Beware of easy credit, for it can cause more grief than no credit.

Summary

Earning interest is marginal to a financier; first and foremost, smart investors assure their principal will be safe. Earning interest is easy after the money is safe—as one wise investor stated, "What interests me is the principal, not the interest."

There are many sources of finance available, indeed, sometimes too many. Getting the right match means not only finance, but the business savvy of the

---

57. A useful study would be just how many people use the easy credit of bank cards and fail in business.

entity who is successful enough to have money to lend. The right match can be tricky, and we can waste much time in this area. We must show we can sell the merchandise we buy with the money borrowed, that we can protect that money from theft or loss, and that we can repay any loan.

We must understand that finance is never the problem in business. Ask ten people what the most important step is in starting your business; five will tell you it is getting financed; three will say writing a business plan; one will say getting the right product (close…); and maybe one will say "get a customer." Of course, without a customer you have no business, so naturally the most important step is always get your customers first. And, as I have laid out in this book, that is exactly what we do.

---▼---

CHAPTER EIGHT:

EXPORTING AS A
SELF-EMPLOYED AGENT

The United States is the largest exporter in the world, with agricultural, machinery and equipment, and petrochemical products our leading export items. Exporting is truly "big business," yet there is exporting work to be done at the small business level as well. The trick is to know the value you can provide and the role you can play.

All the lessons learned so far apply to exporting as well. The differences are small and begin with our role. Let's revisit a diagram adapted from an earlier chapter (Fig. 34):

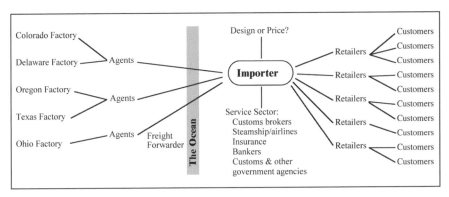

Fig. 34. Exporting as a self-employed agent

You know this diagram well. In importing, the agent is overseas and the importer is in the USA; in exporting what is new is the importer is overseas and the agent—you—is in the US. To work in exporting at the small business level your role will be as the agent between the factories in the United States and the importers overseas. And, necessarily, the value you provide will be one not otherwise available in the market.

As an exporter, all you have learned about importing will be performed by your customer overseas. As an exporter, you will perform here in the US all you have learned so far about the export agent overseas. Particular care must be made to recall that, as in importing, it is your cupidity that drives the product to the market and your irascibility that overcomes any obstacles in your way. In this chapter we will expand on that role, define the value, and point out the differences, so you may know how to buy and sell as a small business export agent.

Problems to Avoid

Many US government entities promote exports with assistance and subsidies. There is no evidence export assistance leads to an increase in exports, but export assistance and subsidies certainly leads to more people trying to export. At any given time in history, there is a volume of exports that makes economic sense. To promote exports by subsidy and assistance is to try to export more than is economically sensible. We are in such a time, so we have far more people trying to export than demand warrants. This makes for much malinvestment in time and money.

Some will object that they know a seller in the US or a buyer overseas, or both, so who cares if the deal makes "economic sense" or not. Subsidies and assistance also create what the economists call "moral hazard," or a reduction in caution because the work is so cheap or easy. Deals that do not provide a solid value are ones that will not happen, or will not endure. When people come to me and say, "I am afraid the buyer and seller will go around me and cut me out of the deal," or, "I am worried about getting paid," or, "How much should I charge in this deal," I become certain, from experience, the deal will not happen, or worse, the exporter will lose money. The questioner is in a deal that does not make economic sense.

To make money and to avoid wasting time with deals that make no economic sense, we need to focus on what value we can provide, and what role we play. Some people would like to sell a few container loads of some known commodity like Hershey's chocolate bars or Walla Walla sweet onions, and make a few per cent commission, from the buyer or seller or both. For the same reasons we as importers are not likely to sell to Wal-Mart, we as exporters are not likely to get such deals. Efficient, professional, competent entities are in place now to move such products, and no one with any sense will trust us with such a large value shipment just so we can earn a little money.

Another possibility is to be an expert in a narrow field, and earn a per cent as a commission agent. A friend of mine who grew up next door to me is a very successful self-employed exporter, working as an agent. After a specialized education in the early 1960's, he went to work for a small Seattle company which wanted to export its "multimeters," a product that measures activity in electronic components. The item is critical in high-tech electronic engineering.

The company became quite successful, and my friend came to know all of the buyers and sellers in the narrow field of high-tech electronics worldwide. Eventually he went on his own, exporting as a self-employed agent, and found great success. The last deal he told me about was a Japanese hospital group looking for electrocardiogram (ECG) machines. He searched for the best place in the world to have such machines made, and found it to be Mexico. He put the deal together, and the Japanese were delighted.

My friend is invited to give pep talks to students at the University of Washington who are considering a career in international business, and they envy his lifestyle, perceived to be one of traveling worldwide to exotic locales, eating sushi and drinking Mai Tais, making 5% commission on multi-million dollar deals, working about 45 minutes a year, living la dolce vita. Naturally they want such a job.

What is not realized is such work is only given to those who are well known in the industry, trusted by both parties, and who are knowledgeable about the product in question. It takes a veteran to even know what sources to tap into to first hear about the Japanese request for ECG machines, and to have been aware of Mexican initiatives in the high-tech medical equipment field. The simple reality is no novice will ever be trusted to handle such deals. We are simply not in a position to reasonably provide a value in such transactions.

Another approach people will take is to organize around a resource, such as I mentioned in earlier chapters relating to importing. Someone will know of a factory or a buyer overseas, and try to build a deal based on this resource. If the resource is a US factory trying to sell their present line of goods, why are they approaching you? A serious exporter wants to deal with established and proven marketers. If the resource is a buyer overseas, do they have a market ready for an established product? If so, again, why will they buy from you? To say "because they know me," or "I am trustworthy," or "hard working" is to miss the point. If your resource overseas was level-headed they would go to the best source in the world, the established best source, who is necessarily also known, trustworthy and hard working.

If not these kinds of deals, then what? We can be the best source in the world in certain circumstances. Essentially, if we are willing to provide a product or service no one else seems willing to bother with. This area is very large indeed.

Casual Exporting

As an importer, inevitably your customers ask you for US-made products. This is the simplest and most likely entree into exporting. Whether it is allied to something you import, or a component, or something unrelated, your suppliers will ask you for US-made product. For example, on some glass candles I import from Taiwan, the rod and tube used as raw materials is actually made of Pyrex, a Corning brand of glass, from the United States. The Pyrex rod and tube is exported to Taiwan, to be fashioned into candles and imported by me into the United States. It is not unheard of for US importers to ship components of products to their suppliers overseas to be incorporated into the ultimate item.

Although I import drinking glasses, I have exported some Libbey glass with my designs to Switzerland. Why? Because there is one category of glass, out of hundreds, that is best made in the US. That is serve ware, bar ware, the kind used in the hospitality industry, such as restaurants. The US makes the best, and I ended up exporting it without any prior intention. As part of the research steps I mentioned in the chapter on finding the best source in the world, naturally I surveyed the US sources. Ultimately I found the best overseas, but in my work I had toured factories in California and the Ohio Valley. I made myself familiar with what innovative work Libbey glass was doing in manufacturing, decorating and, indeed, marketing. When a Swiss buyer requested in New York that my designs on a foreign made glass be put on domestic glass for export, I was ready, willing and able to work up an order on the spot.

An agent of mine for Chinese baskets in Hong Kong asked me once to get him cigarette filter material from the US (completely out of my product area; I haven't dealt in cigarettes since the fifth grade). He had sole distribution rights for a certain non filtered brand of Chinese cigarettes, and people were demanding filters. The US is the best place in the world for cigarette filter material, and he could certainly make the effort to track down a supplier, but with me here in the US, I can do it faster for him.

You may even turn the inevitable into the ideal, and import as a proactive means to develop an export business. In the mid-1970's I had the pleasure of discussing market strategies with representatives of the 3M Corporation while we were trading in China. He was a buyer on a scouting mission, and I asked what products he was looking for. He said it did not much matter, perhaps some magnetic material for their cassette tape business. His real purpose was to do any business with China, exactly what did not matter. The 3M strategy in entering export markets was always to buy from the country first, learn about the culture and business processes, make contacts and build goodwill. By being an excellent customer of the Chinese, they would later become, as it was hoped, excellent vendors to the Chinese.

A decade later at a international trade conference on China, I was delighted to see a professor use as a model for others to copy the strategy of 3M Corporation, who by then was paramount in success of selling to China. Under the reforms a few years earlier China allowed joint ventures with foreign concerns as long as four conditions were in place: 1) China was the majority owner; 2) everything the joint venture manufactured was to be for export sales only; 3) all profits must be retained in China (no repatriation of profits); and 4) an obscure item relating to technology transfer. By this time there were thousands of joint ventures in China, but only 3M Corporation had managed to do so with all four conditions waived in their case. Of course I was aware of certain companies such as Fujitsu who were making televisions in Anhwei for export that were instead being siphoned off for local sales, the fact is only 3M was able to eventually do business on its own terms.

On a separate occasion I queried a front line US Commerce Department officer in the International Trade Administration as to which is easier to start, import or export, and it was his strong impression importing was the more likely. Nonetheless, even although I had no intention of exporting myself initially, it is the flip-side of importing on the international trade coin, and you are likely to engage in it one way or another.

The Opportunity

Problems make for opportunities. The US Department of Commerce, International Trade Administration specifically refuses export assistance to any business that neither manufactures nor warehouses. The reason is that with a limited budget, they have to draw the line somewhere, and the above is another way of saying "don't help small businesses, or new businesses." Large businesses, such as Boeing, get government help but usually at the "Commerce Secretary" level. So the government targets mid-sized businesses for help.

The US Commerce Department claims if all mid-sized companies in the US with "world-class" products were to export, the trade deficit would disappear. The same studies found those very mid-sized companies also refuse to export. The companies research the export possibility, and quickly realize that exporting would be a bad business decision. Can you guess why?

By definition, a mid-sized company has not penetrated the entire United States market. A mid-sized company in Portland can pursue new business in Kota Kinabula, or pursue new business in Atlanta. With the language problems, credit risks, paperwork hassles, learning required, and extra legal requirements, US mid-sized companies simply pass on the opportunity. Herein lies the opportunity: buying exportable products from mid-sized companies too smart to export themselves, and export them working off your kitchen table. Work with a variety of companies selling similar products. The value you provide to the US company is your order is just another domestic order (for it appears to be so to the US maker), and your provide access to US production for foreigners who otherwise are turned down by mid-sized US firms.

Work in any industry you wish, and no doubt your research will uncover opportunities. For example, I once lived in Wenatchee, a small agricultural town. I met with one company making fruit-sorting equipment that flat out refused to export anything for any reason, simply because they said they could not service their products overseas. Another company, a fruit grower, exports over 400 containers of apples and pears a year, all through US-based agents (two of which are local, working off kitchen tables) simply because they do not want to get into "exporting." This is over $100,000 in fees per year paid by one company that simply does not want to learn how to make three phone calls (we'll look at that in a minute). There are hundreds of such companies in central Washington alone. Multiply this by the other states and many other industries and you have tremendous potential.

By looking at anachronistic practices, we may find opportunities. For example, with many New Deal programs of the Roosevelt administration, Stalinist programs were widely admired and copied. One still in place is the Perishable Agricultural Commodities Act of 1933, or PACA. PACA was meant to assure farmers got paid fairly for what they produced by limiting what brokers could charge on a carton of produce they sold. The price is currently 25 cents per carton. Naturally it did not work in the Soviet Union, nor does it work here. A container load of apples may hold 1,000 cartons, and a broker supposedly earns $250, or 25 cents a box for his service, and the grower pays this. Commonly what happens is the broker will buy the fruit at $10 per box (on credit!), resell it at $12 per box, clearing $2000 profit, and then still charge the grower a $250 broker fee, for a total of $2,250. Since the grower has no idea to whom the broker is selling the produce, the grower has no way of checking. (At maybe $2 a box profit, the grower only earns some $2,000.) Thus the $100,000 quoted above is probably underestimated by some $800,000. The Federal government maintains expensive reporting procedures to track selling prices so growers can match their prices against the voluntarily reported selling prices, but the raw data they receive are clearly false.

What Product to Export?

The best product to trade in is found exactly the same way as importing, for the same reasons. Your own background is where your likely expertise and interest is, and a product for which you have a passion will cause you to "go the distance" in overcoming the problems you will face as you proceed. A difference in exporting over importing is that, as an importer, your customers are fellow citizens; in exporting, your customers are in foreign cultures.

The US is the largest exporter in the world in dollars and volume; it is mostly by big business and mostly in commodities. Small business thrives as well, but on the margins. A problem of selling in foreign cultures was elucidated for me in an exchange of e-mails with one American student of Hindi descent who commented on my exchange with an Indian national. The Indian national was a well-educated lad who was promised financing by wealthy relatives for any business he chose to enter. On this basis I was contacted. "I have finance, now what business should I enter?" To me this was completely backwards, and I tried to explain that the lad ought to proceed from what business most interested him, not from the resource of what finance he had. Theologians call it "invincible ignorance" and valley girls say, "He just doesn't get it." There was no way I was going to get my point across, no matter how I nuanced it.

The American student of Hindi descent explained it for me: in India, finance is nearly impossible to come by. On the other hand, with so many poor, something like a Pyrex measuring cup, something we all take for granted, can be a prized possession. Any interest in a new and improved, innovative measuring cup (at a premium price) is nil, since they never had the old one to begin with. With circumstances rather reversed in India, my arguments are not likely to gain a foothold there.

Two points: first, this is why in exporting many people argue we ought never set up our own sales channels overseas; instead, we ought to always sell to the distributors there, simply because we will never understand the foreign culture well enough to thrive. Second, India is a huge "poor" country, perhaps four times the population of the US. Yet, India does have a wealthy class, and a middle class, and a vast population of poor. By some estimates India's wealthy and middle class are similar in size to that of the US, but you are most likely to hear about demand for some basic commodity, rather than some item of marginal utility. If there is demand for Pyrex measuring cups in India, it is likely to be handled by Corning Glass or some other well-connected trader.

This may explain why the United States tends to export so much in commodity items, such as agricultural goods, machinery and equipment (such as jets) and petrochemical products. In fact, our number one export in volume (space taken on vessels, not the dollar value) is scrap: paper, glass, various metals that are recycled and sent overseas. As a commodity, scrap is about as basic as one can get.

Along these lines is the fascinating business of second-hand clothes, as related to me by a trader in the business. Far more clothes are donated than can be consumed by the poor in the US. As he tells it, the clothes you donate to sheltered workshops such as Goodwill or Salvation Army are then sorted by workers into quality and categories (women's high fashion, good condition; men's work clothes, low quality). Various traders bid for exclusive rights to each category for a fixed period, and then the traders broker the clothes for export overseas, assuring a market for the clothes and a profit for the charity.[58]

58. The politics behind the garment trade greatly restrict importation of goods, causing high prices for the consumer, and a drop in sales of items. A useful graduate student study would be to correlate restrictions on garment imports and the effect on the poor as fewer garments are donated to charity.

Another friend exports used laptop computers to the Philippines, where he finds little interest in used desktop models, although the desktop models with comparable power would be far cheaper. Where electric supply "brownouts" are common, a battery powered laptop is vastly preferred.

Selling domestically to the United States will no doubt have surprises, but selling overseas will require a higher level of flexibility, because the differences in market demand will be greater.

Regardless of what you would like to export, what is unlikely is exporting some commodity item. Just as we are in no position to sell to conservators like Wal-Mart domestically, similarly we are in no position to supply large amounts of any commodity item. Commodities are necessarily price sensitive items, and we are in no position to secure the lowest price. It is common for importers overseas to get prices from many sources, even when they are happy with a USA supplier, since they can use any lower price quoted to encourage their USA supplier to cut prices further. Competing on price gets ugly very quickly, unless you are the best in the business. Since we are not the best source for a commodity item, our business must be elsewhere, and that is being a source for items not otherwise available.

Your best bet for exporting is an item you would love to trade in, and sourcing it for a customer overseas who cannot otherwise get the item. It is either an item a US mid-sized company will not export, or an innovation no US company wants to provide overseas.

Finding the Best Customers

First let me reject out of hand the "international trade leads" featured in catalogs, web sites and world trade associations. These are generally offers to sell by people with no supply answered by people with no customers. These leads are a waste of time. There are serious sources we can approach.

We necessarily are limited in the range of customers we can serve. Grand commission deals are outside our scope, as are commodity deals. Where we are most likely to find business is the customer overseas who is frustrated trying to get something fairly marginal in volume (and likely marginal in value as well). Marginal in volume, since the item is not big enough in volume to interest established traders. And even buyers overseas need innovations to stay competitive in their markets.

There are three basic sources for contacting the best customers overseas for your product, and I will list them with relative effectiveness. At the same time, I will lay out a game plan for gaining customers overseas that works very well at the small business level.

Source one: the least effective, but completely necessary source takes us back to using the National Trade Data Bank. Using exactly the same process as laid out in chapter four, we track information on exports instead of imports, and conduct the same analysis.

Using export data, we arrive at which countries are the most active buyers, and normally what prices are being paid for the exported goods. Here again, contact the commercial attachés for the country you identify as the most active buyer of the product in question that you wish to export. After that country's commercial attaché provides you with the name of some importers in that target country, contact those importers with a summary of your interest and capabilities. Save and follow up on what replies you may get.

Source two: TOP, or Trade Opportunity Program is a service of the United States Department of Commerce. Whenever a trade inquiry is made to any one of the many US government trade bureaus worldwide, a note is made and filed with the Trade Opportunities Program at the US Department of Commerce. The US department of Commerce will explain the details, but it is enough to note here that such trade leads are available to very many people very soon after publication. What naturally occurs is perhaps some Saudi businessman looking for sardines is quickly inundated with offers of sardines from many sources. Most of the sources are "wannabes"—that is, they wannabe exporters, and hope this inquiry is the first big break. Therefore the Saudi requester is obliged to winnow through all of perhaps hundreds of responses, down to the one best possible supplier.

This winnowing may take a month or two, and is similar to what we do as importers, as I laid out in the chapter on finding the best source. Ultimately the customer finds the best supplier (and the wannabes jump on the next trade inquiry).

There is no point in following up on these TOP trade leads, because you, starting out, are not the best source in the world for the product, even if it is in your chosen field. The buyer will figure this out in the winnowing process quick enough. So how is TOP useful?

Not only can you get current TOP leads, you can look up leads that are a year old. With new leads you are just one of many and not the best. Using the year-old leads, you contact the buyer and affirm the needs of the buyer overseas are met by the supplier that was selected. This is most likely the case. Then ask what else the buyer is looking for, that the buyer cannot get. Here is where the difference is: no longer are you one potential supplier trying to sell a product for which you are not the best supplier. You are now offering to sell a product you can get that the buyer otherwise cannot find. At this point you are the best supplier in the world for what the buyer wants. But there is an even better source than this.

Source three: the very best source of export customers is the very companies I mention earlier in this chapter, the mid-sized US companies that refuse to export. As you know by now, the raw data, the improvements and lowered costs in communications all make finding the best place in the world for an item rather easy. Those mid-sized US companies that refuse to export are very often contacted directly by buyers overseas. Normally these inquiries are simply thrown away. To you this news is no doubt astonishing, but to the mid-sized US companies receiving such inquiries, the inquiries are an annoyance.

Our most likely customers are those who cannot effect a purchase from an US factory (because the factory refuses to export), or those who are having trouble finding some minor item no one else will bother with. Our bothering with such items gives us the entree to offer to do ever more valuable work. Our passion for the product gives us the wherewithal to do the work required.

With this we can now "qualify" potential customers overseas. Do they want redesign? If no, then the potential is limited in this deal because they want current product, which inevitably someone else is better suited to provide, not us. If yes, then the item is necessarily "new," and something we might provide. Can they get their redesign elsewhere? If yes, our potential is limited, because "elsewhere" necessarily means someone known and superior to us. If no, then we are still in the game. Can they open a confirmed letter of credit or prepay for the goods? If no, naturally the potential is limited, if not nil. (You can also slyly check credit on a potential buyer by checking to see if a steamship line will deliver the goods "freight collect," meaning "freight paid by the buyer after delivery." If no, then the buyer is likely not of good reputation. But "yes" is no guarantee of creditworthiness). If all seems to point to a qualified buyer, and the buyer can open a confirmed letter of credit or prepay for the goods, then we can reasonably proceed.

Will such mid-sized companies be delighted if you offer to act on those inquiries? Probably not. Even though the inquiries are being discarded, it is possible that the mid-sized company is reticent about sharing the inquiries with you. Who are you, and is there some unforeseen way the good deed of giving you these leads will come back to haunt the mid sized USA company? These are real concerns.

The mid sized companies must have confidence in you. That confidence will not come immediately; it will come over time as you develop a relationship with the US manufacturers whose products you wish to export. The beginning of that relationship is when you contact the factory, inquiring about your own customers, the customers you found through sources two and three above. These customers, plus the work you do developing the business, and your passion for the product ought eventually to inspire the confidence to work with you.

Finding the Best Suppliers

Finding these mid-sized companies is easy enough, every library carries the Thomas Register which is a directory of almost every company that either makes or distributes something in the USA. Their site is online and interactive at www.thomasregister.com as well. This is the easy part.

The problem is getting the suppliers to work with you, and here is where matters become complicated. When exporting, you may or may not want the US company that makes the goods to know that you will be exporting. Let's look at why.

Assume we have identified a US factory as a qualified supplier: It is known to deliver goods on time, at a fair price, to specification. Our only remaining concern is whether the factory will redesign products to our specification. Since what we can reasonably sell overseas necessarily must be altered for those markets, if the supplier will not redesign goods, then the potential for profitable business is too limited to bother with.

If a qualified factory will redesign, will they agree to the goods being exported? If no, then we need to ask ourselves, "Do they need to know?" or, more likely, do we need to reveal? If yes, they need to know (either because they ask or for some reason we tell), then again we have very limited potential.

Here's how we may argue our case for cooperating with us in exporting their goods:

1. We will buy the goods and export them. For all intents and purposes, the sale to us will be just another domestic sale, with no added risk or effort for the factory.

2. Selling overseas, we are a kind of intelligence agency, gathering world trade data in the commodity the factory makes. Should some third country develop an alternative to the US factory's product, we will know this early and report it.

3. Export sales represent some production capacity used up. By exporting, there is less capacity for domestic sales. This can effect the price of the goods domestically, in theory at least, because the less available the higher the price. In practice, for example, federal marketing orders each year decide how much agriculture will come on the market, in an effort to keep prices high.

4. The deal is speculative and rather small, and just an effort to discover what potential there may be in the long run. Since we cannot know yet what is at stake, there is no point in creating any contracts or agreements. We will transact a deal and then study if there is more potential. The seller can always decide to formalize the relationship with contracts later, if we discover there is long term and substantial business to be done. (In international trade, the only thing of value is the relationship. Should the factory ever decide to try to impose a disadvantageous contract on you, you take the relationship with you when you walk.)

Practically speaking, a supplier who does not need to know if the goods will be exported is as good as a supplier who is willing to have the products exported. Sometimes a supplier is not concerned what happens to goods until someone mentions "export," and then the supplier decides to call in the lawyers and the deal is ground down to worthless.

Which brings us to the next decision point: will the supplier demand any export rights? By export rights I mean anything that the supplier might demand as a requirement to do business, such as exclusive territories, minimum sales requirements, or pricing demands. These limit potential because they tie your hands, and likely involve a lawyer who will add costs that crush any potential. If the supplier demands any export rights, the value of the deal is limited; if not, the deal is still possible. If so, will the

US supplier offer credit terms to you, such as 30 or 60 days to pay? If yes, use the factory as your bank to finance the deal. If no, will the supplier take a transferable letter of credit as payment? If yes, then proceed with the buyer overseas prepaying the sale by transferring cash into your bank before shipping the goods.

A Summary Graph

Some say intelligence is measured by the ability to solve problems, and others say it is an ability to spot patterns. Maybe it is best to solve the problem of deciding if an export deal makes sense by graphing it out. The decision process above may be better summarized as a decision tree (Fig. 35):

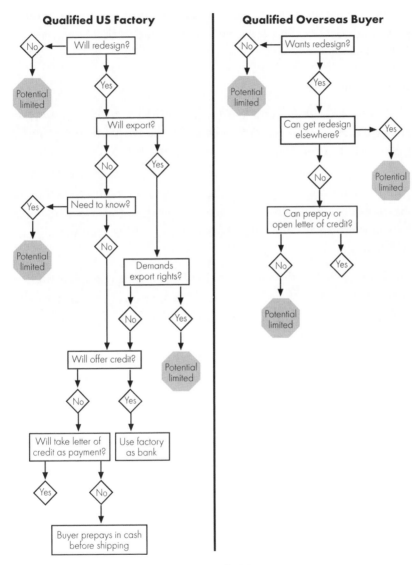

Fig. 35. Export decision tree

Here I juxtapose the decisions that lead us to whether a deal is reasonable or not. You are between the qualified factory in the US and the qualified buyer overseas. "Potential Limited" means the deal is ultimately unlikely to go through. If you can get to "yes" on both sides, then you may have a workable deal.

Structuring the Deal

Of course, as with importing, before you settle on terms, you discover in advance what every requirement and cost is, and work up your price based on that research. Once you have a buyer and a maker for a product, you call your freight forwarder (an export version of the Customs broker, and often in the same company) to handle the paperwork, and to comply with all the rules and regulations, and to arrange the movement or logistics. The freight forwarder you intend to use will advise you and fill in the details all along.

People anticipate that the hardest part of exporting is the logistics, rules and regulations. In fact, it is the easiest, because once you have the buyer and seller worked out, the rest requires a maximum of three phone calls. You call your banker, to assure the payment is secured, you call the factory to place the order, and you call your freight forwarder to book the shipment on a vessel and to prepare all required documents. Of course, as with importing, before you settle on terms, you discover in advance what every requirement and cost is, and work up your price based on that research. An importer gets this information from a Customs broker, an exporter from a freight forwarder. Often these two functions are in one company.

For example, here is a price work-up on 1,029 boxes of apples (a 40' container load) to China:

	Unit cost	Total cost
Ex-Factory Price	$12.17	$12,522.93
+ Cartage to exporting carrier	0.66	675.00
+ Cost of lading on carrier - included in freight		

+ Export documentation fees	0.10	102.90
+ Bank fees	0.17	175.00
+ Profit	2.25	<u>2,405.25</u>
= Free On Board price quote		
(FOB, or the "C" in C&F)		$15,881.08
+ Cargo insurance	0.10	102.90
	plus 10.00	10.00
+International Freight	5.00	<u>5,145.00</u>
= Cost, Insurance, Freight (CIF)		$21,138.98

Each and every cost noted above can be provided by your freight forwarder or banker. There may be costs not noted above peculiar to your item. Your customer overseas will dictate whether you offer a FOB or CIF price (an alternative to CIF is C&F, in which the buyer overseas is arranging the cargo insurance, something the two of you will decide in advance).

All of the items listed above can be gained, but one you must decide upon, and that is "profit." Here we must decide if we want to take title to the goods and add a profit, or take a commission for the seller, or a commission from the buyer, or both. All ways of earning on export will fall into one of these categories.

Commissions are the least likely means for us to be paid. It sounds nice, bring the buyer and the seller together and take a commission, but again the reality is we are compensated based on our value to the marketplace. The commodity deals, or technical deals, or "resource connection" deals are the most likely candidates for commission earnings, but these are the very deals we are not likely to effect. Since we are developing marginal items not otherwise available, taking title to the goods and adding a markup is the most likely scenario. But this still does not answer the question, "How much can I charge?" This is where the art comes in, and there is no good answer available, just a guideline I will offer from experience:

Beginning with what interests you, and whether it is a service or a product, I am always astonished as to what it is people really want—and if you listen, just how easy it is to hear what they want.

I am always amazed at the premium people will pay to have a rather simple solution to a problem (whether the solution is a product or a service). Here is where the money lies, charging a substantial premium to solve a rather small problem no one else will bother with. Such deals tend not to be five or ten percent profit on a substantial risk, but 50% profit on a small deal. And once you make yourself valuable in a small area, inevitably larger, better deals begin to come your way.

Chapter Nine:

▼

Managing the Company

The farther along your plan proceeds, the more ways your business becomes unique. Relatively few people can tell the difference between Calvin Klein and Ralph Lauren when it comes to fashion, but the closer you get to people who know those two, the more explicit the differences. Indeed, between the two men, the belief they are complete opposites makes one chary of ever hiring an employee of the other.

Nonetheless, all businesses have sales and expenses, and the difference between the two is profit (or loss). Certain industries tend to have certain returns expressed as percents, and I mentioned earlier research that shows all businesses, over time, tend towards an average return.

Management is responsible for profit and loss. The goal is profit, and very often the profit is more a result of managing the expenses than the brilliance of the product lines. Calvin Klein is considered the more daring of the two in fashion, but Ralph Lauren consistently is more profitable. The difference is management. Every business goes through cycles of up and down, and a key to success is to be able to ride the roller coaster.

Your primary tool in management is a business plan. You cannot write an accurate business plan, and I doubt anyone ever has. Yet a business plan is necessary for success. A business plan is where you write down your game plan and projections for perhaps the next two years (longer is a waste of time). Then, as you execute, when you are wrong and the plan goes awry, you can adjust the rest of the plan accordingly. And here is the most practical tool for success: being able to adjust quickly when your plans do not work out. You may find sales start nicely and then unexpectedly dry up for 4 months. Some people will do nothing but wait, others may sign on with a temporary work agency to assure income until things can be pushed along again. The difference between the two is success. Of the very many people who thrive in this business that I have talked to, the stories of the "early years" are the most astonishing. The heroics these people performed go unsung, but to the owner of the company it is all "no big deal" or "long ago and far away." I can almost guarantee that if your business is thriving ten years from now, you too will have "war stories" from the early years.

Another fairly common theme is the business for which the owner has a passion normally pays a satisfactory wage, when balancing self-employment, tax write-offs and work enjoyment. (Accountants earn hefty fees showing the self-employed how to work within the law to maximize lifestyle and minimize taxes; for part of this strategy it is common for self-employed people to take very little in actual wages, since it is taxed so heavily). Thriving business owners tend to live as though "business is slow" and watch closely at the margins. And when in fact a boom year occurs due to exceptionally well-received product or a boom in the economy, how do the owners behave?

A pattern I see is they take the exceptional profit as though it was a one-time event (or at least won't happen again for a few years) and with a CPA's advice invests it in something sound, even if it is a summer cabin or another business.

Tinkering at the margins is the work where you constantly review your costs in each of your budget items, and search out efficiencies that can cut costs and improve the bottom line. If you have twenty expenses listed in your chart of accounts, you have twenty areas where you can seek to limit your costs and improve your profits. If on the other hand, you enjoy travel, you may wish to cut costs in some areas so you can direct ever more resources to your travel budget.

Drafting the Business Plan

Assistance in writing a business plan is cheap and plentiful, so I will restrict what I have to say to areas that I think are unique to small business international trade, or I believe are left out of other sources of advice (search the internet for limitless, excellent sources).

Earlier in the book I recommended you create folders for each area of your research and deposit in them copies of everything you learn. Therefore, at this point the raw material for your business plan ought to be ready to use in drafting the plan.

Using any of the widely available templates for composing a business plan, now compose the prose part of the plan with your raw material from your research and meetings. This is relatively simple. For me more of a challenge, and more fun, is to compose the numbers in the plan. Let's look at a pro forma income statement (Fig. 36), sales projections, inventory planning levels, and a collections schedule.

Sales	$2,954,629	100.00%
Cost of goods sold	-1,399,733	47.4
Gross profit	1,554,896	52.6
Other income	19,196	0.7
Total	$1,574,092	53.3
Expenses:		
Commissions	275,186	9.3
Officers' salaries	98,400	3.3
Salaries and wages	368,777	12.5
Payroll taxes	29,096	1.0
Profit sharing and pension plans	66,697	2.3
Health & welfare	24,922	0.8
Rent	46,085	1.6
Utilities	6,107	0.2
Telecommunications	20,212	0.7
Insurance	22,999	0.8
Office supplies & expenses	45,160	1.5
Auto & Travel	23,867	0.8
Advertising & gift shows	69,643	2.4
Catalogs and samples	51,459	1.7
Interest and bank charges	7,988	0.3
Legal and accounting	6,694	0.2
Outside services	28,252	1.0
Bad debts	26,488	0.9
Repairs and maintenance	18,293	0.6
Taxes and licenses	3,121	
Dues and subscriptions	1,020	
Promotion and entertainment	4,376	
Shipping and warehouse supplies	22,504	0.8
Depreciation	12,904	0.4
Miscellaneous	1,575	0.0
Total expenses	1,281,825	43.4
Net income before taxes	$292,267	9.9

Fig. 36. Typical income statement for a small gift and
housewares importing business

This income statement would be typical of a small import company, and serve to give you a better idea than presented in the chapter on costings regarding what you might expect in costs and profits, again assuming you are in the gift and housewares industry. Please be clear that this is only an example, and your experience may be wildly different. In time various cost items go up or down, so even within a single company each item may fluctuate remarkably. These are the items in the chart of accounts for your business that represent the targets for your efforts to manage costs at the margin, and improve profits for your business. Please note the $292,267 essentially belongs to the owner, who is otherwise compensated through the "officers salary" budget item. It is a matter between you and your CPA to decide what strategies result in the best overall compensation for you.

"Other income" noted in the statement above may be profits from an export sale, or perhaps a consulting fee, or profits from investments made with your cash reserves during a slow season that were waiting to be employed in the rush season.

Sales Projections

Sales projections are just that, projections, and unlikely to be very accurate predictions. Since we are merely setting expected benchmarks, ones we can observe and then adjust our plan when our projections prove inaccurate, we need not sweat this task too much.

We can certainly support our projections with some objective information, and some affirmations. Our strategy is to gain at least enough orders from customers to cover the minimum production run of our suppliers. Our sales projections ought to do at least this. Second, we can ask our sales representatives what they can reasonably sell, and see if that independently confirms our estimates. And again, do the sales representatives' sales projections at least cover the suppliers minimum production requirements?

Making the plan realistic requires an understanding of typical annual business cycles, and how they affect your planning.

The Ordering Cycle and Stock Levels

I cannot stress enough the number one rule in importing: never buy inventory without customer orders in hand. Even as your company grows this remains true, but as your company grows you develop a customer base that comes to trust you.

This customer base allows you to risk buying a little extra with the confidence you will sell it anyway. In my days as a buyer in China I commonly heard other buyers ask the Chinese sales representatives what the minimum order was for a given product. The Chinese would reply, and the buyers, mostly representing large, established importers would reply in turn, "Oh that I can sell anyway." Say the minimum order was 500 pieces: the buyer knows he can sell 500, the question is only whether he will sell 5,000 or 50,000 pieces. The buyer has enough trusting customers who will try anything offered, so collectively they will snap up the 500 pieces of the minimum. But as those are sold and more orders come in, the buyer can then decide whether he needs 5,000 or 50,000.

Once you project sales, based on your company's experience, you must work up orders to the suppliers. To assure timely delivery of adequate supplies, I offer some tools to help you write your orders.

Consider this table:

Sales (not orders) by month as a percentage of per annum sales

January	10.4%
February	7.6%
March	7.3%
April	6.1%
May	4.6%
June	4.1%
July	6.6%
August	8.9%
September	9.2%

October	14.0%
November	12.7%
December	8.5%

This table was compiled after studying a five year trend of various importer/wholesalers of gift and housewares companies. If you expect to sell a thousand units of an item for a given year, then the table will give you a pretty good idea of how many you may sell each month.

Keep in mind you can be wrong about your projection, and your supplier can be wrong about production capacity. Plus, there are lead times to produce the goods. Also, the importer shoots for four inventory turns a year, or no more than a three month supply of merchandise to sell. The next tool helps you manage these problems:

		Ordering Cycle	
Order	Ship	Cancel	Inventory Period
Oct 15	Jan 15	Feb 15	Feb, Mar, Apr
Jan 15	Apr 15	May 15	May, Jun, Jul
Apr 15	Jul 15	Aug 15	Aug, Sep, Oct
Jul 15	Oct 15	Nov 15	Nov, Dec, Jan

The order date is the date you need to place an order for merchandise, assuming it takes 90 days for your manufacturer to deliver. Therefore, an order placed October 15 is expected to be shipped by January 15. This merchandise is to supply needs for February, March, and April. If the merchandise is later than February 15, it will come too late to be of use in the period mentioned. To assure the supplier does not ship late, the agreement or letter of credit notes a February 15 cancellation date.

Note this schedule calls for placing the order for the second period before the first period starts, and just as the merchandise is supposed to be shipped for the first period. By ordering more frequently the importer can better manage inventory levels. If a three month supply is less than the suppliers minimum, ask the supplier if they will make the minimum but just ship the ordered amount.

By working with these two charts, as well as the Sales and Marketing Magazine survey of buying power, you can begin to build a variety of useful tables. In addition to planning out orders you can plot out sales as well, such as the table in Fig. 37:

Total Sales Projection		$360,000				
Period %	100%		25.3%	14.8%	24.7%	35.2%
Period $		$360,000	$91,080	$53,280	$88,920	$126,720
	Territory %	Territory $	Jan-Feb-Mar	Apr-May-Jun	Jul-Aug-Sept	Oct-Nov-Dec
Atlanta	13.2	47,520	12,022.56	7,032.96	11,737.44	16,727.04
New York	15.1	54,360	3,753.08	8,045.28	13,426.92	19,134.72
Los Angeles	12.55	45,180	11,430.54	6,686.64	11,159.46	15,903.36
Chicago	9.8	35,280	8,925.84	5,221.44	8,714.16	12,418.56
Dallas	7.1	25,560	6,466.68	3,782.88	6,313.32	8,997.12
San Francisco	3.2	11,520	2,914.56	1,704.96	2,845.44	4,055.04
Seattle	3.7	13,320	3,369.96	1,971.36	3,290.04	4,688.64
Denver	4.0	14,400	3643.20	2,131.20	3,556.80	5,068.80
Miami	5.0	18,000	4,554.00	2,664.00	4,446.00	6,336.00
Columbus	4.0	14,400	3,643.20	2,131.20	3,556.80	5,068.80
Minneapolis	7.2	25,920	6,557.76	3,836.16	6,402.24	9,123.84
Reston	8.2	29,520	7,468.56	4,368.96	7291.44	10,391.04
Boston	5.5	19,800	5,009.40	2,930.40	4,890.60	6,969.60
Honolulu	1.45	5,220	1,320.66	772.56	1,289.34	1,837.44
	100%	360,000	91,080.00	53,280.00	88,920.00	126,720.00

Fig. 37. Sample annual sales plan

Fig. 37 lays out sales by territory by calendar quarter, by dollar amount, assuming projections of $360,000 in sales. Certainly any sales projection you make is a guess, but by breaking down your best guess into what is the scientific likelihood of the distribution of time and place, both your suppliers and sales representatives can examine the document and estimate the likelihood on their part to deliver and sell respectively.

Also, I found in certain items such as ceramics, the supplier was willing to let me change my order within a category. For instance, I ordered a few hundred of a dozen different face masks. As sales progressed I found the ballerina style began to outsell the clown style. I asked the supplier to reduce the number of clowns and increase the number of ballerinas with no change in total units manufactured.

Any business plan template you choose will now have you take the sales you project for each month, use it a a basis for your monthly income, subtract out your expenses each month, and net what your profit or loss is each month. Your negative months demonstrate where your capital shortfalls are, and when and at what level you need financing, if any.

Keep in mind, since most wholesalers give their customers at least thirty days to pay, that your sales and your income will come at different times. Let's say your plan is to make your first shipments (legally known as "sales") to your customers in the month of August. Further, you expect those sales to be $10,000 in value. And your terms are that you expect to be paid in thirty days after you ship, which means the customer is obligated to send you a check at thirty days after you ship. Naturally customers will be liberal with your credit and send the check 30 days after they receive the goods. You can expect the shipment to take a week in transit, and the check to take a week to arrive, add that to thirty days and 45 days may be more realistic to expect before payment. Then there are those who are slow-pay, and other problems. All this means that you are not likely to see income from your $10,000 sales for a while, and then not all at once. A more likely schedule would be as outlined in Fig. 38.

	August	September	October	November	December
Total Sales	$10,000	$20,000	$30,000	$40,000	$30,000
10% cash or COD	1000	2000	3000	4000	3000
40%/30 days		Aug→ 4000	8000	12000	16000
30%/60 days			Aug→ 3000	6000	9000
20%/90 days				Aug→ 2000	4000
Total Cash-In Receipts	$1,000	$6,000	$14,000	$24,000	$32,000

Fig. 38. Cash flow detail

I am only showing the first five months cash flow detail to make the point, and you can build your own projection from this. Note total sales for August are projected to be $10,000, and on the left I note that 10% of receipts may be cash (or prepayment) or COD. We might also see the balance as follows: 40% within 30 days. 30% in 60 days, 20% in 90 days. This means for our $10,000 in sales in August, we may only see $1,000 in that month. The rest arrives over the next 90 days. (I've written "Aug" next to the amounts to show how a month's income may roll in. All of the "Aug" notes add up to the $10,000 sales for August.)

But note the cumulative effect: by December you are actually receiving more in income than your actual sales, and more income than the previous month, even though the sales are less, due to residual receivables being paid.

With these examples you ought to be able to estimate what your sales will be, assure production can cover sales (and vice versa), break down sales by month, break down sales by territory, order enough inventory in a timely manner to maintain efficient inventory levels, and forecast cash income and needs.

The lynch pin in your entire business plan is the mission statement, where in a sentence you describe what you do. This becomes the focus and the guiding light for all you do. With the mission statement, you introduce your business plan and your company to buyers and sellers, and anyone else interested in your company. These are harder to write than you may suppose. Study the mission statements of other businesses so you can get a sense of style and content. For example, for a business that brokers education online I use the following as my mission statement: our mission is to lower the cost and widen the access to education through free trade worldwide, while ever increasing student and teacher satisfaction.

With a mission statement, anyone asking can know what we do, ask more questions if they like, and we can maintain focus.

A Shift in Thinking

To grow beyond the start-up phase, a shift in thinking and actions must occur. Although the fundamentals of listening to customers as a basis for developing new designs remains, more complex issues must also be addressed. The focus widens from "what does the market want" to "how to get more market and what else does my market want?"

Knowing the role of the small business importer allows you to direct your activities to a reasonable goal; knowing the value you provide allows you to clearly help others achieve their goals and simultaneously thrive yourself. But as you perform your role and provide a value, questions constantly arise, problems develop, opportunities present themselves, and the importer is thrown into a quandary: what should I do?

The business schools for at least the last forty years have been teaching how to run the next Xerox Corporation. This is right and proper for those who will go to work for conservator companies, but detrimental to those who plan to start-up and grow a new, innovative and competitive business. Even today as more universities develop "entrepreneurial studies" sections in their business schools, the message hasn't changed. I have looked into the textbooks of such schools and found although the cover of the book says "Entrepreneurial," the contents are the same old conservator message. This is like wrapping a James Brown album cover around an Patsy Cline record—could be disappointing.

But as this book has pointed out, there is a fundamental, albeit complementary, difference between conservators and innovators. This difference is not only in the value they provide and the role they play, but also in how they operate.

A friend of mine started an import business and was complaining about the "flood of problems that come in the door (or over the telephone line) every day, and trying to keep on top of it." Some of these were problems such as too many checks, very many new orders, reorders over the phone, as well as customer complaints and other normal business problems (the kind of problems everyone wants). I gently suggested that his organization too closely resembled General Motors, and if he would stop applying conservator solutions to innovator's problems he would get on top of the workload.

For instance, this importer was installing a new computer system, after his old one had failed to perform adequately. He had hired a computer consultant to modify the programs and specify the hardware. He explained in detail the configuration and capabilities, and I noted I had the same specifications and more in my computer system. He expected to have his system up and working in a few months, and mine had been up and working the first day, and by this time had performed flawlessly for over a year. My friend paid $13,000 up front for his programs alone; I paid $150. With sales per employee roughly equal, I have no trouble handling the daily deluge. The solution he devised was straight out of a conservator's play book: hire a consultant and throw money at the problem.

When computers were first introduced to business, the conservators needed hardware specifications and software capabilities unique to each conservator. Therefore, each computer was in effect built from scratch, each program written from scratch. And rightly so: Aetna Casualty and Life's computer system was useless to General Motors, and vice versa. To this day, such large companies have in-house computer programmers, just as they have in-house lawyers and so on. The first pacemakers were handmade and did not perform so well. Today pacemakers are mass produced and perform very well.

Over the years, off-the-shelf software has become so comprehensive, and computer hardware so inexpensive, that there is no need to pay over $1500 for complete software and hardware, including printers, to run a company as large as $5 million a year in sales. You even can charge such a system and make payments, or pay even less by buying used equipment.

In the real world, as a business begins to thrive, the owner is convinced his is the most important business on earth: the owner dreams, breathes, eats, sleeps, talks and walks the business. Owners truly believe their business is important and unique. Using the best information they have, the example of the conservators, they make decisions like the computerization decision above. And the decision was wrong. The bottom line effect of the decision is to render at least $130,000 in sales wasted. To pay for the software alone, assuming a 10% net profit, $130,000 in sales will generate $13,000 profit, enough to pay for the software. When you make an expenditure (and keep in mind it is an expenditure your competitors do not make), the amount is subtracted straight from the bottom line.

The error was first in following a conservators lead, and second in believing that somehow his business was special or unique and therefore needed software to match.

In another instance, an importer with backing overseas was given the opportunity to buy out his backers with profits from the operation. The price was $100,000, but the importer could not generate the profits. In going over the books post-mortem, I noted in the eighteen months leading up to the loss of control of the company, the importer had paid $100,000 to lawyers to secure worldwide patent rights for the company on his products. He gained control of the products for the company, but lost control of the company. The $100,000, of course, was generated by the company, and would have been profit had it not been paid out to lawyers. The patents are for an item the market no longer cares for.

The Benefit of Your Insignificance

In every seminar I teach, inevitably someone describes a problem and asks about a solution. I have developed a tool, a concept, for entrepreneurs to use when faced with problems. The concept is what I call the "benefit of your insignificance." In essence, the entrepreneur has to realize that nobody knows and nobody cares about his business. Therefore, it doesn't matter what you do, the rules generally don't apply, you're free to act as you see best, and you can make up your own rules as you go along. When I apply the concept of "the benefit of my insignificance" to any problem, the solution becomes obvious and the problem is solved.

I realize this is a provocative concept, but nothing has been more useful over the years for setting right the view of people struggling to establish an import company, and to thrive once established.

Let us list some thoughts in light of the realization of the value of your insignificance:

• To make money, your business only has to be better than the worst company in your field making money. You may knock out the worst company making money, and become the worst yourself, but that is not a bad start. Indeed, you will be far ahead of 80% of the other people who start business and fail. In other words, it doesn't take much to succeed.

• Financing is easy to come by because you don't need much, and it is easy to prove you can earn money. Low capitalization means low risk.

• You can use off-the-shelf software because you do not need any special reports. You don't have anything special to report (I recommend BestWare's MYOB accounting program).

• Your orders will all be small, and if you make a mistake, foul up the order, or fail to deliver, you will not get sued because it doesn't matter. Is your reputation shot? You don't have a reputation!

• No need to prepay taxes, because they are so low.

• No need to ever speak to a lawyer. In over twenty years of business I haven't, simply because nothing I do requires a lawyer's help, and they are trained to help conservators anyway. No need to ever get a patent or trademark, because you will be done with the product long before the cost of obtaining the rights can be amortized.

• Timing doesn't matter. Take your time, enjoy the process. If it is a good idea today, it will be even better after you take time to think about it more.

• Conservators dread and carefully manage exceptions. For innovators, every day is exceptional, and the exceptions are where the money is made. While conservators spend vast amounts of money avoiding and managing exceptions, the innovator welcomes each one that comes in the door.

• You could not possibly violate antitrust laws, and if you did, who would bother with you?

• Your marketing network has time and space for you because there is not a significant amount of you.

• No need for any contracts; in any dispute you will lose anyway. No deal is particularly important, so walk away if it doesn't pay. You may lose in court, but the cost of collecting is prohibitive.

• Licensing your company is easy, because it is rather unimportant.

• Never need to attend small business conferences, "meet the lenders days," or join international trade clubs, or apply to government business assistance programs, because they don't mean you in their advertisements.

• Information from competitors is free because you are not a threat to anyone.

• Image is everything to the conservator. Images are expensive to market. Your image is strictly and precisely your product. You only have to inform people about the product, and spend no money on your "image."

• You don't have to lease office space. Work out of your home and write off expenses instead of incurring new expenses. You probably have adequate office equipment already, or what you need will not cost much. No secretaries, no extra phones, just a fax machine, a computer, some file folders and a good product.

• You need no product liability insurance. Nobody knows or cares about your company. You are not worth suing.

As the problem arises, and you think of solutions, you must think which of the possible solutions are based on and motivated by a feeling of the significance of your company. Recall the value of your insignificance, and rethink the problem. You will come up with an effective decision.

This in no way contradicts the role and value importers provide, nor does it limit income potential or success. Quite the contrary, the concept of the benefit of your insignificance is an excellent tool in the job of building success, and strips all nonsense away from the core value and role.

One of the oldest jokes in wholesaling refers to the price cutter who proclaims that what he loses on each product he sells, he makes up for in volume. Joking aside, I witnessed an actual instance of this when I pointed out to an importer that a souvenir item he was selling to a major tourist destination was landing at 48.5 cents each, and he was selling them for 47 cents. He had to, he said, the competition was tough. The volume was tens of thousands of pieces on each order, and this amounted to half of his business. I pointed out that if he gave up this losing half of his business, his company would be instantly profitable. But unfortunately his ego ruled that his company must not shrink ever, and he could not pass up any business. Eventually his company failed.

These cautionary tales can be useful, but let us learn from some good examples of where things go right.

Pet Rock vs Ty, Fads vs Manias

Fads cannot be profitable, because they are too short-lived, as mentioned earlier. A mania is something else, and can be quite profitable. In essence, a mania is a well-managed fad. The trick is to convert the fad into a mania.

Earlier I mentioned the Pet Rock fellow whose fortunes waxed and waned with that fad. In the rare instance someone has an item that becomes a fad, normally the response is to expand production as fast as possible to meet demand. The better thing to do is counterintuitive; if your item becomes a fad, do not maximize production, rather limit production.

As of the writing of this book, the Razor scooter fad is dying out as well. The company began selling these scooters in 1986, and enjoyed years of profit. Sadly, as the scooter became a fad, they expanded production instead of limiting it.[59]

The fellow behind the Beanie Babies, Ty Warner, shows a better way— that is, how to convert a fad into a mania. Given that the demand for Beanie Babies was massive, and given that competent production was limited, it is clear Ty Inc. managed the fad artfully: by constantly changing the designs. Ty Inc. could limit the amount of product needed to supply the demand, and also limit the amount of production capacity needed. Lower overhead naturally follows.

For example, instead of making 100 million of style "A" Beanie Babies to meet demand, Ty Inc. can make 5 million style "A," then use the same production capacity to make 5 million style "B," and so on. The result of having made and sold 100 million Beany Babies anyway, although of many different "designs" and with limited production capacity, is to leave the market still desperate for more of the same kind of product.[60] Of course, it is a bit more complex than this, but the point is, by "retiring" a given doll after a point in time, demand is excited while production capacity is limited. If and when the fad for the dolls passes, Ty will go back to being a rather small business—except the owner, Ty Warner has, in the

---

59. People use the current plethora of Razor scooters and the knock-offs as evidence that one must patent-protect their idea, keep their ideas secret, use trademarks and all other manner of efforts to block others from competing. Wrong. The Razor has been around for some 15 years and what they are observing now is the end of the process, not the beginning.

60. As of October 20, 2000, the official ty.com website was registering close to 4.5 billion-yes, billion-hits.

meantime, bought the New York Four Seasons Hotel for $275 million with his profits.

This is how *Forbes* describes the owner in an October 11, 1999 report:

> H. Ty Warner| $5 billion| Beanie babies. Chicago. | 55. Single| "Our name brand will not go away. We want to be the Coke of collectibles." That's what the Beanie Babies baron told *Forbes* a few days after his Internet site implied that the company would "retire" its line of cuddly creatures. Likely marketing ploy created just the kind of frenzied buying Ty's become known for provoking. Kalamazoo College dropout, took job selling stuffed toys. Quit to bum around Italy. Came home, designed line of stuffed Himalayan cats and other toy animals before creating Beanie Babies: understuffed toy animals affordably priced for the allowance set. Kids loved the cute names (Snort the bull, fleece the lamb); limited distribution spawned a cult of adult collectors. Beanies hit market at $5 to $7, can reach $12,000 in collectors' circles. Fierce protector of the Beanie trademark, favors boutiques over mass merchants. Low profile: no signage at Ty's Chicago headquarters; prefers cabs to limos. Beanie babies might be a fad, but his Four Seasons Hotel in New York should last.

If Ty Warner had simply made 100 million copies of one doll, the demand for the fad would have been satisfied, and his product would have died out, and his business would have folded into bankruptcy. To make the 100 million dolls in the short life-span of a fad, he would have had to recruit and establish a far larger production capacity, and expanded all other phases of his company to support that level of sales. A company able to move 100 million of one item is organized differently from a company able to move 100 million total of a thousand different items. This insight may be obscure to a novice, but I assure you any experienced manager, or warehouse clerk for that matter, understands this perfectly.

When the fad died out, Ty Warner would be the proud owner of a vast physical plant and operation geared towards moving a single design in massive quantities in a short period of time. He would have malinvested and found himself with a white elephant of a business infrastructure, inasmuch as his fad had died out, and there is no more product to move through his system.

The pattern endures: nobody special, loves plush toys, designs own, first tries not so hot, prefers small stores to large, not afraid of a profit (margins must be astonishing on those dolls—perhaps "Fleece the Lamb" is really a joke for "Fleece the Kids"), eventually has a hit, lives humbly and invests profits well. I give an example that everyone knows about to make the point. I worked for a fellow who immigrated to the US with nearly nothing, and within 20 years had a custom home on the waterfront in the San Francisco Bay Area's most prestigious neighborhood, his sailing yacht out front, Mercedes and Ferrari in the garage, and extensive land and stock holdings. Yet as a wholesale business, almost nobody ever recognizes his name, or the name of his company. And like most such people, he does not mind.

Nordstrom

A friend of mine is an independent sales representative for Baccarat Crystal, one of the most coveted brands. As Nordstrom[61] expanded its giftware department they called him in to write an order. After working up an order they presented it to him; he examined it, and then declined to accept the order. The Nordstrom buyer was astonished. My friend explained what would be a proper display and selection for Nordstrom, and maintained that image and sales would suffer with such a small selection; he would accept an order only if Nordstrom were to take a stand-

---

61. I use Nordstrom as an example because they have a well-known name. With a recent change in management, Nordstrom has begun to accept, indeed seek, government subsidies for store locations and expansion. I predict here Nordstrom will begin a long decline since this represents a shift in focus from the needs of their customers to the needs of the government.

alone Baccarat display, with a certain selection for which my friend would regularly provide service and write re-orders. The buyer replied that she would have to consider his counter-offer, and would get back to him.

Although my friend knew he was right and giving the Nordstrom buyer the best advice, nonetheless the Nordstrom buyer might contact Baccarat directly, place an order and complain about my friend.

Eventually the buyer called my friend, agreed to his terms, and Baccarat is sold in all Nordstrom stores. My friend was called to France as a hero to tour the Baccarat factory and the wine country.

Bambergers

Bambergers is an East Coast department store chain. When I was managing an import company in San Francisco, the New York sales rep called and informed us that Bambergers wanted to place a $60,000 order with my company. I had dealt with Bambergers for years, and we were delighted, until the rep told us Bambergers wanted a quantity discount. My sales manager came to me with the news that we would lose the order if we did not give them the discount. Naturally I declined, since we do not compete on price.

The sales manager informed the rep, who in turn informed Bambergers. Bambergers made their final offer: full freight allowance (we pay the freight from San Francisco to New York), or they take their business elsewhere. The sales manager declined, and the rep, very angry at the idea that they would lose a $9,000 commission over a freight allowance, demanded to speak with me.

I backed up the sales manager's decision, very much aggravating the New York rep, and I reminded the rep that I refused even Macy's any such blandishments. The sales rep demanded to go over my head to the owner of the company, noting that this disagreement might affect our relationship. It took some doing to find the owner, but he backed me up, telling the New York rep that I could sell $60,000 worth of goods to smaller stores who would pay faster without any discounts. The rep replied it would take a hundred and twenty $500 orders to match a $60,000 order, and also noted the Bamberger order was easier business. The owner offered to let the reps give Bambergers a concession out of their commissions; say $6,000 as a ten percent discount, but the $6,000 would be taken from the reps commission. The rep declined, and did not disguise his disappointment.

I would be happy to report that I did get plenty of smaller orders, the rep got over it, and all's well that ends well. But two weeks after I thought the issue was dead, I received a $60,000 order from Bambergers, no discounts, completely in compliance with our terms and conditions. My sales manager called the New York rep and asked what happened. The New York rep told her Bambergers all along very badly wanted the merchandise. It sells very well, and the rep never doubted Bambergers would order with or without any discounts. Astonished, my sales manager asked why the rep was so insistent and tough, and the rep replied it is his job to get the best deal possible for the customer (remember, you pay the rep, but the rep works for the customer, and any buyer worth his salt will aggressively pursue any and all concessions he can get).

As an alternative to getting discounts, some buyers will ask a vendor to pay a kickback to the buyer if the order is placed. Instead of my company giving a 10% discount, or $6,000 to the department store, I give 5%, or $3,000 to the buyer directly, mailed to his home. As long as the department store doesn't find out, everybody is happy. Let us make clear this is a crime and I have never engaged in this activity, and it is a rare problem, but aggressively monitored by retailers.

Therefore, a $60,000 order with no concessions attached would suggest to the VP finance for the department store that the buyer was stealing from the store. Any order that large without any concession is very rare. Buyers must have copies of a vendors terms and conditions, memos going back and forth showing how hard the buyer tried to get concessions, telephone logs to support the buyers position, all to protect the buyer from any suspicion.

Ultimately, the buyers can buy what they want for their departments, with or without discounts. Our item's designs were so superior to the competition that we could sell them without any concessions. If not, we would redesign until we reached that happy position.

As a legal matter, what you offer any one store, you must offer to all stores. It is not uncommon for Macy's, who may have been paying full price all along, to hear through the grapevine, or a newly hired buyer, that you give 5% discounts to other stores. Macy's, like any other department store, will simply figure what the value of such a discount would be on their purchases from you for the last year, and just deduct that amount from your next invoice.

A Store that Shall Remain Nameless

It took years for us to unravel this mystery. A Store that Shall Remain Nameless placed a large order with us and asked us to inflate the invoice value by 10%. An item normally a dollar must appear on the invoice at $1.10. Certainly, I replied, if they would pay the 10% more. The buyer made it clear this was no joke, and affirmed they would ultimately pay only the regular dollar price. I refused the order, but left the door open to possibly working with them if they would just explain why. They refused to explain, but again the owner was called in to mediate. I argued accommodating this request was going to be a computer nightmare, and the mischievous paperwork was going to be the grounds for dispute and slow pay. The owner overruled, and I shipped the goods with invoices 10% above regular list price, and the store eventually paid regular list price. It wasn't until years later, in a seminar, when I related this story, that an automobile dealer raised his hand and explained what was going on.

Like automobile dealers, retailers get loans based on their assets. Inventory is one of the retailer's assets. Accounts payable, or what is owed on those assets is a liability. If a department store has $30 million in merchandise assets at cost, inflated by 10% to $33 million, yet the invoices show a net liability of $30 million, the store just created on paper a $3 million increase in net value, against which the store can borrow money. The automobile dealer affirmed he commonly ran this ruse. It is a short term fix that must be straightened out before the fiscal year ends or the auditors find out, and fraud may be charged.

Of course to this day I have no idea what the department store was doing, but this seems the best explanation to me.

Spiegel

Our Chicago rep called with the good news that Spiegel was carrying a hand carved wooden item of ours in their catalog. We normally shipped them bulk, 24 pieces to a case, but Spiegel was offering them as individual items. Spiegel's order was large, but they wanted us to repack each hand carved item in a box that would be suitable for sending the item through United Parcel Service, and marked with their item number and purchase order number.

I declined instantly, knowing the cost would be substantial, and probably wipe out any profit. The rep said I can't just say no, I must say no, unless...; that is, under what conditions would I sell the items? I asked a sheltered workshop (charitable workhouses for the handicapped and developmentally disabled) to cost out the time and materials to repack the item to Spiegel's specifications. They would do the work for 50 cents an item. I decided that since I take a 100% markup on everything I do, that Spiegel would have to pay $1.00 more per item. I informed the Chicago rep, and rested easy believing that was the end of it. Again, the order came through to my requirements. The business was very profitable, the sheltered workshop brought on many more workers, and the rep enjoyed a hefty commission.

General Foods

The largest single order I ever encountered was a $175,000 order for 17,500 country motif mugs, set of four, placed by General Foods. The mugs were to be featured in a Sunday morning all-newspapers insert advertisement for Maxim coffee, and guaranteed to have 23 million impressions (advertising lingo for how many people will read the ad). The mugs could be had normally at retail for $22.00 the set of four, but with a proof of purchase they could be had for $13.00 from General Foods.

The order came my way when the General Foods buyer spotted the mug in my New York showroom and fell in love instantly. Although the reps were delighted at the idea of a $26,000 commission on one order, they were terrified at the impact the ad would have on the market, and unsure if I could ship within a reasonable amount of time.

I first ascertained the factory could meet the delivery schedule. Then I contacted an acquaintance who was Vice President–Product Development at a major liquor conglomerate. I relayed the facts of the case and asked what impact this order would have on our business. He asked how many customers I had, I told him 5,000 spread throughout the United States, and he said I might get two complaints, but no noticeable effect on business, long or short term.

He was right. The factory went into 24 hour production, the mugs were shipped directly from Nagoya, Japan to Kankakee, Illinois without us touching them.

Most remarkable to us was that I could put into the market, which I assumed I had covered fairly well, 17,500 sets of our most popular item, and in no way affect our business negatively. This was a powerful lesson in the reality of the size of the U S market, and how unlikely any of us will ever fully tap into it.

Liquidators

Every industry has its bottom fishers, people who buy what is generally considered junk and fix it up to resell at a tidy profit. Real estate, the stock market, automobiles, computers - all industries have such people. In retailing the bottom fishers are called liquidators.

As your company grows, inevitably you will find yourself with some product that no longer sells. You misjudged the market, or perhaps you have a few thousand left of something of which you have sold hundreds of thousands. The best thing to do is call a liquidator and unload the product as quickly as possible. The worst thing is what most people do: reject the liquidators offer and hold on to the item waiting for a better price. Hell will freeze over first.

Liquidators look at the item and the quantity you have and figure at what price could they move that quantity through their stores in one month. If they figure they can move your $2.00 item, which normally retails at $4.00, in a month at 25 cents, they liquidator will offer you five cents. Insulted, most wholesalers decline. And the goods rot in the warehouse, costing the company rent, insurance, adverse balance sheet and so on.

Accepting the liquidators offer gives you a nickel that you can put back to work, making you far better off than before the liquidator appeared.

In time, you will have your own stories with happy endings as long as you make sure you know your value, offer the best products, always require just compensation for your efforts, and never be afraid to accept your mistakes.

These examples show how some people who have immersed themselves in the culture of their market are able to take difficult situations and develop positive results. This is the result of taking the job seriously, observing, practicing and providing a value.

All of these examples relate to business in the US, and the results of learning about your market. Although knowing the United States market for your product is critical to your success, knowing about conditions overseas can be the most fascinating part of the business. Fig. 39 takes the import/wholesale structure and adds on the extraction/export structure:

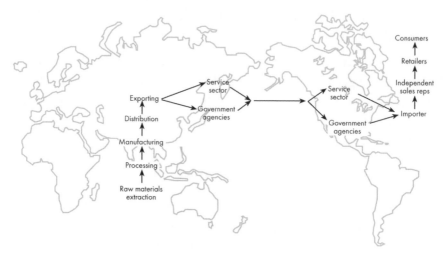

Fig. 39. Steps from raw materials to consumer

Starting with the extraction of raw materials from the source (minerals from the earth, wool from the beast, wood from the forest, coral from the sea), a product evolves from a process of refining and manipulating until the end product is achieved. It is knowledge of these many steps that can become important to your success. Rug merchants know that the altitude a sheep wanders, when wool is shorn, how long it is stored, and how processed and dyed (if at all) greatly affects the quality of the end product, not to mention the workmanship. Your customers will expect you to be knowledgeable about your product, and your trips overseas ought to greatly expand your knowledge and understanding.

Processing Orders

An earlier chapter mentioned the independent sales representative's concern for your ability to handle the paperwork involved in product wholesale and distribution. The procedures are quite simple, but if handled incorrectly or even sloppily, the results can be disastrous. There is no source I know of that addresses the prosaic process of order processing, but it cannot be overlooked.

The first document in order processing is the order itself. Here are the steps in order processing:

1. Log in the order. An "orders received log" is kept by day, every day (note the date across the top of the sheet), listing every order received. List the name of the customer, the dollar amount, the purchase order number if any, and the source of the order (mail, phone, sales representative, etc.). This log will prove invaluable when a customer inquires regarding the status of an order. The first thing you will want to know is, did you receive the order? The order log provides a starting point.

The other purpose for the log is to help weed out duplicate, triplicate and quadruplicate orders. I have had four identical orders shipped to a retailer when the customer only ordered once. The problem occurs when a major customer calls in an important order directly to you to assure prompt delivery. The order is taken over the phone and order processing begins. That is order number one. The buyer calls the independent sales representative to let them know they have placed the order the independent sales representative has worked so hard to gain. The independent sales representative later calls in the order to your company as well, but is written up by a different employee. That is order number two, the duplicate. A few days later in the mail comes a confirming copy of the order from the major buyer: order number three, the triplicate. By this time, a shipment is heading out the door against the original phone order, but the problem goes on. The independent sales representative sends in a confirming copy on his order form to remind everybody he is to get a commission for the order. This is order number four, the quadruplicate, the order from hell.

As the major buyer receives a duplicate shipment, he calls to let you know. An investigation reveals there is a triplicate order on the way to the retailer and one more, the quadruplicate, is being loaded onto a UPS truck as we speak. This has occurred more than a few times.

If you often review the orders received against the log, you cut down on the likelihood of useless repetition tremendously.

2. Check credit. The customer file is pulled for old customers, and files are made for new customers. The credit and collections clerk reviews the payment history of the old customer and checks creditworthiness on the new customers.

3. After clearing credit, the orders are sorted by ship date.

4. Those orders to be shipped immediately are matched against available inventory. If there is not enough inventory to make a worthwhile shipment, the customer is notified of the delay.

5. Packing lists are generated from those orders able to be shipped. The packing lists are used to select inventory, with notations made by the shipping crew confirming what was packed, the weights and measures noted for the shipment, and the name of the carrier that received the goods for delivery to the customer. One copy of the packing slip (unless otherwise directed) is put in the shipment, the other is sent back to the order processor for invoicing.

6. An invoice is generated against the information on the packing list. The original is mailed to the customer, and copies are retained for distribution as follows:

   a. accounts receivable

   b. customer file

   c. invoice copies–numerical file

   d. invoice copies–alphabetical file (having both allows swift reference in case of a question)

   e. notification copy to independent sales representative (and the basis for commissions paid)

7. Customers make payments against their invoices, and any event that results in a net reduction in the invoice amount paid is covered by a credit memo to the files. The credit memos to the customers are debit memos to the commissions paid the independent sales representative.

Essentially, this is all there is to order processing, the matter of such great concern to the independent sales representatives. Naturally there are as many permutations to this procedure as there are import companies; everybody has his own special way to track orders and pay the independent sales representatives.

Make News, Enhance the Image, Grow the Business

A newsletter can be a medium to announce upcoming trade shows, to introduce new products, to explain and educate your customers regarding technical terms or processes relating to your products. David Ogilvy has written excellent books on advertising that are essential reading for anyone going into any business. His agency handles the American Express advertising. Every bit of American Express advertising has three components: the ad makes news, enhances the image of the company, and grows the business (verifiably results in more business). These three simple criteria ought to guide anything you write regarding your company. Consider publishing a newsletter, and distributing it to customers over the internet via e-mail.

Expanding Your Lines

Expanding your line is a matter of finding out who your customers are and determining what else they buy. Taylor and Ng is a Bay Area importer that grew rapidly after introducing the wok to the United States. People buying woks would naturally be interested in accessories for the wok: cooking chopsticks, fry-paddles, tempura drying racks, lids and rings; once the wok is accessorized, then come the wok cooking ingredients and cookbooks. Finally the wok chef needs Asian tableware upon which to serve the meals created: rice bowls, soup bowls and tureens, oval plates, teacups and pots, chopsticks and serviettes. Year after year Taylor and Ng brought out more and more, growing stronger each year. (Having eaten dog myself, I know it is a delicacy in many South East Asian countries. Walk is a homonym with wok. Never ask anyone to walk your dog in South East Asia; the results may be at variance with your desire.)

Farm It Out

Now that I have products, sales representatives, suppliers, and customers I need to organize my operations to command and control this activity. Fig. 40 shows the organizational chart for an importer of consumer goods at approximately $4 million dollars in sales, and employing approximately 24 people:

National Sales Manager	Operations Manager	Accounting
Sales	Warehouse operations	The books
Liaison with reps	Computer operations	General ledger
Sales projections	Order processing	Accounts payable
Advertising-promotion	Inventory control	Accounts receivable
Product development	Credit & collections	Payroll
	Customer service	Budget maintenance
	Traffic	& projections
	Communications	
	Logistics & support	
	Physical plant	
	Research	

(Owner / General Manager above all three columns)

Fig. 40. Organizational chart

Naturally, all of these functions must be performed by you on day one when you start your business. As your company grows, you will certainly need help running the company. A healthy ratio of sales per employee in the gift and housewares industry is $156,000. That is to say, until you reach $156,000 in sales, you ought to be able to handle the company yourself. After that, bring on a part-timer until you hit $312,000 in sales, when that person can become full time. As sales increase, bring on another part-timer, and so on. By studying the chart, you can spot the areas in which you are not particularly strong. That would be precisely the area in which to look for help. You can follow this advice, but certainly I have even better advice: never hire any employees.

Due to the improvements in communications and transportation, the simplification and drastic price reduction in computer systems, and the staggering increases in liabilities associated with having employees, there is simply no reason to ever hire help.

Half of the 24 employees mentioned above would be warehouse people. My warehouse is in Sparks, Nevada. To be precise, I have no warehouse; all of my products are shipped to a private company in Sparks that runs a "pick and pack" operation.[62] For a variety of companies like mine, the Sparks warehouse company stores my inventory, receives orders from me, ships the order including a packing list, sends us a list of what was shipped to whom, and I in turn bill the customer directly. The customer pays me directly, and I have yet to find a customer at all concerned about this arrangement. For my part, I never physically touch my products, and the cost of letting a professional warehouse fulfill my orders is far cheaper than I could do it myself. It would cost me a minimum of 30 cents per square foot to rent substandard warehouse space in Seattle. State of the art warehouse space in Sparks, in the quantity the warehousing company rents out, costs about 15 cents a foot. I am charged a 66% premium, or 25 cents a foot, but this is far less than what I would pay. Also, in the busy season when I need 30,000 square feet, I pay for 30,000 square feet. In the slow season, when I need only 19,000 square feet, I only pay for 19,000 square

---

62. The mail order companies use these but call them "fulfillment houses." I daren't tell my wife I am going to Reno to visit a fulfillment house.

feet. Warehouse expense becomes variable instead of fixed! So much for half of those 24 employees.

Computers used to take three people to operate, but now the job can be done by less than one, due again to the improvements. Sales is certainly farmed out to reps, and I know of one importer who simply designated his Chicago rep as National Sales Manager, giving him an overage percentage to lead all the other reps to ever increasing sales and profitability. The accounting area again is greatly simplified. Every transaction is so comprehensively posted I could print a Balance Sheet and Profit and Loss Statement after each item I record.

The reduction in demand of management time due to fewer employees is so profound that much time is freed up for you to focus on the remaining areas where once employees were required.

Nonetheless, your company may continue to grow and you find that you are being overwhelmed with "unfun" parts of the business; still, resist hiring. In this case, clearly define the area where you need help, and bring on a partner who has those skills.

It is commonly held that the only good partner is a dead partner. I too feel this way, but the fact is, studies overwhelmingly support the idea that partnerships out-perform and out-survive sole proprietorships. Hewlett and Packard, Wells and Fargo, Jobs and Wozniack, Gates and Allen, Burger and King, Gilbert and Sullivan, Lennon and McCartney all admit they could not have achieved their success without the other partner. Ditto for names generally unknown, such as Roy Fong and Ron Rubin in San Francisco, who have reintroduced the tea emperors once enjoyed with their company Imperial Republic. And consistently the successful among us touchingly honor the spouse, that essential partner, for the good results.[63] There are many reasons for this: competitiveness, synergy, two-heads-are-better-than-one, the

---

63. Careful not to assume the opposite, that failure can be laid at a spouse's feet.

appearance of reliability to the outside world, and so on. I have done this with happy results.

As you build your business, you will be tripping over other talented, aggressive people who like you are building their businesses. You will quickly spot their complementary strengths. Keep in touch with these people. Eventually you may find a merger to be an excellent business move. And by far most important, you are free to focus on the fun part of the business, the only part that matters: the buying and selling.

Summary

This book is the first to recognize that the relationship between large business and small business is symbiotic, each with an important role to play, especially in relation to each other. Essentially, small businesses are the innovators introducing new and better products. Large businesses are the conservators who "appropriate" the innovations of the small businesses and apply the economies of scale not only in manufacturing, but also in finance and distribution to make the innovations available to a much wider group of consumers—a group that was unable to pay the premium price the innovator had to charge.

The innovator does not lose out in this paradigm, because the time lag between introduction and abduction is always long enough for the innovator to realize tremendous profits (remember Apple and IBM). Furthermore, the innovator, with one success, is very well positioned to add on successes, given the fact that no innovator is a one-trick pony. The problem for the innovator is not, "What do I do next?" but, "Which one of these 500 great ideas do I work on next?"

We agreed without a customer we have nothing. We've defined a good customer, and agreed that at the small business level it is the better stores, upper-end retailers, that make our best customers.

We explored which comes first, the customer or the product, and learned how those companies we see thriving came up with their product, very often started on the basis of a problem solved, a problem experienced by the founder—and the founder having the "why don't they just…" experience.

We visualize which stores in our area would sell such an item, and then we test our bright idea by asking, as a customer of the store, if they have the item which we have conceived.

If they do have it, we buy it, and move on to another idea.

If they do not have it, we push up through the clerks to the buyers to make sure. We keep pushing until we are told our idea is good, but does not exist.

This process also yields, naturally, more ideas for us to fold into our original concept, improving yet more.

Eventually we leverage the retailers' confirmation of our idea as good and nonexistent into samples of our item from the best source in the world. We learned that for a small business, the best source is inevitably overseas. These are leading suppliers, and as such feel pressure from competition on their main lines, and are always searching out new product lines to produce. We offer that to suppliers overseas.

We return with our samples of our item which was identified as good and nonexistent, and we surprise the retailers by switching from their "customer" to their potential supplier of a needed item. When we return with the samples, we are a boon to the retailer. We have a new item to offer, one they already believe to be a good idea—but it now exists!

One of the values we provide in business is to buy the supplier's minimum order requirement, and break it up among various stores from which we've received orders. This is our main strategy. Of course, we are only speaking with maybe a half dozen retailers locally to get started, and that is not enough business to cover the supplier's minimum production requirement.

Small orders are normal, and make our business rather likely and easy. Small orders are normal, and no retailer in his right mind wants the risk and capital encumbrance of the minimum order requirement of a supplier overseas.

Reflect on the value you provide in the market place, the role you play: you introduce new items to stores desirous of such items, you help overseas makers expand sales to the United States.

Exporting as a self-employed agent is essentially the same work, but reversed, with you acting as the "overseas agent" here in the United States for an importer overseas.

To progress in this business you repeat two steps over and over: prove it with orders and buy only what is warranted by orders. At zero cost to you, you can find out immediately, before you invest a dime, if there is any interest in what you believe will sell. Simply contact the customers you expect to sell the item, ask the buyer or owner, and see what they say. Act on customer feedback.

And, once you have the supplier and customer established, the rules, regulations, logistics, finance, organization, license—all become exceptionally easy. Also, having read this book, you may want to visit www.johnspiers.com, my website devoted to small business international trade. Here you'll find current links to resources, plus a community of small business international traders you may join to seek answers and share ideas about small business international trade.

Although this book is based on experience as well as what I've been taught, no book can explain how to do something in every instance; the why allows you to focus your energy and resources on the goal given your particular circumstances. Knowing why allows you to act creatively in the face of the unique opportunities and choices every businessperson experiences. Knowing why reduces tremendously the uncertainty involved in starting an international business and allows the small businessperson to actually enjoy the process of building a small business, in spite of the tribulations inherent in any business start-up.

*　　　　　*　　　　　*

Where were you five years ago? Think about it, and how time flies. How much have you accomplished? How much closer are you to doing what you want to do with your life? If you start your international trade company today, where will you be in five years? Join us.

BIBLIOGRAPHY

Suggested Reading

1. *Human Action: A Treatise on Economics* (Scholars Edition) by Ludwig von Mises (Ludwig Von Mises Institute; ISBN 0945466242). If you want a comprehensive and correct book on economics, especially economics of international trade, this is the book.

2. *Rick Steves' Europe Through the Back Door 2001* by Rick Steves (Avalon Travel Publishing; ISBN 1566912288). Before you travel get some tips from the master of travelling inexpensively.

3. *Ogilvy on Advertising* by David Ogilvy (Random House; ISBN 039472903X). This man will teach you much about business, from the perspective of an advertiser. He's a bad boy in the business, and 25 years after reading his insistence on putting coupons in advertisements for Rolls Royce motor cars I still recall his ideas when deciding what matters and what works.

4. *Building a Mail Order Business: A Complete Manual for Success* (4th Ed) by William A. Cohen (John Wiley & Sons; ISBN 0471109460). My book for clarity sake assumes one distribution channel, when in fact there are dozens in the United States. Dr. Cohen explains mail order, and it may be usefull to compare and contrast for deeper understanding. You may not sell via mail order, but you will likely sell to mail order houses.

5. *Innovation and Entrepreneurship: Practice and Principles* by Peter F. Drucker (Harperbusiness; ISBN 0887306187). This seminal book provided many insights to me, and is referred to regularly in my text.

6. *Letters of Credit under International Trade law: UCC, UCP & Law merchant,* by Matti Kurkela, (Oceana Publications, Incorporated; ISBN 0-379-20679-X). Kurkela excels at surveying the reality of letters of credit, and then arrives the exact opposite conclusion than I did. I recommend it highly.

INDEX

0-595-19955-0